This Wired
Home

The Microsoft® Guide to Home Networking

Alan Neibauer

PUBLISHED BY
Microsoft Press
A Division of Microsoft Corporation
One Microsoft Way
Redmond, Washington 98052-6399

Library of Congress Cataloging-in-Publication Data
Neibauer, Alan R.
    This Wired Home : The Microsoft Guide to Home Networking / Alan
  Neibauer.
        p. cm.
    ISBN 0-7356-0847-4
    1. Local area networks (Computer networks) Amateurs' manuals.
  I. Title.
  TK9969.N45   1999
  004.6'8--dc21   99-42530
                                                         CIP

Printed and bound in the United States of America.

  2 3 4 5 6 7 8 9   QMQM   4 3 2 1 0 9

Distributed in Canada by Penguin Books Canada Limited.

A CIP catalogue record for this book is available from the British Library.

Microsoft Press books are available through booksellers and distributors worldwide. For further information about
international editions, contact your local Microsoft Corporation office or contact Microsoft Press International
directly at fax (425) 936-7329. Visit our Web site at mspress.microsoft.com.

Sharing a program or Internet account is subject to the terms of your software license agreement or ISP member
agreement.

This book describes the author's opinions about products and services that can be used to create a home network.
Publication of this book does not imply an endorsement by Microsoft of any specific approach or product.

For Microsoft Press
Acquisitions Editor: Christey Bahn
Project Editor: Sandra Haynes

For Studioserv
Development Editor: Joseph Gonzalez
Copy Editor: Gail Taylor
Technical Editor: Steve Sagman

Contents

Part 2

Installing the Hardware

Chapter 4
Installing Network Cards   67

Chapter 5
Running the Cables   83

Chapter 6
Networking Without Cables 99

Part 3
Setting Up the Software

Chapter 7
Installing the Software 111

Chapter 8
Creating Profiles   129

Chapter 9
Learning to Share   143

Part 4

Running the Network

Chapter 10
Printing Across the Network   **177**

Chapter 11
Communicating Over the Network   **193**

Chapter 12

Going On Line Through the Network 231

Chapter 13

Playing Games 247

Part 5

Extending the Network

Chapter 16
Your Future Home Network

Acknowledgments

There are many people who deserve my thanks and appreciation for making this book a reality. My thanks to Sandra Haynes who served as project editor, coordinating everyone's efforts and keeping the entire process on track, and to Steve Sagman who served admirably as project manager and technical editor.

I wish to thank Joseph Gonzalez who served as development editor, and Gail Taylor, who acted as copy editor. My appreciation to Sharon Bell, compositor, for her work in creating the attractive pages that you will soon be reading.

My thanks to Christey Bahn, acquisitions editor, who brought me on board, to Claire Horne, my agent, for knocking on the right doors and calling the right numbers, and to Lucinda Rowley, managing editor.

I could not have completed this, or any, book without the devoted love and support of the remarkable woman I am blessed to call my wife, Barbara. Since we walked down the aisle in 1966, she has managed to charm me with her smile and take my breath away with her beauty.

Introduction

Try to imagine a future in which you can share files, printers, a telephone line, and a modem from every room in your home. Whether you're at home or somewhere around the world, you can see and talk to other members of your family on a video display without getting out of your chair or making an expensive phone call. You can play family games and help your kids with their homework even when you're away on business. But this really isn't a vision of the future. It's the present, and it's made possible by something called computer networking.

Connecting your home computers in a network is neither difficult nor expensive. Anyone can do it at very little cost. In fact, you can get some of the benefits of setting up a network just by purchasing a single cable that costs less than $20. You can get almost all of the benefits of a network for under $100. And if you have Microsoft Windows 95 or Microsoft Windows 98, you already have all the necessary software, and the networking capability is free (what a nice word!).

In the old days—maybe as far back as 10 years ago—networking was indeed expensive and difficult. You had to know a lot and spend a good deal of money to set up a network. But that was then. Today, if you hear someone say that setting up a network is too complicated, point out that it's the new millennium and things have changed.

In this book, you'll learn all about connecting your home computers in a network, from simple file-sharing solutions involving a single cable to more advanced systems that hook up your entire house. You'll also find out about networks that run with cables and without and you'll learn how to harness the free networking capabilities of Windows. With the information in this book, you'll be able to choose the networking solution that is best suited to your own home and needs.

Chapter 1 shows why it pays to connect your home computers in a network and it describes the main benefits of networking, such as sharing printers and files, sending and receiving e-mail, and playing family games. In Chapter 2, you discover some quick and inexpensive ways to share printers and files even without a network (this is where the $20 cable comes in).

In Chapter 3, you find out about different types of networks and the different ways in which you can connect computers—with and without cables. With this information, you'll be able to start making some initial decisions about your future home network.

Chapter 4 covers the selection and installation of an important piece of equipment called the network interface card. If you don't feel comfortable opening the case of your computer to install a new card, you'll find out how to choose the correct card and then have someone else install it for you.

In Chapter 5, you see how you to connect your computers with cable. Here, you'll learn more about the types of networking cable and how to run cable from room to room within your home.

If you decide that you don't want to connect your computers with cable, you can read about the alternatives to cable in Chapter 6. In this chapter, you find the pros, the cons, and the how-to's of connecting computers through your home's existing phone lines, power lines, and even via radio transmission using a wireless network.

Chapter 7 guides you step by step through the process of installing the software you need to get the network up and running.

Sharing a computer with other members of the family is the subject of Chapter 8. You learn how to create and use profiles that let family members maintain their own custom settings on each computer.

One of the best reasons to set up a network is to share files. In Chapter 9, you find out how to share documents, graphics, programs, and other files over the network, and how to back up files through the network for safekeeping.

Chapter 10 is a guide to sharing printers. Thanks to your network, you'll be able to use any printer in your home without having to move disks or printers from room to room.

Chapter 11 is all about family communications—using the network to send and receive messages to one another. Among other things, you learn how to send quick popup messages and create a home post office.

In Chapter 12, you discover the ultimate in network sharing: how to set up your network so that every member of the family can surf the Internet at the same time through a single modem and telephone line.

In Chapter 13, the accent is on entertainment with computer games on the network that encourage communication and competition and that are great fun to play.

Chapter 14 contains all the information you need to set up a family Web. Each family member can create a Web site with a home page and other pages using the software that comes free with Windows. Anyone in the family can then use a Web browser to surf the family Web, just like surfing the Internet.

If you travel for business or pleasure, you certainly want to read Chapter 15, in which you learn how to use a laptop or office computer to stay in touch with the family and access your home computer and the network while you're on the road.

Finally, in Chapter 16, you explore the exciting future of networking. You find out what's happening in home automation, learn about alternatives for high-spee Internet connections, and discover what the future may have in store for your home network.

Use this book as your personal guide to creating and making the most of your family network. And have some fun while doing it. If you have any questions about setting up your network, you can contact me at alan@neibauer.net.

Part 1

Getting Started

Chapter 1
Why Set Up a Network?

It used to be that families fought over which TV program to watch or who would get the car on Saturday night. Now they struggle to get the phone lines. Your kids want to chat with their friends on line, you want to do some research, and your spouse wants to sell some concert tickets on an online auction site. Your family might fight over the color printer or who gets to use the Zip drive to store a large file.

With a television, the kids can watch one set in one room while you enjoy your favorite program in another. But when you have more than one computer in the house, the solution is not quite as simple, because only one person at a time can get on the Internet or play that great new game on CD-ROM.

In this chapter, you'll learn how you can avoid these problems by *networking*— that is, connecting two or more computers to the same system. You'll also learn about other advantages of networking. For example, your family can play computer games together, you can help your children with their homework, and you can foster communication and a sense of family, even when family members are away from home.

See Also

In Chapter 16, you'll look ahead into the future and see how networking will change the way you live and work.

Sharing an Internet Connection

If you have only one phone line and one Internet account, you know what it's like when several people in the house are competing for the same dial tone. Try to access the Internet while someone else is on the phone and you won't be able to connect. Even if you have two phone lines, you still have a problem. Most Internet service providers (ISPs)—the companies through which you connect to the World Wide Web (see "The Buzz on ISPs," below)—let only one person per account log on, regardless of the number of screen names or e-mail accounts you have. You'd need to set up a second ISP account as well, and that starts to get expensive: two phone bills each month and two ISP charges.

Note

Sharing an Internet account is subject to the terms of the ISP agreement. Please check your member agreement before sharing an account.

When you connect your home computers to a network, everyone in the house can share a single phone line and a single ISP account. You can have everyone chatting on line, browsing the Web, and even downloading software, all at the same time. Unfortunately, there are some drawbacks:

- Browsing and downloading might be a little slower when someone else is connected. However, at least you're on line, and you don't have to wait all night for the phone to be free.

The Buzz on ISPs

To connect to the Web, you need an Internet service provider (an ISP), whose phone number your modem dials to go on line. There are countless providers; some of the largest are America Online, AT&T Worldnet, CompuServe, and MSN.

While there are many types of ISPs, they generally fall into two categories: those that require special software and those that don't. Some ISPs don't require special software because they use a Microsoft Windows feature called Dial-Up Networking. This means you can dial up to connect to a network—in this case, the Internet. Other ISPs make you use their own special software and their own dial-up services. Once you're connected through these ISPs, however, you have full access to the Internet through their *customized* menus. A few other services actually give you a choice of whether to connect by using Windows Dial-Up Networking or by using their software.

- Sharing an Internet connection may not work with some Internet providers. Some require their own special software and won't let you connect using the Dial-Up Networking feature in Windows.

- You may need to buy special software or hardware to let you share a phone line and Internet account. The good news, however, is that the software is inexpensive, and may even be free if you have the latest version of Windows.

Note

Microsoft Windows 98, Second Edition, and Microsoft Windows 2000 both have modem-sharing features built in. With these programs, you don't have to buy any additional software or hardware to share a phone line and an Internet account.

Don't Worry If the Line Is Busy

Nearly all new computers come with built-in modems, so you'll probably have a separate modem for each computer in your home. But to avoid dueling over a dial tone, you can connect your home computers in a network and designate a modem on one of them to be shared—that is, used by family members on other computers connected to the network. If one modem is faster than the others, such as an ultra-fast cable modem, it makes sense to share the fastest connection. You'll learn how to share modems and Internet accounts in Chapter 12, but for now let's see how sharing a modem on a network can help.

Suppose your computer has the modem that's being shared. Here's what can happen. Another family member working on a computer connected to the network opens a Web browser or uses an e-mail program. The browser or e-mail program actually goes on line using your modem. If your modem isn't connected to the Internet, it dials in and becomes connected. It's as though the other family member reached into your room and dialed the phone with your modem.

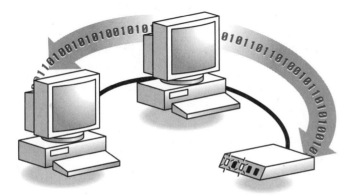

If you are already using the shared modem, other family members on the network just share the ride. They don't have to dial in because the connection to the phone company is already made. When they go on line, they won't hear a phone dialing; they just connect.

What if your computer is not turned on? No problem. Other family members can still go on line using their own modems, as long as the line is free.

Getting the Most from Your Monthly Bill

Because of the way sharing works, a second or third person connecting to the Internet doesn't even have to log on to the ISP. The person would not have to enter a user name or password, and would not have to wait until a connection is made. The browser or e-mail program just slips in line with others that are already connected.

As far as the ISP is concerned, you are using only one account, so you pay for only one account. If your ISP offers unlimited use, you don't have to worry. But if your ISP gives you only so many hours for free and charges for additional time, sharing is an even better idea. If two people are on at the same time for one hour, their use only counts as one hour, not two.

The Bottom Line

The easiest way to share a phone line and modem is to get a free or inexpensive program and install it on your computer. You'll learn how to get and use such programs in Chapter 11. With Microsoft Windows 98, Second Edition, and Microsoft Windows 2000, the software is built in.

Sharing Printers

Suppose you have a laser printer connected to your PC, but the kids have a color printer on theirs. If you were not on a network and wanted to print in color, you'd have to:

1. Put the file on a disk
2. Take the disk to the kids' computer

3. Print the document on their machine—assuming, that is, that their computer has the program needed to print

The other option would be:

1. Unplug the color printer from the kids' machine

2. Carry the printer over to your computer

3. Unplug your printer and plug in the kids' printer

4. Print the document

5. Reverse the procedure to return the printer

There must be a better way!

When you've set up a network, anyone on the network can connect to any printer, even if the printer is attached to another computer. There's no need to transfer files or printers from computer to computer.

- If you have only one printer, everyone on the network can use it.

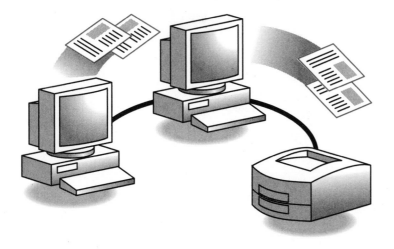

See Also

You'll learn how to share printers in Chapters 2 and 9.

- If you have more than one printer, you can just pick the one you want to use.

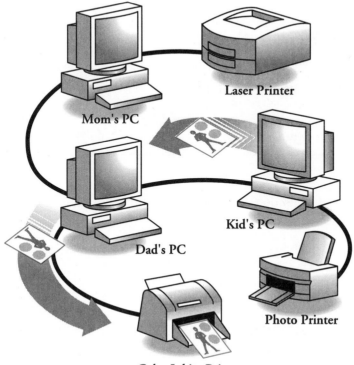

Laser Printer

Mom's PC

Kid's PC

Dad's PC

Photo Printer

Color Inkjet Printer

When your computers are on a network, your kids can print their document on your color printer by just doing the following:

1. Selecting Print from the File menu.

2. Choosing the printer they want to use.

3. Clicking OK.

If your printer is in use, their document just waits in line until the printer is free.

Putting the Printer On Line

Normally, a printer is connected to a computer through its printer port. By connecting the printer to the network, however, everyone can access the printer through the network.

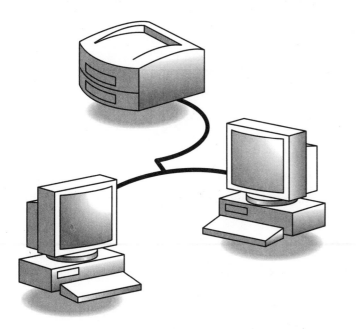

What's the benefit of connecting a printer directly to the network? As long as the printer is turned on, anyone on the network can use it. When a printer is attached to a computer, that computer must be on as well.

Connecting a printer to the network also saves you from dreaded "parallel overload." In addition to a printer, you may have an Iomega Zip drive, scanner, and other hardware connected to the printer port, which is also called the parallel port. Usually, everything works fine. But if you try to use two devices at the same time, you're asking for trouble. If you were to print a document while accessing your Zip drive, for example, your system might freeze up. By connecting the printer directly to the network, you avoid this problem by not having to attach it to the parallel port.

The Bottom Line

Networking can save you the expense of buying another printer and the trouble of shuffling disks and printers between computers. You can use any printer that is attached to a computer on the network, getting the most from your investment.

Sharing Files and Folders

If you have more than one computer in the house, sooner or later you'll need to share files between them. Your spouse might be using your computer to write a letter, for instance, when you'd like to work on a document that you've saved on your hard disk.

If you're not on a network, here's what you have to do before you can begin working:

1. Ask your spouse to stop working for a moment.

2. Copy the file to a floppy disk—assuming it fits on one.

3. Go to another computer in the house and copy the file from the floppy disk.

Avoiding the Floppy Shuffle

When your computers are on a network, though, you can grant other network users permission to access files and folders located on your machine. If others have granted you access, you can get to files on their hard disks, too. You just access the files as though they were on your own system. You can copy or move a file from one system to another, and even delete a file. Not only is there no need to shuffle floppies, but also it's easy to move around files that are too large to fit on a floppy.

Does this mean that all of your personal files are available for everyone to read? Not at all. You can control who has access to your files and whether others can just read them, or also change and delete them.

Making Files Easy to Find

Because files don't have to be moved from one machine to another, you can designate set locations for certain documents. You can store all of the household budget information on the computer in the family room, save investment information on the computer in the spare bedroom, and put miscellaneous files on the kids' machine.

When you need a certain type of document, you'll know exactly where to find it. And if you can't remember which computer the file is stored on, you can search for it on the network using the handy Find command on the Start menu.

Keeping Documents Current

But it's no big deal to copy a file to a floppy, you might be thinking. Maybe not. But even if the inconvenience of copying the file doesn't bother you, you might end up with *version nightmare.* Here's a scenario that might sound familiar.

You have your budget on the computer in the den and you want to work on it in the spare bedroom. So you copy it to a floppy and move it to the hard disk in the bedroom computer. You make some additions, a few changes, one or two deletions, and then save the budget on the bedroom computer's hard disk. As you're working, your spouse decides to make a few changes to the version of the file in the den. So now you have three versions of the budget: the one on the bedroom computer, the one on the floppy, and the one in den. And of course none of them match.

When your computers are on a network, you can just access the computer in the den from any other computer in the house, making changes to the budget in its original location. If someone else tries to access the file while you're working on it, that person gets a message saying that the file is in use. Once you're done with the file, you can be sure that anyone who uses it after you will be working with the most recent version.

Working Together

Because networking allows you to share files, you can collaborate with other family members. After you make changes to the budget, for example, your spouse can review what you've done. You can take a look at your child's homework, suggest some improvements, and then let your child make the corrections before printing it out.

Most word processing programs help you collaborate by tracking revisions. Revision marks in the document show the text you think should be deleted, rather than actually deleting it. They can also indicate—with a color and formatting—text you've added. As you can see in Figure 1-1, on the next page, which shows a document that's been edited with revision marks, changes are easy to see, and they can quickly be incorporated into the final document. You can also add a *comment,* a short note that doesn't appear on the screen but is indicated by a color or an abbreviation. To display the comment, you simply point to the color or the abbreviation and the text appears in a small pop-up box.

A comment

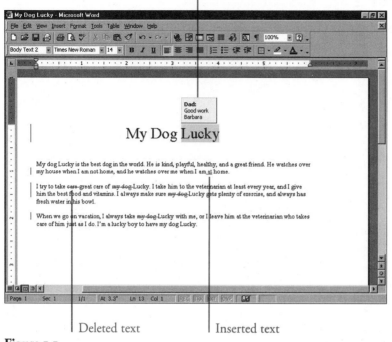

Deleted text   Inserted text

Figure 1-1.
Collaborating on a document on the network.

Safeguarding Important Documents

While you want only one *working* copy of a file, you can make *backup* copies on other machines. That way, if a hard disk goes berserk and the original file is corrupted or lost, you'll always have a safety net.

You should always back up important files. You can copy them to a Zip disk or, if they're small enough, to a floppy disk. If the original file gets damaged, all you have to do is retrieve the backup. When you're on a network, you can also back up files to another hard disk on the system, taking advantage of the larger disk drives found on newer computers. Moving a file from one networked computer to another is faster than making backups on a tape or a series of floppy disks. In addition, the backup version is available to everyone on the network.

The Bottom Line

When you set up a network, you save time and trouble by sharing files, while maintaining privacy and security. You can avoid multiple versions of the same file, locate files easily, and back up files for safekeeping. As your disk becomes full, you can avoid upgrading to a larger disk by storing your files on a computer that has extra room, a money-saving and time-saving feature.

See Also

You'll learn how to share documents in Chapter 9.

Sharing CD-ROMs and Removable Drives

CD-ROMs and removable drives, such as Zip drives, are a real boon to computer users. They store vast amounts of information, and they're fast, safe, and convenient. These days, most computers come with CD-ROM drives and many also come with removable disk drives.

Escaping the CD Shuffle

Many folks keep an encyclopedia or some other reference CD in their CD-ROM drive at all times. When they need to look up a word, find a map, or do some research, the information is quick and easy to access.

Most computer programs, such as the Microsoft Windows program itself, are supplied on CD to save space. (Windows 98, for example, would fill hundreds of floppy disks.) When you're working with a program, or doing some magic on the computer, you may need to access the CD. Take Microsoft Office 2000, for example. When you install Microsoft Office, just the main parts of the program are usually copied to your hard disk. When you want to use a feature that hasn't been installed, Office automatically looks for the information on the CD. This would mean removing the encyclopedia or other CD from the drive and inserting the Office CD. When you finished installing the Office function, you'd once again have to swap CDs.

With a network, you can access any CD on any computer in the network. So that means you can leave the CD for your encyclopedia or other program in the drive of one machine, and access it from any other.

Adding Zip to Your Life

A Zip drive is one of the greatest add-ons you can get for your computer. The newest Zip disks can store up to 250 MB of information—all on a cartridge small enough to fit in a shirt pocket!

Removable disks are great for backups and for transferring files that are too large to fit on a floppy. They're also terrific for storing those files you don't need often but still want to have around. Anyone on the network can access a removable drive that's attached to one of the computers. They can get files from the drive and save files to it.

Some removable drives are built into the computer. When the drive is attached to the computer's parallel port, though, you have to be careful. No one can access the drive while that machine is printing.

See Also

You'll learn how to share disks in Chapter 9.

The Bottom Line

You can save money by buying one removable drive and sharing it with other members of the family and you can access files on a CD without swapping CDs in your own machine.

Communicating with Others

With everyone on a separate computer and, perhaps, connected to the Internet, you may think that there will be less personal communication in the family. While that is a possibility, people have complained about that sort of thing since the invention of the record player (now the CD, of course), the television, and the video game.

While networking may not bring the family physically closer together, it does foster its own brand of communication.

Using an Electronic Intercom

By using a system known as instant messaging (IM), you can find out if a friend across town—or around the world—is on line, and send a message that pops up on that person's screen. You can also send pop-up messages within the family network, as a sort of electronic intercom. The software for this comes with Windows.

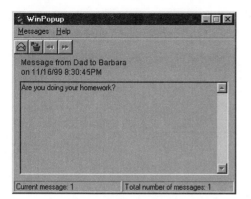

If your computer is equipped with microphones and speakers, you can also speak to each other through the network, and, if your computers are equipped with cameras, even see each other.

Sending Mail, Messages, and Reminders

But what if the people you want to send messages to are not on line? In the old days, you'd send them letters or leave messages on their answering machines. With networks, you can send or receive e-mail between networked computers by simply creating a Microsoft Post Office (the software comes with Windows). Just as you send e-mail to someone over the Internet, you can send e-mail to another computer in your home so your message appears in the inbox on the other computer.

You can also leave electronic "sticky notes" on other peoples' computers, as long as their computers are turned on. The notes appear right on their desktop.

![Sticky note: Barbie -- Call Adam as soon as you get in. Dad — 4/27/99 1:34 PM]

Staying in Touch

It's never been easier for traveling family members to stay in touch. By using a laptop computer to dial in to the network at home, they can send and receive e-mail, transfer files, even update their calendars. And once again, the software used to make the connection comes with Windows.

The Bottom Line

Networking opens all sorts of channels of communication that might otherwise be closed. You can send quick notes that appear directly on the screen of other computers, and you can create a more sophisticated post office for sending and receiving home e-mail—just like Internet e-mail. The family can share a calendar to keep track of important events, birthdays, and other family happenings. And when someone is on the road, or away at school, the family connection can be maintained.

See Also

You'll learn how to communicate over the network in Chapter 11.

Playing Family Games

The family that plays together, goes the old saying, stays together. And that's another strong case for networking. Play is a form of communication, and families can actually use computer games to enhance their quality time together. Kids love to play action games on their computer, while parents may enjoy more cerebral pastimes like bridge, hearts, or chess.

Setting Up for Multiplayer Gaming

On a network, family members can go head-to-head in games of all sorts, many of them inexpensive or even free. Each member of the family can be sitting at a different computer, but interacting in a virtual environment in which you can see each other, compete against each other, or even cooperate with each other against a common foe. You can all be racing on the same track or moving around some science fiction landscape trying to mutually solve a puzzle.

Games on the network can also keep score for you automatically, so there's no arguing over who's right or wrong, who shot first, or who's cheating. Many games will even remember the score, enabling you to pause and pick up later on where you left off, or keep a running record for everyone to see.

The Bottom Line

Through interactive game playing, the entire family can share adventures without leaving the house. You'll draw the family closer together even when you're all playing in different rooms. You can compete individually or in teams, and you can have more than one game going if not everyone wants to play the same one.

See Also

You'll learn how to play games on the network in Chapter 13.

Making It Educational

By networking your computers, you'll also learn more about computers and software. You'll become familiar with the role networks play in society because all networks, large and small, enjoy the same benefits, but just on different levels. If you have children who are old enough, let them share in the process of setting up the network. They can help make decisions, run wires, even help install software. The experience will give them an edge in school and maybe even toward a career.

One way or another, networking your home computers is a time-saver, a money-saver, and just a smart thing to do. In the following chapters, you'll learn how to design, install, and use a home network, but first, you'll learn how to accomplish some basic networking tasks without having to set up a network.

Chapter 2

Getting Connected Without a Network

Now that you're all hyped up about networking, here's a small surprise: sometimes you may not need a network at all. Perhaps you are interested in sharing a printer, and occasionally transferring some files between computers, but you don't want to play games or send and receive e-mail among the family. Maybe you'd rather communicate in person, the old-fashioned way. While you'd be missing out on the many other benefits of using a network, you can still share printers and files, which is the subject of this chapter.

When Sharing a Printer Is Enough

If you're considering sharing a printer, take a look at the distance between the computers and the printer. If they are all located in the same room, sharing the printer will be a piece of cake. You won't need to purchase expensive devices that help you share printers and you won't need to run wires from room to room.

If the computers and printers are in different rooms, your options will be a bit trickier and more costly. Printer cable is thick and not that easy to fish through walls or hide along the baseboard. In addition, because a standard printer cable should not be more than 15 feet long (any longer and the signals fade on their way to the printer), you'll need to buy extra hardware if the devices you're linking are far apart.

See Also

If the computer and printer are far apart, see "Extending Your Reach," on page 26.

Using Printer Switches

When two computers and a printer are near each other, the easiest way to share the printer is with a printer switch. The least expensive type is a manual switch box with a knob that you turn by hand. As shown in Figure 2-1, you connect a cable from one computer to the A side of the switch, and a second cable from the other computer to the B side of the switch. You then connect a printer cable from the printer to the printer connection on the switch. The printer connection is usually labeled *common* because it is connected to the device shared by the two computers.

Figure 2-1.
You can connect two computers and a printer with a switch box.

When the knob is in the A position, the job you're printing flows from the A computer, through the box, and into the printer. When the knob is in the B position, the job flows from the B computer, through the switch, and into the printer. Some switch boxes can link three, four, or more computers to the same printer.

There are a few drawbacks to manual switches, however. You must locate the switch so that users at both computers can reach it easily, preferably from their chairs. In addition, if either person forgets to turn the switch before trying to print a document, assumes the document has gone through to the printer, and then exits the word processor without saving the file, the document might be lost. Although Microsoft Windows will soon tell them that there has been a problem with the printer, it might be too late to retrieve the document by then. Similarly, if you turn the switch while someone else is printing, you can cut off a print job in the middle. This can cause an error message and generate some angry stares. Wait until the printer has stopped printing completely before turning the switch.

Some people used to believe that turning a manual switch while the printer was powered on could damage some printers. This may have been the case in the early days of computers and printers, but it's no longer a concern with newer, more robust printers and switch boxes. Of course, if you worry about such things, just shut off the printer before turning the switch, and then turn the printer back on.

Finally, as printers become more sophisticated and complex, you must make sure of the quality of the electrical signals going to them. Printer cables should be labeled *bi-directional* and *IEEE 1284 compliant*. *Bi-directional* means that the cable is capable of carrying signals both to and from the printer. This allows the printer to keep the computer informed about its printing status. *IEEE 1284 compliant* means that the cable meets industry standards for quality. When you connect the cable, make sure that all connections are tight and that they can't slip off. Switch boxes not only extend the path that the signals must travel to get to the printer, they also introduce additional connections that have to be checked. Make sure to check them regularly.

On the upside, a switch box for two computers and one printer (called a 2-to-1 switch) costs less than $15. Use the existing printer cable to connect the switch box to the printer, and buy two additional cables (approximately $15 each) to run from the printer ports of the computers to the switch box. These cables have 25-pin male connections at both ends, as shown here, to fit the female connections at the back of the computer and at the switch. So for $50 or less you can share a printer between two computers.

To link your computers to a printer via a switch box, see Figure 2-2 and follow these simple steps:

1. Make sure the computers and printer are turned off.

2. Disconnect the printer cable from the computer and plug it into the "C" or "common" connection on the switch.

3. Connect either end of one of the new cables to the printer port on the back of one of the computers.

4. Connect the other end of the cable to the A connector on the back of the switch.

5. Connect one end of the other new cable to the printer port of the second computer.

6. Connect the other end of that cable to the B connector on the back of the switch.

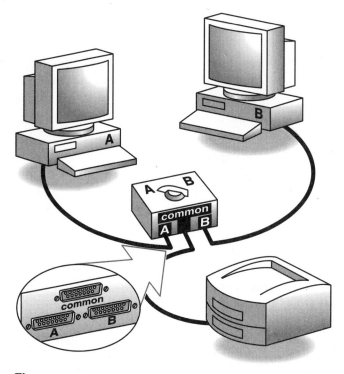

Figure 2-2.
Connecting two computers and one printer to a switch box.

You can use the same type of switch, by the way, to connect two printers (a laser printer and a color inkjet printer, for example) to one computer. You'll need to use the Add Printer Wizard in the Printers dialog box (click Start, choose Settings, and then click

Printers) to install the same printer to the same port of both computers, and then hook up the switch box as shown in Figure 2-3. With the computer and printers turned off, connect the printers to the A and B connectors on the switch box and the computer to the C connector. It's that simple. Before you print a document, select the correct printer in the application's Print dialog box and turn the switch to that printer.

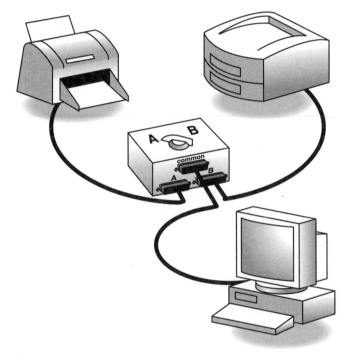

Figure 2-3.
A switch box can connect two printers to one computer.

Putting It on Automatic

Automatic switches hook up like manual switches, but there's no switch to turn. They are like a traffic officer in the middle of the intersection, managing the flow of print jobs to the printer. The switch electronically watches the incoming cables for a document that needs to be printed. If the printer is busy and a document comes in from another computer, the switch holds up its hand and says, "Wait." When the printer is free, it says, "okay, it's your turn," and sends the next print job through.

At about $50 or more, automatic switches are more expensive than manual switches. Some models can handle just two computers and one printer; others can link several computers and several printers. The JetDirect auto switch, for example, made by Hewlett-Packard, can accommodate four computers sharing a single printer. To install it, you connect a cable from each computer to one of the four ports on the switch, and then connect the common port to the printer.

You can place the switch in manual or automatic mode. In manual mode, you have to press a button on the device to change printers. In automatic mode, however, the switch constantly scans the incoming lines for activity to the printer. It then sends the documents to the printer in the order they are received.

The same switch can be used to connect up to four different devices, such as a printer, a scanner, and a Zip drive, to one computer's printer port. In this configuration, you connect a device to each of the four ports on the switch, and then connect your computer to the common port on the switch.

When you use a switch to connect several devices to one computer, it's useful to be able to specify which device you want to use from within Windows. The JetDirect auto switch comes with the software shown here.

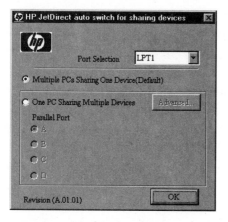

With this software, you can specify whether you're sharing one device among multiple computers or several devices on one computer. If you select One PC Sharing Multiple Devices, you can click Advanced and specify the device that is connected to each port.

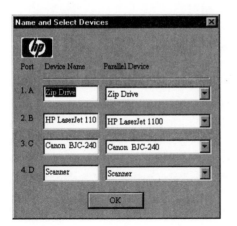

To use a device, select it by clicking the JetDirect icon on the Windows taskbar.

Note

When you add a Zip drive to the switch, you must connect it to port A, so that Windows will be able to detect it properly.

We Need a Buffer Here

Not all automatic switches are created equal. Some of the inexpensive models lack a key feature that can prevent traffic tie-ups. Let's say that Tom sends a document to the printer first. While it is being transmitted and printed, you try to print a document from your computer. Because the printer is busy, your job is held up, waiting in line until the printer is free. This means that until Tom's job is printed and yours begins, you might not be able to exit the application you are using. You'll have the same trouble if you use a switch to connect several devices to one computer. While a job is being printed, for example, you won't be able to access the Zip drive or scan a document using other devices connected to the switch.

The solution is a *buffer*. This is simply a memory-containing device installed between the computer and the printer. Now, as Tom's job prints, your document is fed directly into the buffer's memory. As far as your computer is concerned, the document is off and printed, so you can go on to other work. When Tom's job is done, your document is printed from the buffer's memory.

Some automatic switches come with their own built-in buffers, or you can purchase separate buffer devices that connect between the switch and the printer.

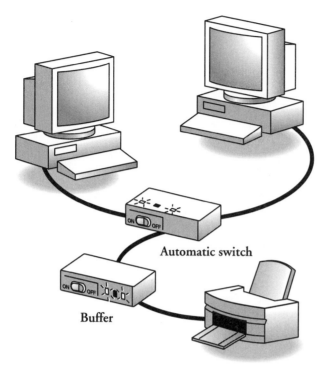

Automatic switch

Buffer

Extending Your Reach

No one wants to get up and walk into another room to flick a manual switch. Fortunately, there's a special type of automatic switch designed for use with computers that are far apart or in separate rooms. The most common model employs transmitters that are plugged into the printer port of each computer and a receiver that plugs into the printer's parallel port. The transmitters and receiver are connected with regular telephone cable. Such devices can link up to 30 computers, with a total distance between them of 2000 feet.

Note

Some of these systems also let you print from a computer's serial port to a parallel printer.

If you need to extend the distance between just a single computer and a printer, install a transmitter on the computer's printer port and connect a receiver to the printer or to one side of a switch, as shown in Figure 2-4. The printer signals can go a lot farther on the telephone cable used to connect the transmitter and receiver than they can on a regular printer cable. To add another computer to the configuration, just buy another transmitter.

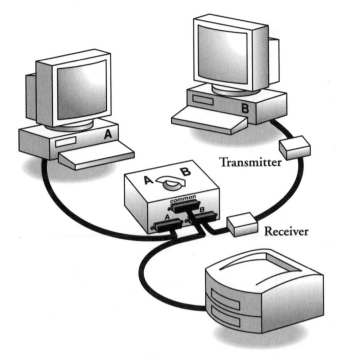

Figure 2-4.
Extending the distance to a switch.

There are also devices that enhance the signals from your computer so that you can link it to a printer up to 50 feet away, using standard printer cable. Most of these devices plug into the computer's printer port to amplify the signal before it is transmitted down the printer cable.

Making a Direct Connection

One great benefit of networking is the capability it gives you to transfer files between two computers. But if you only need to do this occasionally and the two computers are close to each other, there's another way to hook up your computers and save some money in the process. Both Windows 95 and Windows 98 let you connect two computers with one simple cable. That's why it's called a *direct cable connection*. With this system, you can transfer files between two non-networked computers or between a networked and a non-networked computer.

One Simple Cable Is All It Takes

To set up a direct cable connection you need a cable, of course. Windows can use any of four types of cables:

- A null modem serial cable
- An Extended Capabilities Port (ECP) parallel cable
- A Universal Cable Module (UCM) parallel cable
- A Standard or Basic 4-bit parallel cable

Of these four options, the Extended Capabilities Port (ECP) parallel cable is probably your best bet. Information flows faster though parallel cables than through serial cables, and the ECP cable is cheaper and easier to find than the UCM cable. The Standard or Basic 4-bit parallel cable was popular in the past, but it's no longer easily available, and it's slower than the ECP cable anyway.

Cables used for a direct cable connection have the same type of connection on both ends, because they are going into the same plug on both computers. If there's a cable connecting your parallel port to a switch box, you can try that cable, in a pinch, for a direct cable connection; but it probably won't work. The cable may look like the one you need, but it might not be able to handle the transfer of files.

When you buy the cable at the computer store, ask for "a parallel cable to use with a direct cable connection in Windows." You'll probably be given LapLink cables, named after the program that's a popular alternative to a direct cable connection.

Note

If the store doesn't have a cable for a direct cable connection, and you have to transfer files right away, consider buying a file transfer program, such as LapLink, which comes with its own cable. We'll look at such options in "Another Way to Share Files and Printers," on page 39.

Installing the Free Software

Once you have the cable, the software you need is free and built into Windows 95 and Windows 98. Follow these steps to make sure that the software has been installed:

1. Click Start on the Windows taskbar.
2. Point to Programs, and then point to Accessories on the Programs submenu.

3. In Windows 95, look for Direct Cable Connection just under the Accessories menu. In Windows 98, point to Communications on the Accessories submenu.

Do you see Direct Cable Connection on the menu that appears? If you do, skip ahead to "Choosing a Protocol," on the next page. If you do not see Direct Cable Connection, you'll have to add it. You may need your Windows CD to do this, so make sure you know where it is, and then follow these steps:

1. Click Start, point to Settings, and then click Control Panel on the Settings submenu.

2. In the Control Panel window, double-click Add/Remove Programs.

3. Click the Windows Setup tab in the Add/Remove Programs dialog box.

4. On the Windows Setup tab, shown in Figure 2-5, click the word "Communications," but do not click the check box next to Communications or you will remove the check mark.

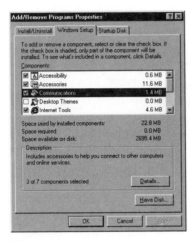

Figure 2-5.
Add Direct Cable Connection using the Add/Remove Programs Properties dialog box.

5. Click the Details button.

6. Click to select the check box next to Direct Cable Connection as shown here.

Components:	
☑ 📠 Dial-Up Networking	1.2 MB
☑ 📠 Dial-Up Server	0.1 MB
☑ ⌨ Direct Cable Connection	0.3 MB
☐ 🖧 HyperTerminal	0.0 MB
☐ 🖧 Microsoft Chat 2.1	0.0 MB

7. Click OK to close the Communications dialog box.

8. Click OK to close the Add/Remove Programs dialog box.

Here is where you may need your Windows CD. On some computers, the files that Windows needs in order to add more components are stored on the hard disk. If so, direct cable connection will be installed and you're ready for the next stage. If the files are not on your hard disk, you'll be asked to insert the Windows CD. Put the CD in the drive and click OK. The direct cable connection feature will then be installed.

Choosing a Protocol

In order for two people to communicate, they must know the same language, or be awfully good at charades. The same goes for computers, but with computers we call the shared language a *protocol*. The two computers use the same protocol to be able to understand what the other is saying.

There are a lot of different protocols, but for home networking, only three are important: TCP/IP, IPX, and NetBEUI (pronounced net-buoy). IPX is the one you need for a direct cable connection, but it's best to make sure all three protocols are installed in Windows, just in case you need them.

If you're running Windows 98, here's how to see whether the protocols are on your computer and how to install them if you need to.

1. Click Start, point to Settings, and then click Control Panel on the Settings submenu.

2. In the Control Panel window, double-click Network.

On the Configuration tab of the Network dialog box, shown in Figure 2-6, look for the big three—TCP/IP, IPX, and NetBEUI. If any of them are not listed, you'll have to add them. Follow these steps to add a protocol:

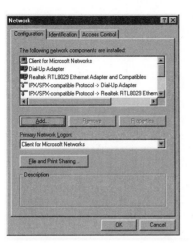

Figure 2-6.

The network components list shows the protocols that are installed.

1. In the Network dialog box, click Add to see this dialog box.

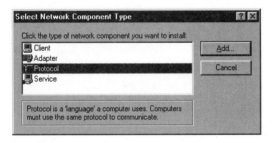

2. In the Select Network Component Type dialog box, click Protocol, and then click Add.

3. Click Microsoft in the list of manufacturers to see the options shown in Figure 2-7, on the next page.

4. In the Network Protocols list, select the protocol you want to add, and then click OK.

5. Repeat steps 1 through 4 to add the other two protocols.

6. When you're done, click OK to close the Network dialog box. A message tells you that you must restart your computer for these new additions to work.

7. Click OK to restart the computer.

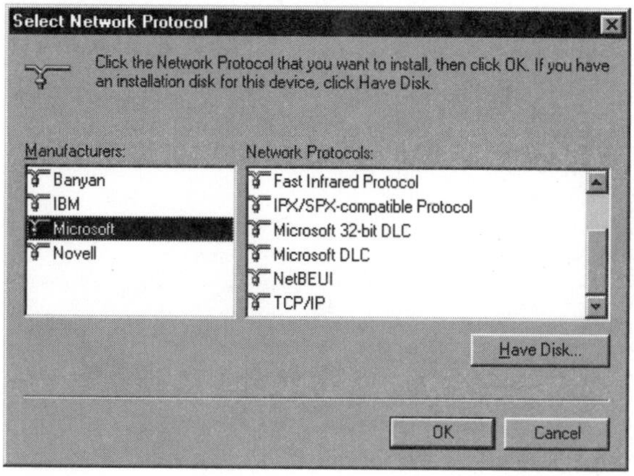

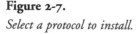

Figure 2-7.

Select a protocol to install.

Setting Up a Direct Cable Connection

Now that the protocols you need are installed, you're ready to set up a direct cable connection. With the two computers turned off, plug in the connecting cable. If you're using a parallel cable, make sure the printer is off, remove the printer cable, and then plug the new cable into the printer port. If your cable is a serial cable, plug it into the computer's serial or COM port.

Now that the hardware is set up, you need to deal with the software end of things. First you have to choose one computer to be the host and the other to be the client. The host machine contains the information you want to get to. The client is the computer you will use to access the information.

After you've chosen a host computer, you need to allow its files and folders to be shared. This means that other users can view and work with them over a network and over the cable connection.

You can provide access to your entire hard drive or just to selected folders. Sharing your entire drive in one step makes it easy for other users to get to the files they need. If you're worried about security, you can limit another user's access to just reading and copying files but not changing or deleting them. If you want to keep another user from even seeing certain folders on your disk, it's possible to share only those folders you do want to make available.

To allow access to the entire drive on the host, follow these steps:

1. Double-click My Computer on the desktop.

2. Right-click the C disk.

3. Click Sharing on the shortcut menu to open the Properties dialog box shown in Figure 2-8.

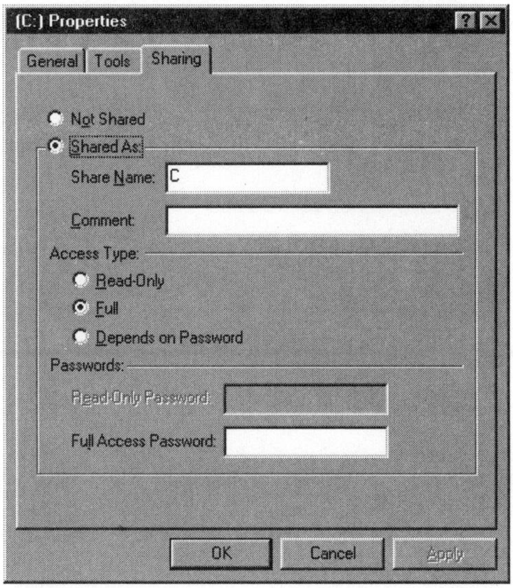

Figure 2-8.
You can change how disks and folders are shared on the Sharing tab of the Properties dialog box.

4. On the Sharing tab of the Properties dialog box, click Shared As.

5. You can leave the Share Name as is, or replace it with another name that will be seen by others connecting to your computer.

6. In the Access Type section of the dialog box, choose the type of access you want to offer to others.

- **Read-Only** means that the person on the guest computer can copy and look at information on the host but not delete or change the information. The person on the guest computer cannot, for example, add a file to the host computer.

- **Full** means that the person on the guest computer can do anything at all to the information on the host, including adding, deleting, or editing files.

- **Depends On Password** determines the level of access according to the password the guest enters, either a read-only or a full access password.

7. Depending on the type of access you've chosen, enter a Read-Only password, a Full Access password, or both. If you don't want to require a password, you can leave these fields blank.

8. Click OK.

9. If you entered a password, a dialog box opens asking you to confirm it. Reenter the password, and then click OK.

A small hand attached to the drive icon indicates that the drive is shared.

(C:)

Note

You can also choose to share only specific folders. Right-click a folder in My Computer, choose Sharing, and then set the folder's sharing properties in the Properties dialog box.

Now start direct cable connection on the host computer.

1. Click Start, point to Programs, and then point to Accessories on the Program submenu.

2. In Windows 95, click Direct Cable Connection. In Windows 98, point to Communications and then click Direct Cable Connection on the Communications submenu.

    If this is the first time you are running a direct cable connection, you'll see the dialog box in Figure 2-9.

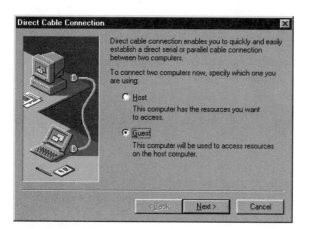

Figure 2-9.
Choose whether the computer you are using is a host or guest.

3. Click Host and then click Next.

4. In the Direct Cable Connection dialog box, shown in Figure 2-10, select the port you are using, and then click Next.

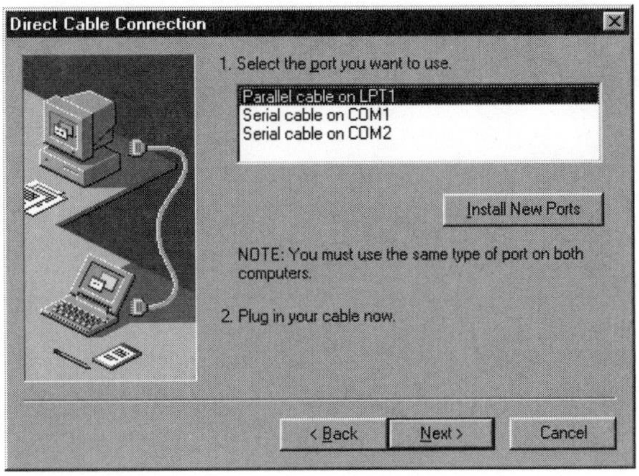

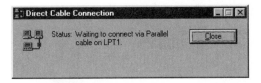

Figure 2-10.
Select the port you are using.

5. If you want to require the person using the guest computer to enter a password, select the check box labeled Use Password Protection, and then click Set Password. In the next dialog box, enter the password in both fields and click OK.

6. Click Finish.
   A message reports that the host computer is waiting for the guest computer to connect.

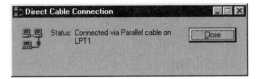

7. Now follow the same procedure on the guest computer, but select Guest in the first dialog box rather than Host.

   When you click Finish, the machines connect. On both machines, you see messages that they are verifying the user name and password. Then the guest computer reports that it is looking for shared folders. Finally, the host computer shows a message, like this, to indicate that both computers are connected.

The next time you start a direct cable connection on the Host, you'll see the dialog box shown in Figure 2-11. Click Listen on the Host and click Connect on the Guest.

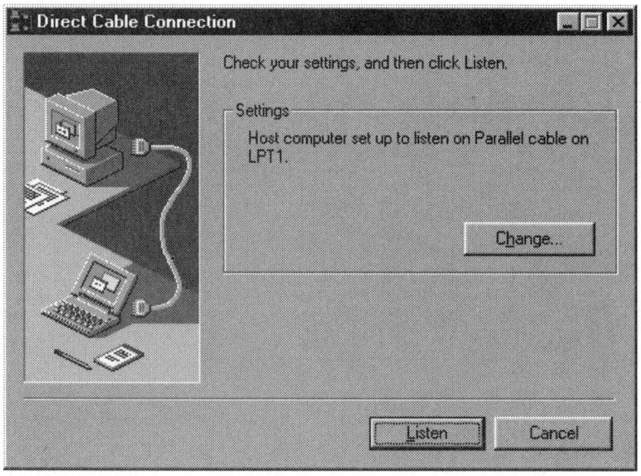

Figure 2-11.
Starting direct cable connection a second time.

Using Direct Cable Connection

After you connect the host and guest computers, the guest computer displays a dialog box showing the shared resources on the host, as shown in Figure 2-12. The person using the guest computer can then open any shared folder to access its files, and move or copy files between the two computers using the drag-and-drop method.

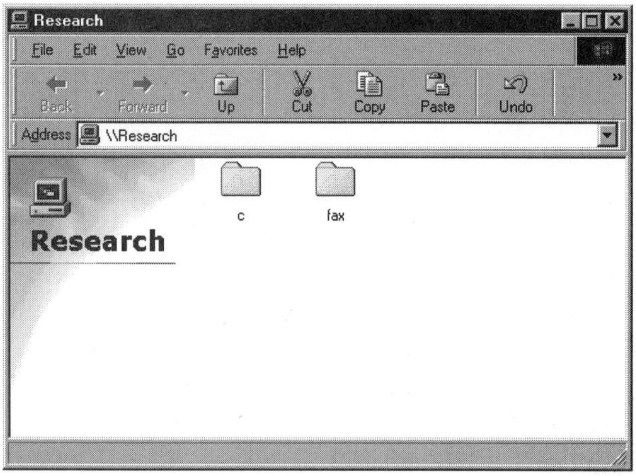

Figure 2-12.
The shared resources on the host computer are visible on the guest computer.

The host computer must leave the Direct Cable Connection dialog box open on the screen. Closing this dialog box stops the connection and causes the guest to receive the error message shown in Figure 2-13.

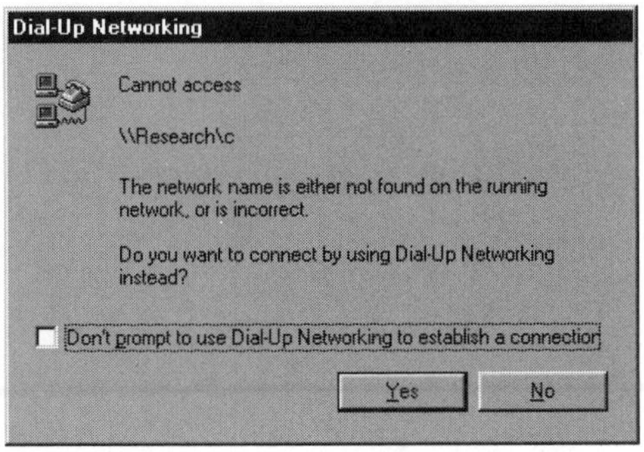

Figure 2-13.
Windows shows an error message if you break a direct cable connection.

Other Software for Direct Connections

With a direct cable connection, one computer must act as the host and the other as the guest. Let's say, however, that you want to change which computer controls the flow of information. The only way to reverse the computers' roles is to break the connection between them and then reconnect.

If you want to switch the host and guest computers on the fly, you might want to consider one of the other programs designed to transfer files directly between two computers via a cable connection. Many of these programs are available free or at low cost over the Internet, so you can download them to your computer and try them out.

FastLynx, for example, can monitor more than one port for a connection with another machine also running FastLynx. This means that you could actually connect two or more computers to yours at the same time. One might be connected to the parallel port, the other to the serial port.

Once installed and connected, FastLynx displays the contents of both machines on a split window with two panes, as shown in Figure 2-14, on the next page. You can transfer files between machines simply by dragging them from one pane to the other.

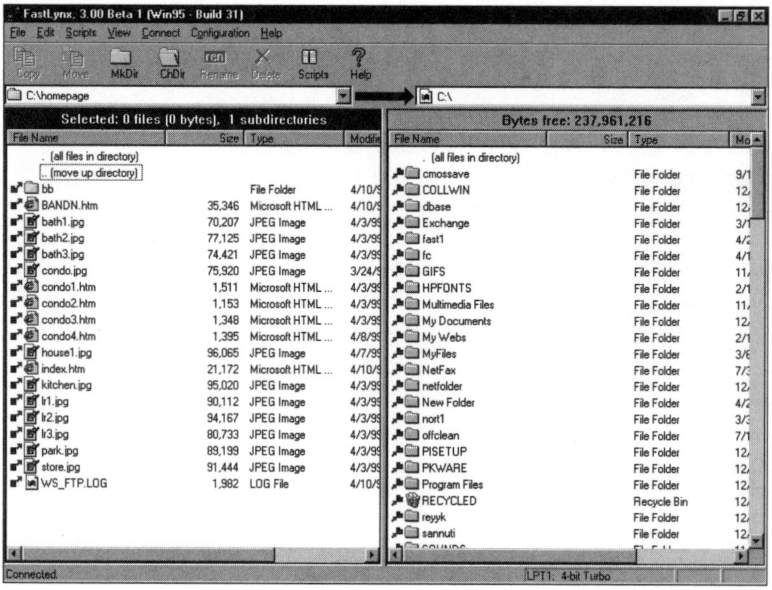

Figure 2-14.
Move and copy files in any direction with FastLynx.

Note

You can get more information about FastLynx at *http://www.sewelld.com/*

Network Paths

You probably know about the convention used to designate the location of a file, called its *path*. For example, your hard drive is C:, the Windows folder is C:\Windows, and the System subfolder is C:\Windows\System.

The path to resources on a network or over a direct cable connection uses a different syntax called the universal naming convention (UNC). Start the UNC with two back-slashes (\\) followed by the name of the computer, as in \\Joe. To access a specific drive or folder on the remote computer, add the path to the UNC, as in \\Joe\C\Budget.

Another Way to Share Files and Printers

So far in this chapter, you've learned how to share printers and transfer files without a network. Here's yet another way to accomplish these tasks without a network.

An entire class of programs lets you remotely control one computer from another. You connect the computers through a serial, parallel, or USB cable, or through a telephone line and modem. Once the connection is made, you can transfer files and print documents on a printer linked to either computer. Some of these programs also let you remotely control another computer by connecting to it via the Internet.

See Also

We'll look at using remote control programs to share information in a network when you're away from home in Chapter 15, "Networking for Road Warriors," page 295.

Using remote control means that you can sit at your system and actually operate another computer you are connected to. Your keyboard and mouse control the other computer, and you see on your screen what appears on the other computer's screen.

Programs that provide these capabilities include:

- Carbon Copy
- Close-Up
- CoSession Remote
- LapLink
- PCAnywhere
- Rapid Remote
- ReachOut
- Remote Desktop
- Remotely Possible
- Timbuktu

As an example of a remote control program, let's take a look at LapLink Professional, shown in Figure 2-15, on the next page.

Figure 2-15.
LapLink Professional allows you to share files and printers remotely.

Your first task with Laplink, and similar programs, is to designate how the computers are to be connected. It's possible to enable more than one port so that you can connect to your computer from another computer in the home and dial in to your computer from the road with a laptop. In Laplink, you select Port Setup from the Options menu to open the Port Setup dialog box shown here.

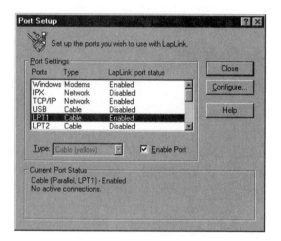

To enable the ports you want, select each one in the Port Settings list, and then select the Enable Port check box.

As with direct cable connection, you must have the proper cable to make the link work. In the Port Setup dialog box, the entry in the Type field shows the type of LapLink cable required. To connect the parallel (printer) ports of two computers, for example, use the yellow cable that comes with LapLink. If you later have problems connecting through the port, you can open the Port Setup dialog box again, choose the port, and click the Configure button to fine-tune how the port works.

Note

LapLink and some of the other file transfer programs come complete with the appropriate cables for connecting computers.

By default, each time LapLink makes a connection between two computers, it lets you copy files between them. You can choose other services, listed below, by selecting Connect Options from the LapLink Options menu and then clicking the Connect tab in the Options dialog box.

- **Remote Control** lets you control the other computer from yours.

- **Print Redirection** lets you print a document from your computer to the printer attached to the remote machine and from the remote machine to the printer attached to your computer.

- **Text Chat** lets you exchange messages with the person using the remote computer, just as you would in a chat room on line. In fact, a chat window pops up on your screen automatically whenever the remote user sends a message, as shown in Figure 2-16.

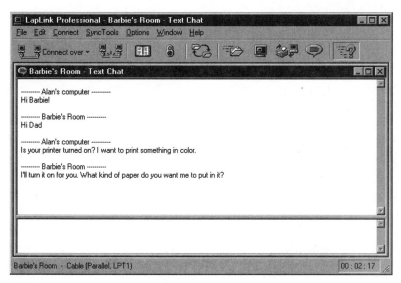

Figure 2-16.
LapLink's Text Chat feature lets you exchange typed messages between computers.

When you're ready to make the connection, start LapLink on both computers. The program automatically detects the connection you've established with the other computer and displays the disks, folders and files of your computer and the remote computer side by side, as shown in Figure 2-17.

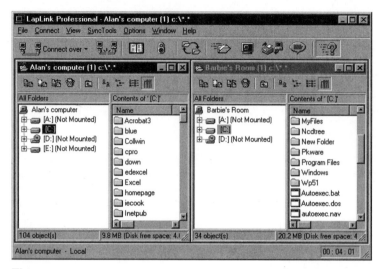

Figure 2-17.
LapLink displays the disks, folders, and files on both computers.

If Laplink is unable to detect the connection automatically, you may need to click the Connect menu and choose Connect Over Cable. This opens the Connect Over Cable dialog box, shown below, in which you choose the remote computer to which you want to connect and the combination of services that you want available: File Transfer, Remote Control, Print Redirection, and Text Chat.

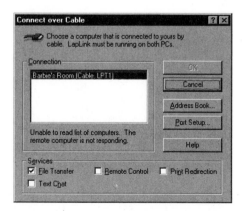

To transfer a file, open the folder on either computer containing the file as you would in Windows Explorer, and then drag the file to a folder on the other computer. In addition to moving and copying files, you can synchronize them using a feature called Xchange Agent. This feature keeps track of changes to files and makes sure that both computers have the most recent version by automatically copying that version to both computers.

Going Wireless with Infrared

Another way to transfer files among laptops is to connect them through their infrared ports. This process is easy because laptops can be connected without wires, and the software you need is built into Windows.

Follow these steps to make sure that infrared communication has been enabled on both computers:

1. Double-click to open the Windows Control Panel and double-click the Infrared icon.

2. In the Infrared dialog box, click the Options tab, shown in Figure 2-18.

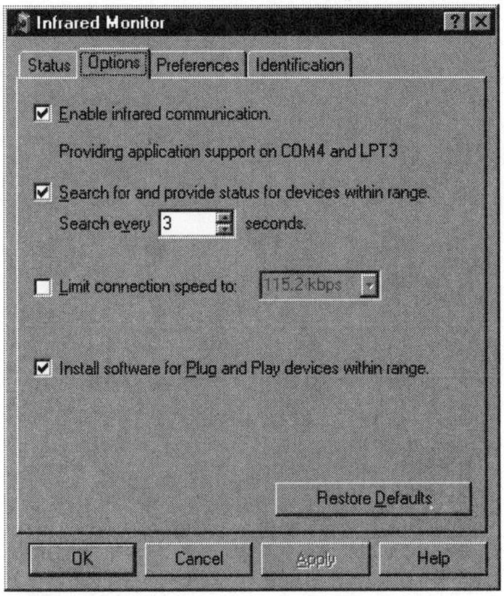

Figure 2-18.
Enabling infrared communication.

3. If the Enable Infrared Communication check box is not selected, click it now.

4. Click OK.

5. Repeat the procedure on the other laptop to enable infrared communication.

When you are ready to transfer a file between two computers connected by infrared, follow these steps:

1. Position the computers so their infrared ports are facing each other.

2. On the computer containing the file you want to transfer, double-click My Computer on the Windows desktop and double-click the Infrared Recipient icon, shown here.

Infrared
Recipient ...

Windows opens the Infrared Transfer dialog box, shown in Figure 2-19.

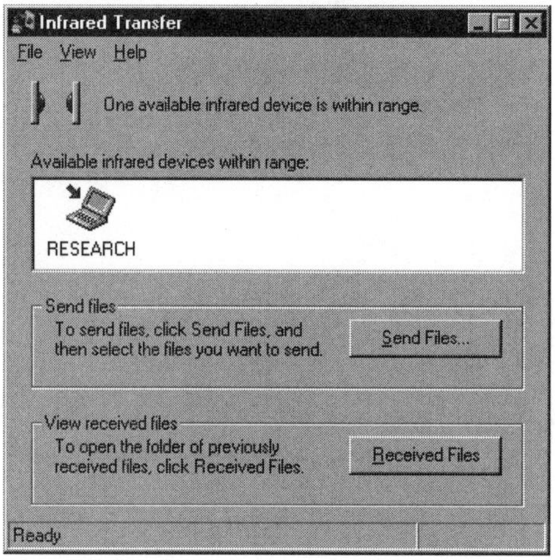

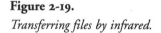

Figure 2-19.
Transferring files by infrared.

3. If more than one computer is shown in the box, click the one to which you want to send the file.

4. Click the Send Files button, select the file you want to send, and then click Open. The file will be transferred to the other computer and saved to a folder named My Received Files.

On the other computer, you can click Received Files in the Infrared Transfer dialog box to see which files have been sent to that computer by infrared.

In this chapter, you learned a number of ways to share files and printers, even when your computers are not connected through a network. You can share printers with an inexpensive manual switch box or with an automatic switch. You can share files using the software built into Windows, and with some additional software and hardware, you can share both printers and files at the same time.

In the next chapter, we'll return to the subject of networks. You'll learn how to get started when you want to do more than just share a printer and transfer an occasional file. You will learn about the types of networks you can set up and the hardware and software you'll need to connect your home computers in a network.

Chapter 3

Planning a Network

You know it's time to set up a network when just sharing a printer or transferring an occasional file doesn't cut it anymore. Networking doesn't have to be complex or expensive; you won't have to learn the history of networking or study arcane subjects such as network layers. But before you run down to the computer store and part with your hard-earned cash, it's a good idea to take the time to make some basic decisions about your networking needs.

This chapter will help you decide on the type of network you want and how best to connect your computers. You'll learn the difference between a *peer-to-peer* network and a *client-server* network, and you'll learn about four ways to move information between the computers on the network. But first, here's a little network preamble.

A Little Network Preamble

Before we look at ways to connect computers, you need to know about an important piece of hardware called the network interface card, or NIC, for short.

In order to connect to a network, a computer needs a NIC to handle the flow of information to and from the network. Some computers come with the NIC already built in, but most don't, so you'll have to order one when you buy your computer or add one afterward.

Most NICs fit inside a computer; others come on PC cards that plug into laptops. There are also external devices that perform the same function as a NIC, but connect to a computer's USB, parallel, or serial port, as shown in Figure 3-1, on the next page. As you'll learn later on, there are even special NICs for wireless networks and for networks that use the telephone and electrical lines in your home to transfer information between computers.

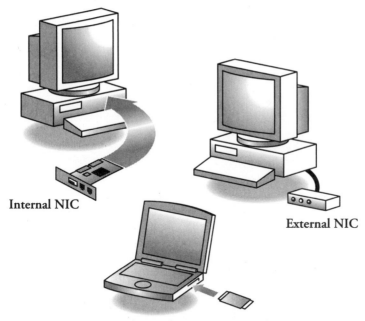

Internal NIC

External NIC

Network Interface on a PC card

Figure 3-1.
Network interfaces can be internal, external, or on a PC card.

Because the type of NIC you'll need depends on how you want to connect your computers, read the rest of this chapter before you go out and buy one.

Not every NIC on your network needs to be made by the same company or even installed the same way. You can use internal NICs on some computers, devices that connect to the USB ports on others, and a NIC on a PC card for a laptop. But in order for the computers to be linked in a network, they all must have NICs with the same type of connectors.

Deciding on Network Control

One of the first decisions you have to make when you're deciding how to set up your network is whether or not to give someone control of it. In one type of setup, called the *client-server network*, a single computer controls access to the network and serves as a central storage area for files and information. But before you decide to go this route, consider these points:

- Putting someone in charge of your network means spending more money on additional computer resources and on software that doesn't come free.

- Putting someone in charge dramatically increases the complexity of creating a network and the likelihood that you'll run into trouble.

It certainly sounds like there's a downside to this option, so before you make your choice, consider the alternative.

Setting Up a Level Playing Field

When no single computer acts as the controller, you have a *peer-to-peer network*. This means that everyone on the network is equal—all are peers. Any computer on the network can communicate with any other computer on an equal basis. It also means that information flows directly between two computers without being controlled by any other, as shown in Figure 3-2.

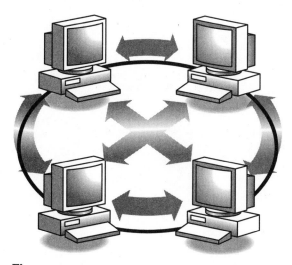

Figure 3-2.
Computers on a peer-to-peer network communicate with each other directly.

A peer-to-peer network, however, does not eliminate all forms of control. Each person on the network can use a password to protect files and folders. You don't have to let people share your files or use your printer or modem. How other people can access your computer is entirely up to you. In fact, you can create a password that controls who has access to your computer, which files they can access, and how they can use them.

For example, you can allow only certain folders to be shared. In fact, to protect critical Microsoft Windows files, you'd always want to prevent the Windows folder from being shared. You can also grant *read-only* rights to a folder. This means that others on the network can look at a file in a shared folder on your computer and copy it to their computers, but they won't be able to change or delete it.

It's possible, too, to grant full access, which means that everyone on the network can read, change, and delete files just as you can. Grant full access only to people you really trust and only to those folders that you want to be totally accessible.

A peer-to-peer network can also have an e-mail system. Your family will be able to send and receive e-mail within the network, just as they can on the Internet. But one person has to set up the e-mail system and control who has access to it.

In a peer-to-peer network, if any one computer is down—is turned off or not working—everyone else on the network can still communicate. In Figure 3-3, for example, even though two of the four networked computers are turned off, the other two computers can still share files and printers. The printers attached to computers that are off won't be available to others on the network, but you'll still be able to use the files and resources of those computers that are on.

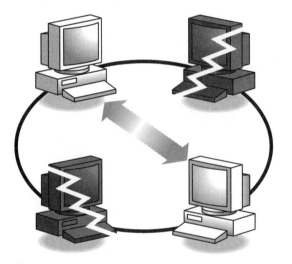

Figure 3-3.
Peer-to-peer networked computers can still communicate when other computers are turned off.

Of course, to use a printer connected to any computer on the network, the computer and printer must be turned on and working properly. Some computers, especially laptops, have a suspend state. After a certain period of inactivity, they save information about all open programs on their hard disk and turn off automatically. When you later turn the computer back on, the screen appears exactly as it was. If a computer on the network goes into suspend, its resources will not be available. Other computers have an energy-saving feature that turns off only the display or the disk drive after a period of inactivity. The resources of such computers may also be unavailable when they go into energy-saving mode. Because there are so many different kinds of computers, you'll have to experiment to see how a particular computer reacts on your network.

A peer-to-peer network has no central storage location for everyone's files. If you're looking for a file that's not on your machine, you'll need to know where it is on the network or search all of the computers on the network to locate the file. And if the computer that has the file is turned off, you're out of luck. You'll have to wait until it's back on to get to the file.

Still, the advantages of peer-to-peer networks—they're inexpensive and easy to set up, run, and maintain—clearly outweigh the disadvantages, particularly for home computers.

Putting Someone in Charge

As you've seen, when you want tighter control over a network, the solution is a *client-server* network. The server is a single computer equipped with special software that supervises everything on the network. The clients are the computers that connect to the server. Communication among the clients must go through the server, as shown in Figure 3-4.

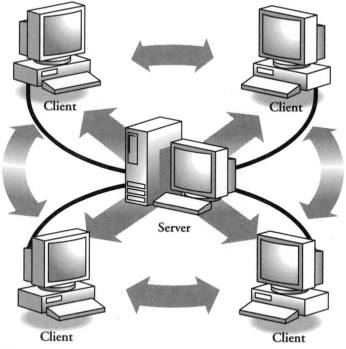

Figure 3-4.
Client computers connect through a server in a client-server network.

You'll need either Windows NT or Windows 2000 to create a client-server network. The server can't use Windows 95, Windows 98, or Windows 98 Second Edition, although the clients can. Windows NT and Windows 2000 also come in two flavors—server and workstation. To set up a client-server network, you'll need the more expensive server version of the program, which is never given away free with a new computer.

In most client-server networks in large offices, the server computer is usually dedicated to the task of being the server and is not used as a regular workstation for everyday jobs. The tasks the server has to do, and the information stored in it, are just too important to take a chance on. If the server is down, the network is down and none of the computers can communicate, as shown in Figure 3-5.

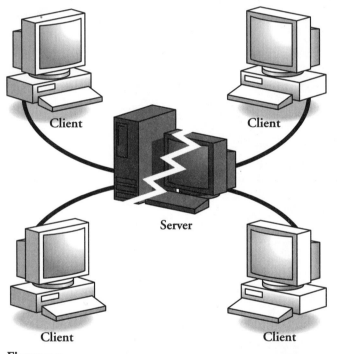

Figure 3-5.
When the server is down, the entire network goes down with it.

The server computer doesn't have to be dedicated, however, especially in a small home office network. You can still use it as a workstation for ordinary tasks, but it's not the best idea. Server software is much more complex than workstation software and requires more effort and patience to keep it running. It also may not include the software needed to run scanners and other devices. On the other hand, operating a Windows 95 or Windows 98 client computer on a client-server network is a piece of cake. You pretty much just turn it on and start working.

A client-server network offers a number of advantages in addition to control. For example, the server can act as a central storage location that everyone on the network can reach. Because the server is always on, you can use it to store graphics, downloaded files from the Internet, and other documents that you want everyone to share. The files are always available and accessible to everyone.

It's also possible to load and run applications from the server instead of installing them on every computer. This way, you can be sure that everyone on the network is using the same programs and can easily share files. When you want to update a program, from version 6 to version 7, for example, you only need to install the update on one machine.

And finally, the server can act as a central message center for e-mail and discussions. As with an Internet newsgroup or bulletin board, you can leave messages on the server for everyone else on the network to see and respond to, as shown in Figure 3-6.

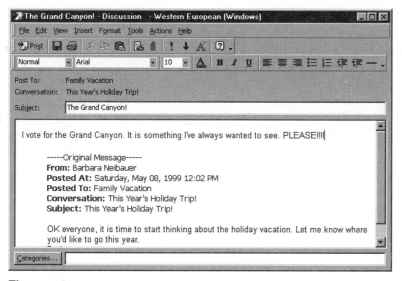

Figure 3-6.
The server computer can also be used as an e-mail message center.

A client-server network offers many advantages to the business user. But for the average home network, the two major disadvantages of the client-server set-up—cost and complexity—usually outweigh the advantages. For this reason, we'll leave the client-server option to large businesses and concentrate in this book on peer-to-peer networks using Windows 98 or Windows 95.

Deciding on the Connection

Your next decision is how to connect the computers so that information can flow between them. Your choice depends on several factors:

- The number of computers
- The distance between them
- The speed you want
- How much work you want to do
- How much money you want to spend

In this chapter, we'll briefly look at four different types of network connections and describe the benefits and drawbacks of each:

- Home phone line
- Home power line
- Network cable
- Wireless

Table 3-1 summarizes the major differences among them.

Table 3-1. **Comparing Network Connections**

Network connection	The good	The bad	The ugly
Home phone line	Requires no cables; plugs into existing telephone wiring	Requires a phone jack in rooms in which you want to connect to the network	Much slower than network cable
Home power line	Requires no cables; plugs into a wall outlet	Slower than network cable	May be subject to electrical interference, which can break contact between network computers and result in data loss
Network cable	The cheapest, fastest type of network connection	Requires running cable between computers	May require running cable through walls, ceilings, and floors; extra jacks and special hardware may also be needed

(continued)

Table 3-1. *(continued)*

Network connection	The good	The bad	The ugly
Wireless	Requires no cables; "broadcasts" network over the air	May be subject to interference from large electrical appliances; computers may have to be moved to improve performance	Generally much more expensive and slower than network cable

Connecting with Cables

Most networks are connected with cables, which transmit information faster than any other type of network connection. As long as the cables are connected, there is very little that can interfere with the flow of information. In home networks, information can travel through the cables at speeds of 10 million bits per second (Mbps) to 100 million bits per second, depending on the speed of the NIC.

These numbers might not mean too much to you unless you've waited on line for a file to download. The fastest telephone modems today can download files at about 53,000 bps, if you have a great phone line. A file that takes 10 minutes to download from the Internet takes only a few seconds to transfer from computer to computer on a network.

The problem with cable is that you have to physically run it to each computer. This is not a problem if the computers are in the same or adjacent rooms and you don't mind drilling a hole in the wall. But when your computers are spread throughout the house, running cable can be a problem, unless

- You're lucky enough to find ways to run the cable without having to pass through too many walls

- You're building a new house

Types of Cable

The two most common types of cable are twisted pair, also known as 10BaseT cable (named for its maximum speed of 10 Mbps), and 10Base2 Thin Ethernet coaxial cable. A network whose computers are connected with either of these types of cable is known as an *Ethernet* network.

Twisted pair cable looks like telephone cable on steroids. It's a thick round cable with connectors that look like pumped up telephone connectors, as shown in Figure 3-7. Twisted pair connectors, called RJ-45 connectors, and telephone connectors, called RJ-11 connectors, cannot be used interchangeably.

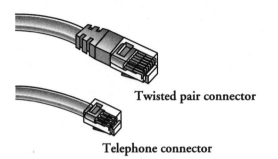

Twisted pair connector

Telephone connector

Figure 3-7.
Network cable connectors resemble oversized phone connectors.

Twisted pair cable comes in two types and several grades. The higher the grade, the better and more reliable the cable, but quality comes at a price. *For more about wire grades, see "Making the Grade," on page 85.*

The two types of twisted pair cables are unshielded twisted pair (UTP) and shielded twisted pair (STP). As shown in Figure 3-8, UTP cable consists of eight insulated wires, twisted together in pairs within an insulating sheath.

Figure 3-8.
Twisted pair cable contains four pairs of insulated wires that are twisted together.

STP cable is similar to UTP but has a layer of metal around the wires within the plastic sheath to shield them from extraneous household electrical signals. STP cable is more expensive than UTP, but fortunately, you don't need it for a home network unless you have some powerful appliances that may create electrical interference.

In most cases, when you wire a network with either type of twisted pair cable, all the cables must converge at a device called a *hub*, as shown in Figure 3-9. The hub acts like a traffic intersection, where all roads come together and traffic can flow in any direction. This means you have to run all of the network cables to a central location in the house, and the hub has to be turned on for any of the computers to communicate.

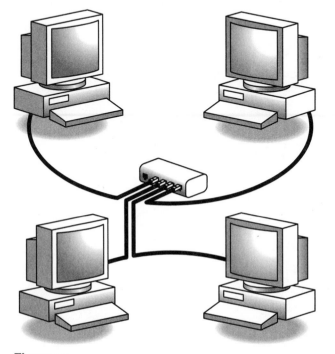

Figure 3-9.
In a network wired with twisted pair cable, all the cables converge at a hub.

See Also

If you're only networking two computers, you don't need a hub. (See "Hubless Networking," on page 86)

The 10Base2 Thin Ethernet coaxial cable is an alternative to twisted pair cable. It looks like the cable from your VCR or cable box, only a little thinner, which is why it's called Thin Ethernet or just ThinNet. As shown in Figure 3-10, on the next page, ThinNet is a round cable with a solid insulated wire at its core and a layer of braided metal under its external sheath. Although thinner than other coaxial cables, ThinNet is thicker than twisted pair cable, so it's slightly more difficult to fish through walls and lay along baseboards.

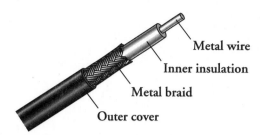

Figure 3-10.

10Base2 Thin Ethernet coaxial cable is an alternative to twisted pair cable.

A coaxial cable network does not require a hub. As shown in Figure 3-11, you simply run the cable from one NIC to another. The absence of a central hub reduces the amount of cable you need to run from room to room and between floors. You can join two lengths of coaxial cable to make a longer cable, and two lengths of coaxial cable joined with a coupler are more reliable than two lengths of twisted pair cable coupled together.

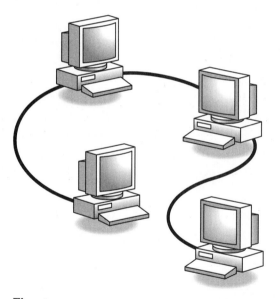

Figure 3-11.

Coaxial cable connects computers directly, without a hub.

Whichever type of wire you select, some sort of wire—either twisted pair or coaxial—is recommended over the other choices described in this chapter, as long as you can physically run the wire between computers. Wire is faster than the alternatives and can connect almost any distance in a house.

Note

You can mix twisted pair and coaxial cables in the same network, but you'll need additional hardware. See "Expanding Your Network," on page 94.

Networking over the Air

If you do not want to string cable throughout the house, consider a wireless network, called HomeRF, for Home Radio Frequency. Just like a wireless phone system, a wireless network transmits information via radio waves to other computers in the house.

Wireless systems use a special NIC that takes the information you want to send to other computers and transmits it over the air. It also receives the signals coming from other computers. In some wireless systems, the NIC connects to a transmitter/receiver installed outside of the computer. The transmitter/receiver has a little antenna that sends and picks up the signals.

Sophisticated wireless systems designed for businesses are very expensive. Home wireless networks are cheaper, but still more expensive than Ethernet. Speed is another consideration. Although wireless networks are slower than cable networks (about 2 Mbps, or just a fifth the speed of the slowest Ethernet network), they are still fast enough for most home network applications.

Wireless systems are also susceptible to interference from a variety of sources. For example, you can't have large metal objects or huge containers of water, such as fish tanks and water coolers, between computers. And then there's the distance factor. Computers on a wireless system can be no more than about 150 feet apart. This shouldn't be a problem, unless, of course, you live in a mansion or castle, but it's something else to consider.

See Also

For more on wireless systems and other alternatives to Ethernet, see Chapter 6, "Networking Without Cables," on page 99.

Networking Through Phone Lines

Your home telephone lines are yet another alternative to cable. Since you probably have phone jacks all over the house, you can network a computer from just about anywhere as long as there's a phone jack nearby.

Home phone networks, called HomePNA (for Home Phoneline Networking Alliance), require a special NIC that connects to a regular telephone jack, which the network shares with the phone line. Adapters, such as the one shown at the top of the next page, allow you to connect both a phone and a NIC to the jack.

You can use the phone to make a call and send information over the network at the same time because the network hardware operates at frequencies above the standard voice frequencies. You just can't make a phone call to connect to the Internet at the same time.

If you have more than one computer in the same room, you can usually connect their NICs with phone cables directly, as shown in Figure 3-12.

To connect a computer in a room without a phone jack, use a regular telephone extension wire to connect the computer to a networked machine in another room. Telephone wire is much easier to hide along baseboards and under rugs than twisted pair or coaxial cable.

If you need more jacks, you can install them yourself or have the telephone company do it for you. The phone company will charge you, of course, but it's easier than doing it yourself and easier and cheaper than running computer cable.

The downside of phone line networks is slow speed. Most phone networks operate in the 1 Mbps to 2 Mbps range.

Note

Some HomePNA network cards include a 10/100BaseT port in case you want to convert from a phone network to Ethernet. Connecting a cable to the port disables the telephone network capabilities of the NIC.

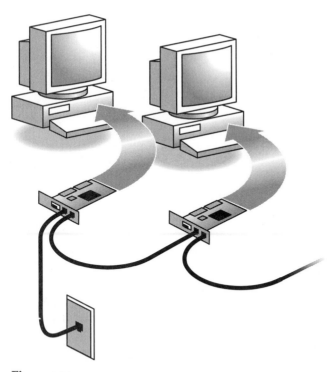

Figure 3-12.
Computers can be linked directly with HomePNA cards.

Networking Through Power Lines

Another type of network uses the electrical system in your house to transmit information. Such systems are called HomePLC (for Home Power Line Cable) networks. In theory, you can connect a computer wherever you can plug it into a wall outlet. The information traveling to and from computers is added to the electrical waves running through your house wiring. HomePLC is slower than cable and slower than some phone line systems.

Most power line networks employ a special device that plugs into a wall outlet, as shown in Figure 3-13, on the next page. A wire from that device connects to a special NIC linked to the computer. Some HomePLC networks connect directly to a computer's parallel port, which saves you the cost of buying a NIC.

Figure 3-13.
Most power line networks require a device that plugs into a wall outlet and a special NIC.

Still in their infancy, home power line networks are slower than Ethernet and are subject to interference. They are not recommended, for example, for use in apartments where your signals can get mixed with those from adjacent units.

Understanding Networking Software

Once you decide on the type of network and connections you want, you'll need two basic types of software:

- Network drivers
- A network operating system

Network Drivers

Your NIC will come with a floppy disk or CD that contains *network drivers,* the special programs that Windows needs to access your specific NIC. The disk or CD may also include drivers for MS-DOS (the disk operating system that preceded Windows), and for other types of operating systems.

Complete instructions for installing the drivers come with the interface card. *To learn more about installing drivers, see "Installing Network Drivers," on page 111.*

An increasing number of NICs now adhere to the Universal Plug and Play initiative (UPnP). Instead of requiring different drivers for different types of NICs, computer manufacturers are working toward a universal standard. The goal is "one size fits all." When you install a new card in a machine running Windows 95 or Windows 98, the Windows system will recognize the card and load the universal drivers from the Windows CD. If the drivers aren't on the CD, you'll need the disk that came with your card.

Network Operating Systems

In addition to the network drivers, you'll also need a network operating system (NOS). This software contains the programs necessary to perform network tasks and to share files and printers. For home networks, the choice is easy. If you have Windows 95 or Windows 98 running, you have everything you need in Windows; you don't need to buy any other software. Windows 98, Second Edition, even has software that lets you share a modem over a network. You can also download free or inexpensive networking utilities over the Internet.

The Bottom Line

In home networking, the bottom line is clearly a peer-to-peer network using Windows 98 or Windows 95. You'll get the network drivers you need with the NIC, and Windows supplies a network operating system and other networking programs for free.

To hook up your network, your best choice, in terms of speed and performance, is an Ethernet network using either twisted pair or coaxial cable. If you can't run cable from one computer to the other in your home, consider a HomePNA (home phone line), HomeRF (wireless), or HomePLC (power line carrier) network.

In the next chapter, we'll get down to the real nitty-gritty of purchasing and installing your network hardware.

Part 2

Installing the Hardware

Chapter 4

Installing Network Cards

The next step toward getting your home network going is to purchase and install the networking hardware: the network interface card (NIC), the hub, and the cables. If you're lucky enough to have computers that have network cards built in, you can just skip this chapter. Unfortunately, as mentioned in Chapter 3, most home computers do not come with a NIC built in, so you'll have to install one yourself.

Are You Network-Ready?

Before going any further, you might want to check to see whether your computers are already equipped with a NIC. Your machines have NICs if you purchased computers ready to be connected to a network, or if you inherited used computers that had NICs installed when you received them. If a computer is new, on the other hand, check its documentation or the specifications on the box the computer came in. Chances are, if your computer is network-ready, the box will say so prominently.

With a hand-me-down or used computer, check the back of the case for an RJ-45 connector, which looks like an extra-large telephone jack, or a small, metal barrel that sticks out. The large, telephone-like jack is for a twisted pair Ethernet connection; the metal barrel is for 10Base2 Thin Ethernet coaxial. You can see the typical network connections on the back of a network card illustrated on the following page.

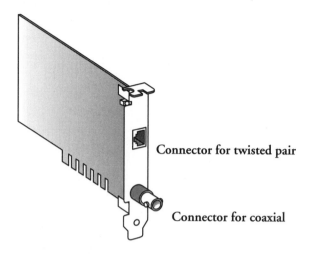

Connector for twisted pair

Connector for coaxial

If you see neither type of connection, your computer is not network-ready. If you see both, you're in good shape. If you see only one type of connection, it must be the correct type for the cable you'll use. Let's say you have inherited an older computer that has a NIC with just a coaxial connection. You cannot connect your computer to other computers that have twisted pair connections without replacing the NIC.

Working Without Cards

Perhaps the one aspect of setting up for networking that may make you uncomfortable is installing the NIC. As you'll learn in "Playing the Card Game," later in this chapter, installing a NIC inside your computer is easy, but if you'd rather not open your computer case, you can either pay someone to do it for you or consider one of the alternatives.

You can find NICs that don't have to be installed in your computer. They just plug easily into your computer's USB or printer port. Many of the USB devices are Ethernet and connect to twisted pair wire just like an internal NIC. They have a USB connection at one end and a twisted pair connection at the other. You plug the adapter into the USB connection on your computer and connect a cable from the adapter to the network hub, which joins all the cables from all the NICs. To use a USB network device, you must be running Windows 98 and have at least one USB connection on your computer.

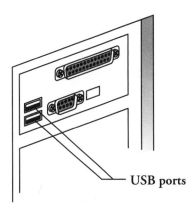

USB ports

Most of the printer port devices, however, are not Ethernet. They do not use either twisted pair or coaxial cable but instead transmit information through the telephone line, your home's power lines, or over a radio frequency without any wires. Printer port devices are usually slower than Ethernet networks, but they're easier to install.

Note

You can also find network interfaces that are serial port devices, but they are more expensive and can be complicated to set up. Serial port devices are recommended for businesses with older computers, but not for home networks.

In Chapter 6, "Networking Without Cables," you'll learn all about USB Ethernet devices and printer port alternatives.

Cook It Yourself or Order Out?

If you decide that the speed advantages of using networking hardware that includes an internal NIC are for you, consider installing the card yourself. There's nothing difficult or mysterious about the inside of a computer—it's just a collection of wires, circuit boards, and other paraphernalia. Lots of folks insert network cards, sound cards, and other kinds of cards themselves. They save a little money and they get the satisfaction of having faced the computer monster and triumphed.

Other folks wouldn't operate on their computer, even if you paid them. They'd rather have a professional do it. They save themselves the frustration if something goes wrong, and they have the comforting feeling that they can just take the computer back to the professional who installed the hardware for them.

Installing a Network Card Yourself

You don't have to be an electronics expert to install a NIC in your computer. You just need some patience, common sense, and the ability to use a screwdriver, which is about the only tool that you'll need.

Of course, whenever you open a computer, you are exposing a lot of sensitive and expensive equipment. Certainly, pulling or poking the wrong part can damage your computer, but if you're careful, nothing will go wrong. There are also a lot of wires and cables running around inside your computer. You can safely move wires out of the way as long as you're careful not to disconnect them.

Just keep in mind that you should not open your computer with wet hands, when the computer is plugged in, or while the kids, the spouse, the television, or the telephone are distracting you.

If you have more than two computers to network, start with just two of them. Buy enough hardware for the two and no more. Setting up a network is not difficult, but it takes some time, and it's best to get two computers communicating before you invest your whole bankroll. Starting with just two gives you time to concentrate on the basics.

If you're not comfortable taking apart your computer to install the card yourself, however, you should consider having a professional install the hardware for you.

Finding Someone Else to Do It

If you decide not to install the hardware yourself, you'll need to have someone do it for you. That person can also set up the software drivers for your network card and configure Microsoft Windows for the network. Network drivers are the programs needed for your computer to access the NIC. If you install the card yourself, you can learn about drivers in Chapter 7, "Installing the Software."

The main drawbacks of having someone else install the hardware:

- You'll have to carry the computer to the store.

- You'll have to do without your computer for a while.

- You'll have to consider deleting any sensitive material you have on your hard disk before you take the computer to the shop.

If you take your computer to the store, you'll have to unplug all of the cables connected to the computer. You won't need to take the keyboard, mouse, or monitor—just the computer case itself. The shop will connect a keyboard and monitor for the installation process.

Some stores may be able to install the NIC while you wait, but others will make you drop off the computer and come back another day. It doesn't take long to install the card, but some shops are very busy, especially during holiday seasons. If you can't do without the computer for long, ask when they are least busy and try to schedule your visit for that time.

I'd also suggest that you go back to the same store where you bought the computer; you might get a price break on installation. When you purchase a computer at a computer superstore, for example, you can usually have a network card installed for a small, flat rate that will be worth it for the peace of mind.

Note

Purchasing hardware by mail order can be a money-saving alternative if you want to install it yourself.

Buying and Installing a Network Card

You'll need to decide what to buy, where to buy it, and whether you should buy separate components or obtain everything in a kit.

It's All in the Cards

In Chapter 3, you learned about the various types of NICs and how to connect your computers. When you select hardware that includes an internal NIC, whether it works through Ethernet or the telephone line, you'll have to make sure you get the correct NIC for your computer. If you decide on an Ethernet network, the NIC you buy must be either twisted pair or coaxial cable. To recap the choices:

- **Twisted pair** looks like telephone cable on steroids, and it's by far the most popular type of cable. You'll need a hub to which cables from all of the computers connect. The hub must be turned on for any computer to communicate with another.

- **Coaxial** cable (also known as Thin Ethernet) looks like cable television wire and does not require a hub. You run the wire from one computer to the next.

When you buy a network card, make sure it is designed for the type of cable you select. You can play it safe by purchasing *combo cards*, which are NICs that have connectors for both coaxial and twisted pair cables.

Next, consider whether you'll be satisfied with the regular 10 Mbps network speed of regular Ethernet or whether you want a 100 Mbps network (also called Fast Ethernet). For home networks, 10 Mbps is fast enough for now. But when the price of 100 Mbps hardware drops in the near future, slower 10 Mbps cards and hubs may become obsolete.

Fortunately, you can mix 10 Mbps and 100 Mbps cards on the same network so you can always upgrade the parts of the network that you'd like to have become faster.

Catching the Right Bus

The *bus* is the part of the computer that moves information around between all the components. The signals flowing in and out of the NIC and other parts of the computer flow through the bus, like traffic on city streets.

The NIC plugs into an expansion slot on the bus that's not already occupied by a video card, modem, or other device. The metal contacts in the slot mesh with the contacts on the card so that electronic information can pass between them.

There are three types of slots in most computers today, and they're shown here.

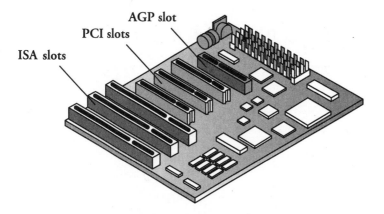

- **Industry Standard Architecture** (ISA) slots are the type used in older machines, but they're still around today. They are usually black and they have a plastic divider across the slot about two-thirds of the way from the end. The card fits into the slot and has a space to accommodate the divider.

- **Peripheral Component Interconnect** (PCI) slots are usually white. They are shorter than ISA sockets and have a divider about three-quarters of the way along.

- **The Accelerated Graphics Port** (AGP) slot is shorter than the PCI slots. It also has a divider, and it is set back further than the other slots. The AGP slot is used for a high-speed graphics card, so you can't use it for a NIC.

Note

Some older computers may have Extended ISA (EISA) sockets, which look like ISA sockets except that they are brown.

You must purchase the correct type of NIC for the type of slot that is open and available in your computer. You can often determine which slots are free from a photograph or illustration in your computer's manual that shows the inside of the computer. It should show you which slots are occupied and by what.

If the manual doesn't help, you may be able to tell by looking at the back of the computer for unused slots. You'll see a series of metal plates covering openings. Some of these will have connections for items such as the monitor, modem, and sound card, and others will be empty. If the computer manual shows what each type of slot is for, match up the blank plate with the slot to determine the type of slot that is empty.

If you still can't tell, open the computer and look around inside to find an empty slot on the main circuit board. If your computer doesn't have any empty slots, you'll need the type of NIC that connects to a port on the back of the computer, such as the USB port. You'll learn about these in Chapter 6, "Networking Without Cables."

Note

If you need help opening your computer, read "Installing the Card" on page 77 of this chapter.

PCI cards are the easiest type of NIC to install inside a computer because they require the least software configuration. In most cases, they will configure themselves when you plug them in and turn on the computer because they are *plug and play* compatible. This means that Windows senses that the card is installed and either installs the correct software by itself or prompts you to insert the disk that came with the NIC.

ISA cards are usually more complicated to install, even those that are plug and play. With ISA cards, you may have to worry about changing their settings to avoid conflicts with other cards in your computer.

Connecting Laptops

Although a few laptop computers have built-in NICs, laptops normally do not have internal slots into which you can plug a NIC. You can still connect a laptop to a network by using a network interface device on a PC card or an external network interface device that connects to the laptop's USB port.

PC cards are about the size of credit cards; they slide into a PC card slot on your laptop and they work just like other NICs. The network cable connects directly to the end of the card sticking out of the computer or to a smaller cable that plugs into the card. Some cards use only twisted pair cable but others have adapters that can accept either twisted pair or coaxial cable.

Installing a PC card NIC is a piece of cake. The label on the card is on top and the end of the card with the small holes fits into the PC card slot, which is usually on the side of the computer. Figure 3-1, in the previous chapter, shows how a PC card network interface fits into a laptop.

Most laptops have two PC card slots, an upper and a lower slot. If one slot already has something in it, like a modem, slide the NIC into the other slot. Then push the card in firmly. This pushes out a small tab on the side of the slot that you can press to remove the card.

Getting to the Hub of the Matter

If you decide to use twisted pair cables to connect computers to a network, you'll need a hub and a twisted pair cable for each computer. The hub serves as a central connection through which all network signals flow. The least expensive hubs are probably all you'll need for a home network. They have ports for up to five computers. You can also get hubs that handle more than five computers, but they are more expensive.

A five-port hub may also have a sixth connector called an *uplink port,* which lets you connect hubs and link them in a chain. When you need to add a sixth or seventh computer to your network, you can purchase another hub and add it to the chain.

You can get 10 Mbps hubs, 100 Mbps (Fast Ethernet) hubs, and dual-speed 10/100 Mbps hubs. The dual-speed hubs are perfect for networks that have both 10 Mbps and 100 Mbps NICs attached because you'll get the maximum speed of each NIC.

Note

As an alternative to a hub, you can use a more expensive device called a *switch*. A switch gives each connection on the network its own path to travel for faster performance.

In Chapter 5, we'll look at installing and locating hubs in more detail. You'll also learn that you can avoid using a hub altogether if you only want to connect two computers together.

The Whole Kit and Caboodle

Because of the growing popularity of networking, many manufacturers package all the essentials for setting up a small network in one box: the network kit. Ethernet kits, for example, usually include two network interface cards, a hub, and a couple of network cables.

The kits are a good value because they often cost less than the components purchased separately. For $50 to $100, you can buy a complete kit that gives you everything you need to connect two computers. If you need to add computers, you can purchase additional cards and cables separately. Also, you can be relatively certain that all the parts have been designed to work together. Many network kits, including the home networking products co-developed by Microsoft and 3Com, even come with a program that sets up Windows for networking, so you don't have to do any software configuration. In addition, most of the kits come with software that lets you share one Internet connection among all the people on the network. This means that everyone on the network can actually browse the Internet at the same time, using one phone line and Internet account.

See Also

You'll learn how to share Internet accounts in Chapter 12, "Going On Line Through the Network."

There are some disadvantages to kits, however. While you may be able to find a kit that includes one internal NIC for a desktop and one PC card for a laptop computer, almost all the kits offer two cards of the same type. That's fine if that's what you need, but otherwise, you may have to purchase a card of a different type separately. The other disadvantage is that if one of the cards is defective, you may have to return the entire kit, which means you'll have to remove both cards and the hub, even if only one component is bad.

As an alternative to a kit, you can purchase each component separately. You can then buy different cards for different machines and return individual pieces if need be. Because all Ethernet cards work together, you can even purchase NICs and hubs from different manufacturers.

Where to Shop?

Now that you've made some basic decisions about the type of components to buy, you're ready to get out the charge card and go shopping. But where?

You'll find the best prices at computer superstores—those large stores that only carry computer hardware and software—and through mail order. The superstore will have a good selection of kits and individual components, you'll be able to purchase the kit and take it home the same day, and you'll have a local place to go if you must return anything. If you can't find items locally, you should opt for buying them through mail order.

Mail-order companies, and online retailers such as PC Connection, CDW, Insight, and others, also offer great prices and often a better selection than local stores. While you have to pay for shipping, most mail-order companies don't charge sales tax. They offer the same return policy as local stores and often provide overnight or two-day shipping. You will have to install the hardware yourself, however, and it will take longer if you have to return or exchange something.

As an alternative, you can purchase hardware at large chain appliance stores, electronic boutiques in malls, and independent computer stores. But while the prices at appliance stores may be good, you'll rarely get the sales help you need. Expect to pay slightly higher prices at electronic boutiques in malls that carry computer games, magazines, and some hardware. Again, the salespeople are usually not computer experts, although they will know a lot about the most awesome computer games. Also expect to pay slightly higher prices at local independent computer stores. However, it's at your local computer store that you'll probably find the most knowledgeable salespeople and most helpful technical support. Try to pick a shop that's been around for a while. There are plenty of little computer stores that pop up, only to go out of business by the time the stop light on the corner changes. There's nothing wrong with these places, but it's nice to have a place to go down the road if something goes wrong.

There's one other place you should consider as a source for computer hardware: computer shows. If you live near a metropolitan area, look for computer shows periodically at convention centers, schools and colleges, or other meeting grounds. You may have to pay a small entrance fee, but you'll have access to a wide selection of vendors and products. While some vendors simply travel from show to show, look for those from local computer stores. If you need support, you may have difficulty tracking down a traveling vendor, or one from out of town.

My recommendation? Purchase a kit from a computer superstore in your area. Check the return policy, and install and test the hardware before the return period ends. If you do not want to install the hardware yourself, have the techies at the superstore do it for you.

If there is no superstore in your area, find a local computer shop that's been around for some time. Tell them what you want and that you want to spend as little money as possible.

Playing the Card Game

If you've chosen to install the network cards yourself, a little preparation will make the job easier and faster.

See Also

If you are installing an ISA network card, refer to "Installing ISA Cards" on page 80 of this chapter before attempting the installation.

Make sure you have a Phillips screwdriver; a small one will usually do. Do not use a magnetic screwdriver because the magnetism in the screwdriver might scramble information stored in computer chips.

Find a small container, such as a paper cup. You'll be removing small screws and you'll want a place to put them so they don't get lost.

While it's not necessary, you may find it handy to have needle-nose pliers available in case you drop a screw and need to fish it out of the computer. You may also need a flat-bladed screwdriver to pry off a cover plate. And you will need a scalpel and forceps (only kidding of course).

Next, remove rings, necklaces, and any other metal jewelry that might hang down or make contact with the inner workings of the computer. Metal is a conductor of static electricity, and necklaces can get caught inside the computer.

Next, find a place to work. You should have plenty of room on all sides of the computer, so pick the center of a room or a hallway where you won't be disturbed by foot traffic. It's best to find a spot near a phone line, because many manufacturers supply a telephone number that you can call for support. With the phone close to your workspace, you can describe to the support technician what you see and what you're doing.

Make sure the work area is as free from static electricity as possible. Rub your hands on your pants or skirt and touch something metal. Did you get a shock? If so, static electricity is present, and it's a danger to the components in any computer. Try working in a room without a carpet and discharge any static electricity by touching the computer case before working inside. You can also purchase an anti-static band that wraps around your wrist and connects to the computer case. Any static flows through the band to the case rather than through the delicate electronic equipment inside the case.

Leave the NIC in its anti-static packet until you're ready to insert it. Never touch the surface of the card or the metal connectors on the bottom, and only handle the card by its edges.

Installing the Card

When you're ready to start, work on just one computer at a time; don't take two or more computers apart at the same time because you might mix up their parts.

Follow these steps:

1. Unplug the computer.

   Note

   Don't just turn off the computer or turn off the power strip it is attached to. The computer must be unplugged.

2. Unplug the wires from the keyboard, mouse, printer, scanner, and any other device. Think of this as a good opportunity to dust behind the computer and straighten out all the cables.

3. Move the computer case to a work area. Don't try squeezing in beside the desk or balancing the computer on your lap.

4. Remove the computer's cover and put any screws that you remove into the paper cup.

   If you have a desktop computer, you may only need to remove the top panel. Some cases have tabs on the back that you press to release and lift off the cover. In other cases (pardon the pun) you must remove several screws at the back of the computer and slide the case forward to remove it. If you have a tower computer that sits on the floor, you can often remove one or both side panels. Look carefully at the case to determine whether the two side panels appear to be separate from the rest of the case. If they are, you only need to remove the screws on one side and slide the panel away. Which side? Sometimes you just can't tell. If you take one side off and you don't see the row of cards and slots, replace the panel and remove the other side.

   The screws you need to remove are probably near the edge of the case. Don't remove any screws from the middle, especially ones near the power supply, where you plug in the power cord, because they might hold the power supply in place.

5. Remove the metal slot cover behind the empty slot in which you plan to place the network card, as shown in Figure 4-1.

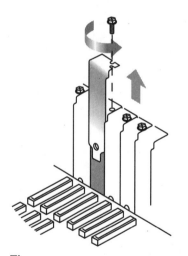

Figure 4-1.
Remove the cover plate for the slot.

You may need to either remove the screw that holds the cover in place or break off the small tab that holds the cover. Use a flat screwdriver to gently pry the cover away and then work the plate back and forth until it comes out.

6. Position the card so the connectors are toward the back of the computer. The metal back of the card will replace the blank slot cover that you've removed.

7. Line up the bottom edge of the card with the slot and confirm that they match. (Some ISA cards will not fill the entire ISA slot, just the front section.)

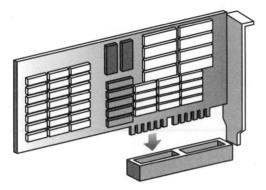

If there are any wires or cables in the way, gently move them aside without disconnecting them. Although most cables inside the computer are connected snugly, make sure you do not dislodge the smaller and more delicate cables, such as those that connect a CD drive to the sound card, while moving them aside to access the slot.

8. Push the card down into the slot, exerting steady, firm pressure. As the card goes into the slot, the metal back should slide down and fit where the plate cover was. The top of the back should rest on the screw hole. If it doesn't, the card is not down all of the way.

Try not to bend the card to either side, rock it back and forth, or touch its surface. Just hold the card by its edges and apply firm, downward pressure.

9. Being careful not to drop the screw into the computer, screw the metal back of the card into the frame of the computer. This screw is important because it keeps the card firmly seated in the slot.

10. Replace the computer cover and be careful not to trap any wires.

11. Before putting the computer case back in its place, clean around the area, straighten out the cables, and make sure you have no extra screws in the container.

12. Plug everything back in. Plug in the power cord last.

Installing ISA Cards

Using ISA cards often requires that you change special settings on the card, such as its IRQ and I/O address. IRQ stands for interrupt request. Imagine the IRQ as a telephone number. Each device in your computer has a different IRQ number that it uses to communicate with the computer. Your computer scans each IRQ line to see which device is requesting service—that is, to send or receive information through the computer bus. Only one device is allowed on an IRQ line at one time. If more than one ISA device uses the same IRQ, their signals may conflict.

Note

Some devices, such as PCI cards, can share an IRQ.

The I/O address is the location in your computer's memory where the signals from the device are stored. No two devices can have the same I/O address or their signals will conflict.

The IRQ and the I/O address of an ISA device are changed either by hardware or software. If the card's documentation tells you that the IRQ and I/O address are set up through software, you can skip this section for now.

On some older cards, you make these settings by changing a small switch or moving a jumper, which is a small device with metal prongs, as shown in Figure 4-2. There will be a plastic cap that fits over two of the prongs. The pair of prongs that the cap is on determines the IRQ that is assigned to the device. The card's documentation will show you which switch or jumper to change.

Figure 4-2.
Positioning a jumper to set the IRQ to 7.

Note

PCI plug and play cards share IRQs automatically, so no special setup is required.

Before you can pick an IRQ setting for the card, you must check to see what's available on your system to avoid a conflict. To check which IRQs are already being used, follow these steps:

1. Look at the documentation on the card for possible IRQ and I/O settings.

2. Right-click My Computer on the Windows desktop.

3. Choose Properties from the shortcut menu.

4. In the System Properties dialog box, click the Device Manager tab.

5. Double-click Computer at the top of the list.

6. Click the Interrupt Request (IRQ) button. The IRQs, usually numbered from 0 to 15, are listed.

7. Look for an unused IRQ or one that is assigned to a device you do not plan to use, such as an unused COM port. Don't worry if some IRQs are used by more than one device in the list. There are devices that can share IRQs.

8. Click the Input/Output (I/O) button.

9. Check to see which of the addresses that your card can use are available.

10. Click Cancel to return to the Device Manager tab.

11. Click Cancel again to close the System Properties dialog box.

Set the switches or jumpers on the card to settings that will not conflict, and then install the card and restart your system.

Your NIC is now installed. If you had it installed by someone, your network drivers and Windows software should also be set up and ready to go. If you installed the NIC yourself, you must still install the NIC drivers and configure Windows, and that's the subject of the next chapter.

If you've had someone else install your NIC, you may still want to go through the next chapter to make sure your network is ready.

Chapter 5

Running the Cables

Now that you have NICs installed in your computers, you are ready to connect them with cable. Just as a chain is only as strong as its weakest link, though, your network is only as sound as the connections between computers, so you'll want to follow the suggestions in this chapter carefully to wire your network.

Running Cables Within a Room

You can often run cable between devices in the same room along or even under the baseboard molding. In some rooms, you may be able to hide the cable by pushing it between the carpet and the bottom of the molding. If not, run the cable on the top of the baseboard molding. Of course, it looks best if the cable is the same color as the molding. When you get to the corner of a room, don't bend the cable sharply, even if it has to stick out slightly from the corner.

Running Cables Between Rooms

Cabling together two or more computers in the same room is relatively easy, but when the computers are in different parts of the house, running cables between them can be more of a challenge.

Running Cables Between Adjacent Rooms

If you need to connect two computers that are in adjacent rooms, you can drill a hole in the wall between the rooms and feed the cable through. Of course, if the computers are on opposite sides of the wall, you won't even have to run the cable along a baseboard. Alternatively, you can run the cable through the ceiling, between the ceiling joists. You'll then have to make two holes, one where the wire enters the ceiling in one room and another where the wire exits the ceiling in another room. If there is a heating duct or a return that runs between rooms, you can also run the cable through it, but if you make holes in the metal to get the wire into the duct, stuff some insulation around the wire to prevent air loss around the holes.

If you want to connect a computer that's directly upstairs, look for a closet. You may be able to drill a hole in the closet ceiling and run the cable through it. Because floors can be eight inches thick or more, you may have to use a coat hanger to fish the cable through. After the cable reaches the other floor, you can run it along the baseboard.

If you'd rather not drill holes in a closet, look for other wires, pipes, or ducts that go between floors. You may find some space that you can use for your network cables next to pipes or other wires. If the space you must go through is insulated, be sure to replace any insulation that you remove. In some localities, the fire code requires that all spaces between floors be insulated as a fire stop.

See Also

Chapter 6 describes how to set up a phone line, power line, or wireless network.

Running Cables Between Nonadjacent Rooms

If the computers you want to connect are not in adjacent rooms, you may need to run cable through an attic or basement. If you have a basement or crawl space, for example, you can run cable between the first floor rooms by drilling down through the floors in both rooms. You can then run the cable down one hole, across the basement ceiling, and up the other hole. Use an attic the same way. Drill up through the ceiling in both rooms. Run the cable up one hole, across the attic, and down the other hole.

See Also

If you need custom cable lengths, see "Making Your Own Network Cables," on page 88.

Using Twisted Pair Cables

When you are using twisted pair cable for the network, you must run a cable from the NIC at each computer to the hub. If you purchased an Ethernet kit, you probably have a hub and two lengths of cable. You plug in the cable just as you would a telephone cable.

Note

Lengths of twisted pair cable with connectors at both ends are called *patch cable.*

If a cable you have is too short, you can join cables end to end with a coupler, which has two female RJ-45 sockets. Couplers for network cable look just like couplers for telephone cable, only they're bigger.

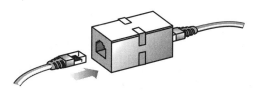

Avoid getting cables that are too long. You'll have to coil up their extra length, and coils actually slow down network connections and make them unreliable.

Making the Grade

You can purchase several *categories*, or grades, of twisted pair cable. The higher the category, the better the cable and the more stable the connection. The standard grade for home networks is called *Category 5*, or "Cat 5." Fast Ethernet, which runs at 100 Mbps, requires Cat 5 cable, but for 10BaseT, which runs at only 10 Mbps, you may be able to get away with Cat 3. Most stores sell only Cat 5 cable because the price difference between categories is negligible for short patch cables. Another category of cable, called Cat 5e, falls between Cat 5 and Cat 6 in price and quality. You won't need to use Cat 6 or Cat 7 cable in a home because they are designed for high-speed networks that must span long distances.

Note

Cat 2 cable is used to wire alarm systems and telephone lines, and Cat 4 is used for networks running at speeds slower than that of Ethernet networks.

You can purchase twisted pair cable in various lengths and colors. Most local stores carry only one or two colors, such as gray and white, but additional colors are available through mail order. You can also get cables that have molded or booted ends; they have plastic or rubberized material that covers the connection between the wire and the plug. This strengthens the connections and makes them more suitable for installations where you'll be frequently removing and reinserting cables.

Hubless Networking

If you want to network only two computers, you can avoid using a hub by connecting their NICs with a special cable called a *crossover* or *cross-pinned* cable. You plug one end of the crossover cable into the NIC of one computer and plug the other end into the NIC of the other computer. No other hardware is required and the cable can even be 100 feet long or more. A crossover cable is inexpensive; a 10-foot cable may cost $20 or less. Unfortunately, crossover cables are not that easy to buy because few computer stores carry them.

If you go to a computer store to purchase a crossover cable, make sure you do not get a regular patch cable, the standard cable for networking. A crossover cable has two of its wires switched, so it's different from a regular network cable.

If you can't find a crossover cable at the local computer superstore, try ordering one from a mail order company, such as Data Comm Warehouse (*http://www.warehouse.com/ datacomm/*). You can also go to a small, local computer store where they might know about such things and make one for you.

Note

Because crossover and regular patch cable look the same, you might want to wrap a small piece of duct tape or adhesive tape on one end of the crossover cable and write *crossover* on it. This will help you distinguish the crossover cable from your regular patch cables.

Locating the Hub

When you want to connect three or more computers or connect a printer directly to the network, you'll need a hub. Consider a hub even when you only need to connect two computers. Hubs are so inexpensive that buying one may cost less than having a crossover cable custom made. Before connecting the hub to the network, however, consider its placement.

Note

You'll need a hub for any Ethernet network of three or more computers that uses twisted pair cable, even networks with computers using external USB NICs.

The hub must be plugged into an electrical source for power, so make sure it is near an outlet. You may also want to connect the hub to an outlet that is not controlled by a wall switch, as you may leave the hub turned on at all times. The hub needs some air circulating around it, so don't put it in a cabinet or drawer and be sure to keep it away from direct sunlight, heat, radios, fluorescent lights, or transmitters of any kind that can cause interference.

The main trick in placing a hub is to make it convenient to all your computers, so that you can easily connect cables from the computers to the hub, passing through the fewest number of walls, floors, and rooms. If you're connecting two computers that are in the same room, just place the hub near an electrical outlet, and run the cables along the baseboard from each computer to the hub. If you're connecting computers in adjacent rooms, locate the hub near the hole you've made between the rooms.

If you live in a one-story house with a basement, consider placing the hub in the basement. You can drill down through the floor in each room that has a computer and run cables down to the hub in the basement.

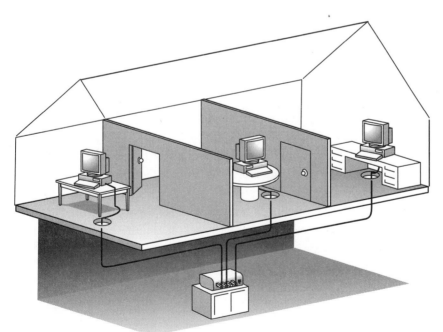

Because you have to run separate wires from every computer to the hub, sometimes the central location where you'd like to place the hub is not ideal, especially when you have to run the cable through walls and along baseboards. Select a location that requires the least amount of cable and the least amount of fishing through walls, floors, and ceilings.

Making Your Own Network Cables

If you have a lot of wiring to do, you may want to consider making your own patch cables. That way, you can get cables that are just the right length and you can save some money too. Rather than purchase patch cable that already has connectors on both ends, you can purchase bulk cable, long lengths of twisted pair wire without any connectors. Although you must usually buy lengths of 250 feet or more to get bulk cable, cable at that length is relatively inexpensive. A 250-foot roll of bulk cable can cost about the same as two 50-foot patch cords. Buying bulk cable in even longer lengths, 500 or 1000 feet, is even cheaper per foot.

Note

You can also purchase patch cable, cut one end off to make it the proper length, and install a connector on the end yourself.

In addition to bulk cable, you'll need a supply of connectors and two special tools—a *stripper* and a *crimper*. The stripper cuts away the coating around the cable so you can place the wires inside in a connector in a specific order. The crimper tightens the connector onto the wires. Complete kits of connectors and tools are not expensive, but some dexterity is required in stripping and crimping the cable.

Another option for cabling is to install Ethernet sockets in the walls. These are like phone sockets, but they're for network cables instead. They help to create a more attractive look and avoid clutter, especially if you plan on selling your home in the future. If you install network sockets, you can even purchase models that do not require a crimping tool. To install them, you'll need only a stripper to expose the wires in the cable and a faceplate that holds the socket on the wall, as shown in Figure 5-1. There are faceplates than can hold two, four, and even more plugs. You'll need one of these faceplates for the location where all the cables connect to the hub.

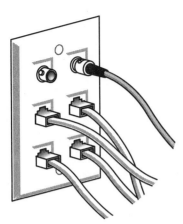

Figure 5-1.
Connecting cables to a faceplate.

Note

If you are running cable along baseboards, you can purchase surface-mounted jacks that attach directly to the baseboard. You then plug the patch cable into the jack.

Using Thin Ethernet Coaxial

When you use coaxial cable, you do not need to connect the network cables at a hub. Instead, you simply connect cables from one NIC to another to form a continuous chain.

At the end of each length of coaxial cable is a male BNC connector (short for barrel node connector). The connector has a pin in the center and an outer ring that rotates. If you look into the end of the connector, you'll see that this ring has two grooves.

The BNC male connector attaches to a BNC female connection, which has two small stubs and no outer ring.

You join the male and female connectors by inserting the male connector into the female connection, so the stubs fit into the grooves, and then rotating the ring on the male connector clockwise to lock the connectors together.

To connect a cable to a NIC, you attach it to a T-connector, and then attach the T-connector to the NIC. The T-connecter has a BNC male connector at the base and a female connection at the end of each arm.

You slide the male BNC connector of the cable onto one arm of the T and then rotate the connector clockwise so it locks into place.

If you are connecting together only two computers, you connect the other end of the cable to the T-connector attached to the second machine. If the machines are in adjacent rooms, you attach one end of the cable to the computer in one room, bring the cable through the wall, and connect it to the T-connector on the other computer.

As you'll see in the diagram on the opposite page, one arm of the T on each computer will not be connected to a cable, but you can't leave it empty because that would cause the electronic signals to be lost. So to each unused arm of the T, you must attach a terminator.

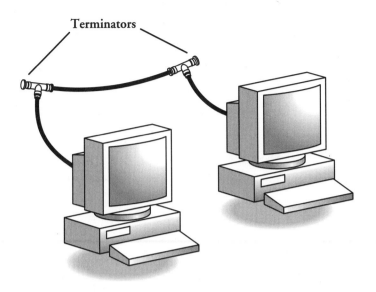

Terminators

After you've connected the cable to the T-connector, slide the T-connector onto the connection on the NIC and rotate it clockwise until it locks into place.

Just picture the network as a chain of computers with a coaxial cable running from the computer at the start of the chain to the computer at the end of the chain. Adding additional computers to the chain is easy. You can add them to the unused connections at the ends of the chain or insert them in the middle of the chain. To insert a computer in the middle of the chain, just take the coaxial cables from the computers on both sides and connect them to the T-connector on the new computer.

If at all possible, use continuous lengths of cable from one computer to the next. Connections are the most common place for problems to occur, so eliminate as many as possible to make sure your network runs well. If you don't have a length of coaxial long enough, you can join cables end to end, the same way you'd use an extension cord. To join them together, you can use the two arms of a T-connector without attaching the connector at its base to anything. You can also use a barrel connector, which is the top part of a T-connector that has the two BNC female connections.

Making Your Own Coaxial Cable

You can create your own custom lengths of coaxial cable by using bulk cable and connectors. There are even "twist-on" connectors that you can attach to the end of bulk coaxial cable without having to do any crimping. These connectors work like the twist-on connectors you can use on cable TV wire. Bulk Thin Ethernet coaxial cable is about $80 for 500 feet, and twist-on connectors are only about $2 each.

If you want to run coaxial through walls, you can also purchase male connectors, sockets, and faceplates, which resemble cable TV outlets.

Good Cabling Equals Good Networking

Now that you're familiar with the basics of cabling your network, here are some overall rules that you should consider.

Use Continuous Lengths

It's always best that the twisted pair cables running from computers to the hub or the coaxial cables running from computer to computer be continuous lengths. Although you can join two cables end to end with a coupler, the connections at the coupler can come loose, and moisture or dust can disturb the contacts. Therefore, the coupler is the first place to look if something goes wrong with the network and the problem seems to be in the cable. Don't place the coupler in a wall, in case it needs to reached or replaced.

Prevent Bends at Sharp Angles

As you run the cable, don't bend it at sharp angles. If you have to go around a corner, for example, don't bend the cable so it folds or creases, and don't pull the cable very tight. The wires inside cables are strong and flexible, but bending a cable back and forth during installation or sharply folding it in the corner of a room can break one of them. Although these wires may not break immediately, they may deteriorate over a period of time.

Keep a Tidy Appearance

To preserve the appearance of your rooms, try to run cable in a wall or above the ceiling whenever possible. Try to avoid running it on the outside of a wall, along the baseboard. Many businesses have ceilings that are dropped just so network and other cables can easily be run from room to room, but you don't usually have that luxury in a home. If you must run cable along a baseboard or up a wall, secure it to the surface. Rather than nail or staple directly into the cable, use U-shaped nails that you've purchased at a hardware store or home center. Never put a cable where it can be tripped over or kicked, and never put it under the carpet where it can be stepped on. Although you may find it tempting to run the cable under an area rug rather than around the perimeter of a room, continuously walking over it, rolling over it with a chair, or vacuuming over it can wear down the cable and eventually ruin it. And no matter how thick your carpet, you'll soon see the telltale sign of a cable bulging through.

Don't Force Cables

If you have to drill a hole in a wall to run the cable, make the hole larger than the connector at the end of the cable. Never force a cable through a smaller hole because you could damage the connector on the end. In fact, always be particularly careful with connectors at the end of the cable. The plug at the end of a twisted pair cable has small metal contacts and a plastic tab that helps hold the plug in place. Don't step on the end or break off that tab. Also, take care to avoid cutting or bending the small wire at the end of a coaxial cable.

Use a Fish or Coat Hanger

The worst part of running wire is fishing it through walls: getting it to go from one location to another when you can't see where it is going. Sometimes fishing cables is easy, such as when you have to run it between two adjacent rooms, but sometimes fishing is so frustrating that you'll want to give up and send mail by carrier pigeon.

If you have trouble feeding the cable through a wall, you can open a metal coat hanger and push one end through. Alternately, you can purchase a fish at a hardware store. It contains a coil of metal that you can unwind as needed. Once you get the coat hanger or fish through the wall, tie the end of the cable to the end of the hanger or fish, and then pull the cable through the other end.

Accessorizing Your Installation

No matter what type of cable you use, you can purchase all sorts of accessories to help hide it throughout the house. The most common of these are raceways and floor cable covers. Raceways, shown on the next page, are usually made of a non-conductive material like vinyl and they attach to walls, ceilings, or floors to hide cable and keep it safe. Most raceways have curves for the corners of rooms to keep the cable from bending too sharply.

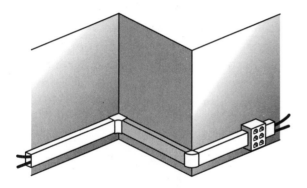

Floor cable covers are plastic or rubber, and they cover a cable that might be stepped on. Depending on their design, you run the cable through them or under them.

Many companies sell bulk cable, connectors, and the other accessories you'll need for a professional cabling job in your home. Unfortunately, most computer stores, even superstores, carry only a small selection of cabling supplies. An alternate source for the parts you'll need is a mail order catalog such as Data Comm Warehouse.

Because you must order the materials and wait for them to arrive, it pays to plan your detailed cable layout in advance. You can run lengths of string where you plan to run the cable to get measurements. You can also make the holes in advance and use the string later to fish the actual cable through walls.

Expanding Your Network

As your needs and your family grow, you may want to add more computers to the network. As you've seen, adding computers to a network that uses Thin Ethernet coaxial cable is easy; just remove the terminator at one end of the chain and connect the cable from the additional computer. But networks connected by twisted pair cable must have enough ports on the hub for all the computers that you want to connect. If you have a five-port hub, for example, you can connect only five computers. When your twisted pair cable network exceeds the hub's capacity, you have two choices. You can purchase a hub that handles more computers, or you can link two or more hubs together by connecting their uplink ports.

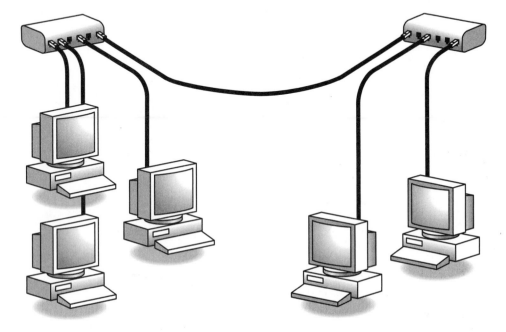

The two hubs you connect are not required to be in the same room of your house, so you can also consider using two hubs to connect different branches of your network where it is difficult to run cables or to avoid running multiple cables along the same path. In Figure 5-2, on the next page, two hubs are used to simplify a household network. With two hubs in different areas of the house, you need to fish only one wire between the areas.

With some hubs, you connect a cable from the uplink port of one hub to the regular port of the other hub. You must connect some hubs with crossover cable and others with regular patch cord. There are even hubs on twisted pair networks that you connect with Thin Ethernet coaxial cable. The documentation for your hub can tell you what type of cable and which ports to use.

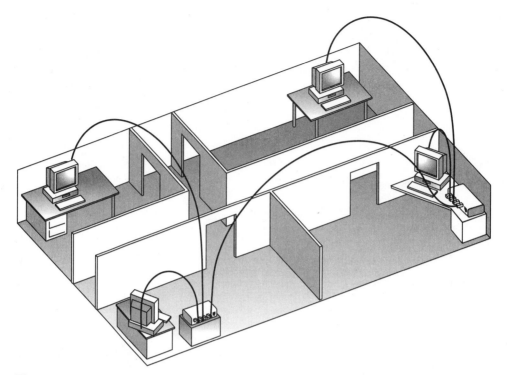

Figure 5-2.

Connecting hubs in different parts of the house.

If you have a hub that contains one or more coaxial connections, by the way, you can use it to combine twisted pair and Thin Ethernet in one network. As shown in Figure 5-3, connect the free end of the coaxial cable to the coaxial port of the hub.

Connecting your computers can be easy, but the location of your computers can sometimes pose some challenges. In most cases, you can find ways to run cables that avoid making too many holes in walls and running cables where they are unsightly. In this chapter, you learned how to connect computers using twisted pair wire, with and without a hub, and how to use coaxial cable.

In the next chapter, you'll learn about some new alternatives that let you set up a network without running cables.

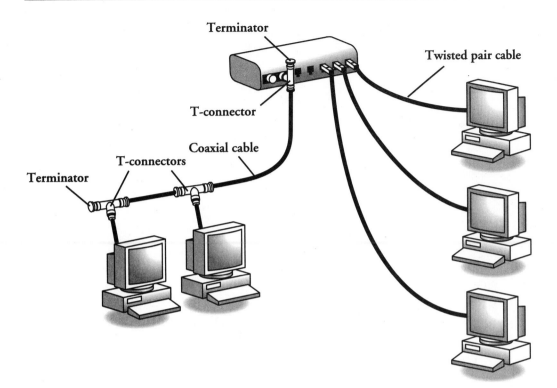

Figure 5-3.
Combining twisted pair and coaxial networks.

Chapter 6

Networking Without Cables

In the last several chapters, you learned how to set up an Ethernet network using twisted pair or coaxial cables that connect the NICs in computers. In this chapter, we'll take a look at alternatives to Ethernet networks that let you avoid running wires through the house. These alternatives provide networks that run through the existing wires in your home, the telephone lines or power lines, and they also include networks that are completely wireless.

Considering the Alternatives

Before looking at the specifics of setting up non-Ethernet alternatives, you should consider how they compare with the Ethernet networks we've already looked at.

The non-Ethernet alternatives are easier to set up and use than Ethernet networks because they don't require you to run any cable, connect to hubs, or worry about terminators. Either they use existing wiring, such as your telephone or power lines, or, in the case of a wireless network, they use no wire at all. They are generally slower than Ethernet networks, sometimes about one-tenth the speed or slower, but are more than adequate for the typical home network.

While startup kits for these systems cost about the same as Ethernet startup kits, they usually lock you into proprietary hardware. With an Ethernet network, you can mix NICs and hubs from various manufacturers without trouble. The hardware that you use with non-Ethernet alternatives, however, is not compatible among manufacturers. If you purchase a telephone network kit from one company and need extra network cards, you'll have to get them from the same company, and that may be a problem if the company discontinues the product line or goes out of business. You may need to start all over with new network equipment.

Some non-Ethernet kits do allow easy migration to an Ethernet network. For example, you might decide to start with a telephone line network to quickly get two computers in your home communicating. Down the road, you decide to connect another computer and printer to the network, but you want the increased speed of Ethernet. There are telephone line interface cards that also have an Ethernet connection. You simply unplug the phone line from the card and plug in your Ethernet cable and hub.

So when would you select a non-Ethernet network? The alternatives to Ethernet covered in this chapter are perfect for renters and homeowners who want to avoid cutting holes in walls to run Ethernet cable from room to room. The external kits are especially useful when you don't want to open your computer to add a card or when you have no slots available for an internal card.

Telephone line networks that use an external device rather than an internal NIC offer the most in terms of terms of ease of use and expandability. They are easy to install and can connect a computer in any room where you have a telephone outlet. If you think you may want to upgrade someday to Ethernet and you have an available slot in your computer for an internal card, consider a system whose card has both a telephone and Ethernet connection.

The general procedures for installing the systems described in this chapter apply to most Ethernet alternatives, although specific products may require special steps.

The focus of this chapter is on the hardware needed to set up a non-Ethernet network, rather than the software. The reason for this is that everything you will learn in Chapter 7 about the software side of getting an Ethernet network up and running applies equally to non-Ethernet networks. The appropriate network drivers must be installed, protocols added, and resources shared. All the network kits discussed in this chapter include software that automates the setup and configuration process. The software installs the drivers needed to run the network and configures Windows for the proper protocols. Most of the kits also include software for sharing your Internet connection with other family members on the network. *(For more on sharing modems and Internet accounts, see Chapter 12.)*

You can choose from many different non-Ethernet hardware combinations when you're setting up a network. With wireless and telephone networks, as with Ethernet networks, you have a choice of using an internal NIC, a USB device, or a parallel port device. Your options are more limited with a power line network. There are no USB power line network kits currently on the market, and you probably wouldn't want to connect an internal NIC directly to a power line because it might directly expose your computer to power surges.

Setting Up a Phone Line Network

Home telephone networks work on the principle that the phone lines running through your home can be shared. The technical term for this is Frequency Division Multiplexing (FDM), which simply means that you have separate signals running through your telephone line on different frequencies. Voice, fax, and modem calls use one frequency; your home network uses a completely different frequency. As a result, network signals can travel through the phone line at the same time as you are using your phone to speak, fax, or surf the Internet.

The Pros and Cons of Phone Line Networks

Phone line networks are convenient for two main reasons:

- You don't need to run any special cable.
- You can connect a computer to the network in any room that has a phone jack.

With a phone line network, the phone jack serves double duty by allowing you to connect a computer to the network as well as to the Internet. If you do need another phone jack in your home, your phone company can install it for you, although they'll probably charge you, of course.

The main limitation of phone line networks is their lack of speed. Phone line networks typically operate at 1 Mbps, compared to an Ethernet network's speed of 10 Mbps or 100 Mbps.

Choosing a Phone Line System

Several companies sell phone line network kits. The AnyPoint Home Network kit, from Intel (*http://www.intel.com*), comes in a parallel port version that includes a small box for each computer. One end of the box plugs into your computer's printer port through a cable; the other end connects by phone wire to a phone jack.

Other phone line network kits, like the HomeLink Phoneline Network in a Box from Linksys (*http://www.linksys.com*), use an internal NIC that connects via phone wire to a jack. The Linksys PCI cards have both a telephone interface and a twisted pair Ethernet jack, just in case you want to change later to an Ethernet network by installing twisted pair cables and a hub.

Diamond Multimedia offers its HomeFree Phoneline Desktop Pac consisting of two ISA phone line cards; you can also purchase PCI cards and a USB device separately to add more computers to the network. All of the devices are compatible with each other.

Using Wireless Network Devices

Wireless networks, called HomeRF (for Home Radio Frequency) networks, send and receive information as radio waves over the air by means of a device called a *transceiver*. So called because it both transmits and receives radio waves, a transceiver is either installed in or connected to each computer on the network. Figure 6-1 shows computers communicating over a wireless network through transceivers.

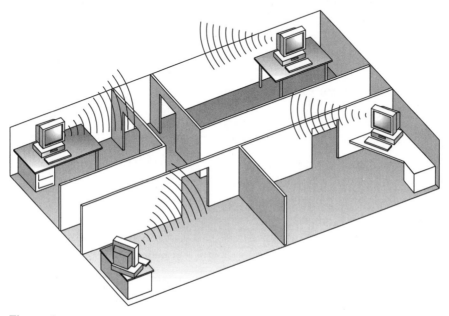

Figure 6-1.
Wireless network transceivers send and receive information as radio waves over the air.

The Pros and Cons of Going Wireless

Wireless networks can be constructed with internal NICs as well as parallel or USB modules. The USB versions are the easiest to set up because you don't have to open the computer to install an internal NIC or share a parallel port with a printer.

Parallel and USB wireless networks are ideal for linking a laptop computer to a desktop because you can situate the laptop anywhere, or move it from room to room, without worrying about wires.

A wireless NIC is installed in approximately the same way as an Ethernet NIC. The only difference is that the wireless version may have a protrusion at the back that serves as the antenna. You might have to angle the card slightly to get the protrusion through the back of the computer before you straighten out the card so that it fits in the socket.

In addition to being slower than Ethernet, wireless networks have two other drawbacks. Wireless networks that are designed and priced for the home function only within a certain distance, usually a radius of about 150 feet between the computers. Although that distance should be enough to accommodate all the computers in an average-sized home, check the documentation that came with your wireless network kit to ascertain its range. If a computer on the network appears to be turned off, it may just be out of range. Try moving the computer closer to the others. If that fixes the problem, leave the computer in its new location.

A more common problem with wireless networks is interference from walls and large metal objects. If a computer on the network is located on the floor under a metal desk, for example, the metal might block incoming and outgoing signals. A wall with metal pipes or studs can also interfere with signal transmission. Try moving the computer to another location, such as on top of the desk or to one side of it.

Note

Watch out for interference from cell phones, pagers, and other wireless devices in the house.

Choosing a Wireless System

A number of companies market wireless network systems. A pair of Aviator network kits from WebGear (*http://www.webgear.com*), for example, contain either two parallel port or two USB port transceivers, which can be plugged into a desktop or a laptop without your having to open up the computer. Because the parallel and USB versions are compatible, you can mix both on the same home network of up to 32 computers. The parallel kit also includes an internal ISA parallel port card that gives you a second parallel port for your computer that you can use for your printer.

Diamond Multimedia (*http://www.diamondmm.com*) markets two HomeFree wireless network kits. One kit includes both a PCI and an ISA NIC; another kit includes one ISA and one PC card for a laptop. You can purchase additional cards separately, including PC cards for laptops, if you need them for other computers. The internal NIC has a small protrusion that sticks out of your computer to serve as an antenna. The HomeFree kits also include the HomeFree Assistant, an easy-to-use program for keeping track of the computers and peripherals being shared on the network.

SohoWare's CableFree wireless network kits (*http://www.sohoware.com*) also come in two versions. One version contains two ISA NICs, the other version has one ISA and one

PC card. The company also offers a product called EtherBridge that connects a wireless network to an Ethernet network.

If you have a really large home and some extra cash, you might want to consider a commercial-quality wireless system. Such systems cost more, but they operate at higher speeds and over a wider area than kits designed for the home. RadioLAN (*http:// www.radiolan.com*), for example, sells a wireless system that achieves Ethernet speeds, but each internal card costs over $300, compared to less than $200 for most wireless kits.

Setting Up a Power Line Network

In a power line network, called a HomePLC (for Home Power Line Cable) network, your home's existing electrical wiring serves as the network cable, relaying information among the computers. You don't have to run any special cables between computers, and you can connect any computer that's within reach of an electrical outlet to the network.

The Pros and Cons of Power Line Networks

Here's how power line systems work.

- A HomePLC plug-in device plugs into an electrical outlet and is connected by cable to your computer's parallel port.

- The HomePLC system sends information through the power lines as a low-frequency radio wave. The frequency of the radio wave prevents it from interfering with, or being interfered by, the regular electric current running through the wires.

- The radio wave travels throughout your house until it is "picked up" by a HomePLC device connected to another computer on the network.

HomePLC networks are the newest of the Ethernet alternatives, so the technology still has some drawbacks, especially if you share an electrical transformer with a neighbor.

A transformer is a device that reduces the voltage of the current flowing through outside power lines to the level required for household wiring. In a power line network, radio waves from a computer on the network travel from the computer's electrical outlet through the household wiring to the transformer supplying current to your house. If, as is often the case, the transformer serves more than one dwelling, your network signals will actually travel through the wires of other houses or apartments served by the same transformer.

Theoretically, if the family in the apartment or house next door shares your transformer and has the same type of power line network device, it could automatically become part of your family's network. Some power line networks, however, include software that let you create a "secure" network that prevents unauthorized users from accessing your network. This is done through the creation of what's called a *firewall*, which limits access to your network to only authorized persons.

The secure network setting, however, is not turned on by default when you install the network software. The PassPort Powerline software, for example, offers a secure network option when you first run the Passport Administrator after installation. Using the Secure Network Wizard, you can identify each of the networked devices and add them to a list of devices allowed through the firewall. Using the Secure Network Wizard is optional, however. If you later add other computers or printers to the network, you have to run the Wizard again to add them to the list of allowed devices.

The other problems with HomePLC networks are electrical interference and power line fluctuations. While the radio waves traveling through the power lines are separate from the electric current, there can be some interference from other electronic equipment in the house, especially other power line devices, such as those for telephone and video. Power line fluctuations can be caused when a large electrical appliance, such as an air conditioner, is turned on. These fluctuations can result in a temporary loss of your network connection.

As an example of a power line network, let's look at the Passport Powerline network kit from Intelogis (*http://www.intelogis.com*).

Passport Powerline

A good example of power line technology, the Passport network kit includes two plug-in computer modules, a plug-in printer module that lets you connect a printer to the network, and a CD containing installation software.

To use a computer module, which is smaller than a paperback novel, plug it into a wall socket, and then plug a cable from the module into the computer's parallel port, as shown in Figure 6-2, on the next page. Because power strips often contain filters and other electronic devices that could filter out network signals, be sure to plug the module directly into a wall outlet and not into a power strip. With this setup, an internal NIC is not necessary.

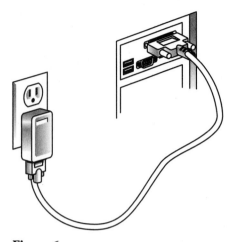

Figure 6-2.
The Passport power line module links your computer's parallel port to your home wiring.

Note

To help avoid power line interference, the Passport Powerline kit also includes two special power strips, which you use to plug in your computer and monitor. This way, the module can occupy one plug of a dual outlet and the power strip the other. The power strip filters out any interference from the computer and monitor.

When it senses the presence of the Passport module, Windows automatically starts a wizard to install the drivers. Rather than use the wizard, however, click Cancel to return to your desktop, and then run the installation program on the Passport CD.

The Passport installation program loads the necessary drivers and configures Windows for the network, installing protocols, setting up network services, and turning on file sharing. After it restarts your computer, it installs the Passport software too, so you don't need to do anything to configure Windows for connecting computers in a network.

To use the Passport kit's printer module, plug your printer's parallel port cable into the module, and then plug the module into a wall outlet. The printer is now connected directly to the network rather than to an individual computer. As long as the printer is turned on, every computer on the network can access it. All you have to do is install the appropriate printer driver on each computer, following the instructions you'll find in the Passport documentation.

Note

Passport also includes Internet sharing software for sharing a single phone line and ISP account among the computers on the network.

Once the hardware is plugged in and the software is installed, you'll be able to access the network through the Network Neighborhood icon on the desktop. You'll also be able to run the Passport Administrator, a useful feature that allows you to see which other devices are connected to the network, as shown in Figure 6-3, and to limit access to the network to include only specified devices. This creates a secure network so that, even if neighbors who share a transformer have Passport networks in their homes, they won't be able to penetrate your network.

Figure 6-3.
Passport Administrator allows you to manage and secure your home network.

Expanding Passport is easy. You can buy additional PC or Printer modules and install them on other computers.

The systems described in this chapter let you create a network without running cables. Although they are slower than Ethernet networks, these non-Ethernet alternatives provide the same benefits as any network, and the day is not far off when the speed of non-Ethernet alternatives for the home will equal that of Ethernet networks.

Now that your hardware is all set up, it is time to install the software you need and to configure Windows to get your network up and running.

Part 3

Setting Up the Software

Chapter 7

Installing the Software

Now that you've installed the network hardware, you're ready to deal with the software. Your network interface card (NIC) won't do you any good unless you configure Microsoft Windows to use it and to communicate with other computers on the network.

In this chapter, you'll learn how to install the software that controls your NIC and that allows your computer to communicate with the rest of the network.

Before you do anything else, however, check the manual that came with your hardware. Some types of network hardware require a number of steps to set them up. Others come with a completely automatic setup program. The home networking products co-developed by Microsoft and 3Com, for example, automatically install all the necessary software and configure Microsoft Windows. Once you've run the setup program, you're ready to connect to your network without any further configuration.

While not every networking system is as automatic as Microsoft's, many have their own special way of installing drivers and configuring Windows. So it pays to look at the hardware manual first and run any installation program the manufacturer provides.

Installing Network Drivers

Network drivers are the first software you have to install. These are files that Windows needs to communicate with your network card. If a disk or CD came with your hardware, it probably contains the network drivers.

Drivers are installed in one of three basic ways, depending on the type of hardware.

- **The Good** Automatically, with plug-and-play devices that are recognized by Windows and that provide the easiest installation
- **The Bad** Manually, with Windows or special software that comes with the hardware
- **The Ugly** Manually, with non–plug-and-play network cards that require special configuration to avoid hardware conflicts.

Loading Drivers Automatically

If you installed a plug-and-play network card, Windows senses that the card is installed and loads the software for it. For some network devices, the drivers are already on your hard disk. For others, they need to be copied from the Windows CD. (Have the CD handy, just in case.) In still other cases, the drivers will be on the disk that came with the hardware.

To install the software, follow these steps:

1. Turn on your computer and watch the screen.

Windows, sensing that a new card has been installed, briefly displays the New Hardware Found message on the screen and then starts the Add New Hardware Wizard. This wizard takes you step by step through the process of installing the drivers.

Note

If Windows does not detect your card, go to Control Panel and double-click Add New Hardware. Keep clicking Next until the wizard finds the card in your system.

The first page of the Add New Hardware Wizard identifies the new hardware that has been detected.

2. Click Next.

Note

Different wizard pages may appear depending on your version of Windows, but the general process is the same as that described here.

The next page offers two choices:

- Search For The Best Driver For Your Device (Recommended)
- Display A List Of All Drivers In A Specific Location So You Can Select The Driver You Want

3. Choose the first option, the one to search for the best driver, and then click Next.

4. On the following page, select the check boxes next to one or more places to look for the drivers. Your options are Floppy Drive, CD-ROM, Microsoft Windows Update, and Specific Location.

5. If your hardware came with a floppy disk, insert it in the drive. Select the Floppy Disk check box to enable it, and then click Next. You can also insert the Windows CD in your CD-ROM drive. Click to select the CD-ROM check box or the Specific Location check box and specify the path to Windows on the CD-ROM (D:\WIN98, for example).

6. Click Next to have the wizard look for the appropriate drivers.
   The next page shows where the drivers are located.

7. Click Next, and then click Finish.

After the drivers are installed, you'll be asked whether you want to restart your computer. The drivers won't be recognized properly until you restart, so click Yes.

Installing Drivers Manually

If the Add New Hardware Wizard doesn't detect your network card, you can load the drivers manually. Follow these steps:

1. Double-click My Computer.

2. In the My Computer window, double-click the Control Panel icon.

3. In the Control Panel window, double-click the Network icon.

4. Click Add to see the Select Network Component Type dialog box.

5. Click Adapter in the list, and then click Add to open the Select Network Adapters dialog box shown in Figure 7-1, on the next page.

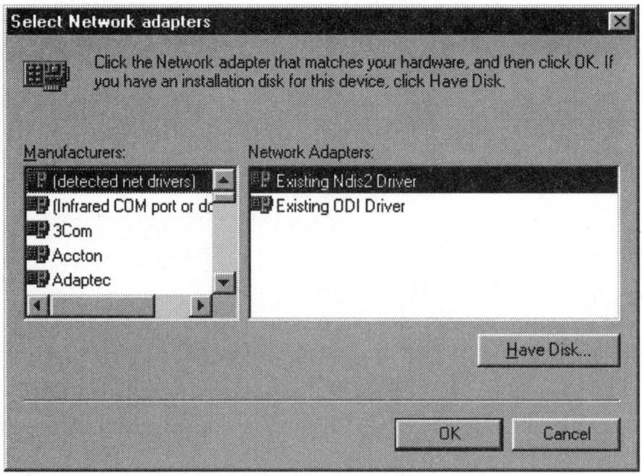

Figure 7-1.
The Select Network Adapters dialog box allows you to select the make and model of your NIC.

On the left in the dialog box is a list of manufacturers whose drivers are provided with Windows.

6. From the list of manufacturers, select the manufacturer of your card.

On the right in the dialog box, you see a list of network adapters made by the manufacturer.

Note

If your manufacturer or card is not listed, but the card came with a disk of drivers, click Have Disk in the Select Network Adapters dialog box and navigate to the disk that contains the drivers.

7. From the Network Adapters list, select your card model.

8. Click OK.

9. When Windows prompts you to restart your computer, click Yes.

Installing Drivers for Non–Plug-and-Play Cards

In Chapter 4, you learned how to install an Industry Standard Architecture (ISA) card and how to set switches and jumpers if the Interrupt Request (IRQ) and Input/Output (I/O) addresses need to be set on the card itself. Some ISA cards, however, let you change these settings using software. Such cards come with a setup or installation program on disk that either makes the settings for you or guides you through the process.

If other devices are already using all your IRQ addresses, you may encounter difficulties when setting up an ISA card. Exchanging the card for another ISA NIC may not solve the problem—you might need a PCI card or an external network device that connects to your USB or printer port.

Run the installation program that came with the software. The program may automatically check out your system and assign the best settings to the card. If the program asks you to select the settings, however, cancel the program so you can check out which IRQs and I/O addresses are free. The NIC manual should include a list of the possible addresses to which you can set your card. Here's a quick reminder about how to find out which of these are actually available:

1. Right-click My Computer on the Windows desktop, and choose Properties from the shortcut menu.

2. Click the Device Manager tab in the System Properties dialog box.

3. Double-click Computer at the top of the list of devices.

4. In the Computer Properties dialog box, make sure the Interrupt Request (IRQ) option button is selected.

5. Look for an unused IRQ. You may also be able to use the IRQ assigned to an unused serial port.

6. Click the Input/Output (I/O) option button.

7. Check to see which of the addresses your card can use that are not already used.

8. Click Cancel to return to the desktop.

Now run the installation program that came with the card and select an IRQ and I/O address not in use by another device. After you install the drivers, it's a good idea to confirm that no hardware conflicts exist. Here's how to do it:

1. Right-click My Computer on the Windows desktop, and choose Properties from the shortcut menu.

2. Click the Device Manager tab in the System Properties dialog box.

    If your network device is not working properly, you'll see an exclamation point or X next to its name.

If your network device has a problem, follow these steps to look into it:

1. In the list of devices on the Device Manager tab, click the name of your NIC under Network Adapters, and then click on Properties.

2. In the Properties dialog box for your network device, look in the Device Status section of the General tab.

If you see a message that says "This device is either not present, not working properly, or does not have all the drivers installed," you have either a bad card or a conflict.

3. Click the Resources tab.

The Conflicting Device List section shows where the conflict is occurring.

Try rerunning the card's installation program and selecting other settings, and if that doesn't work, change the settings manually in the device's Properties dialog box.

Changing the settings yourself is a last-ditch option. There's no guarantee that you'll get the NIC to work, and you could create a new conflict with another device, such as a modem or printer, causing that device to fail as well. If you do want to try changing the settings manually, follow these steps:

1. On the Resources tab of the Properties dialog box, make a note of which settings are being used.

This information will allow you to restore the original settings, if necessary. Restoring the original settings won't do anything for the NIC, but it may restore some other device that you disabled by changing settings manually.

2. Click the Use Automatic Settings check box to deselect it.

3. In the Resource Type list, click the setting you want to change.

4. Click Change Settings.

5. In the dialog box that opens, change the setting, and then click OK.

Restart your computer and test out all your devices. If the new device doesn't work, repeat the process but restore the original settings. Perhaps it's time to take your computer to a shop for the installation or remove the card and exchange it for a plug-and-play PC model.

Configuring Windows 95 and Windows 98

The next step in creating your network is to configure Windows for networking. This involves four procedures:

- Adding the network client
- Installing the network protocol
- Selecting network services
- Identifying your computer on the network

Choosing a *network client* determines how users gain access to the network. You can choose whether everyone who uses a networked computer must log on by entering a user name or by selecting the name from a list. In either case, users must enter a password for access to the network.

A *protocol* allows networked computers to send information back and forth and understand what other computers are saying. A protocol is a sort of language, with its own vocabulary and rules of grammar, that all networked computers have to speak in order to understand each other. If two computers are using different protocols, they are not able to communicate.

Network services are the resources you want to share. For example, you can choose to share your files and to let other network users access your printer.

A *workgroup* is simply a collection of computers that can interact and communicate with each other on a network. Everyone on the network who wants to share resources with others in a particular workgroup must belong to that group and must be identified by a computer name. You must enter the workgroup name for each computer when you set up networking.

Adding the Network Client

The first step in configuring Windows for networking is to determine how members of your family log on to the network when they start the computer or restart Windows. You do this by installing one of two network clients:

- **Client for Microsoft Windows** lets you start your computer and log on to the network by entering your name and password in a dialog box when Windows starts.

- **Microsoft Family Logon** lets you start your computer and log on to a network by selecting your user name from a list.

Follow these steps to select your network client:

1. On the Start menu, point to Settings, and then click Control Panel.

2. Double-click the Network Icon to open the Network dialog box.

3. Look for either Client For Microsoft Networks or Microsoft Family Logon. If one of these is already installed, and you do not want to change to the other, you can skip the rest of this procedure. If neither is installed, or you want to select the other client, continue as follows:

4. Click Add.

5. In the Select Network Component Type dialog box, click Client.

6. Click Add.

7. In the Select Network Client dialog box, click Microsoft in the Manufacturers list.

8. From the list of Network Clients in the Select Network Client dialog box, select Client for Microsoft Networks or Microsoft Family Logon.

9. Click OK to close the Select Network client dialog box.

10. Click OK to close the Network dialog box.

11. Click Yes when you are asked whether you want to restart the computer.

You can have both Client For Microsoft Networks and Microsoft Family Logon installed at the same time. After adding one client, repeat the steps above but choose the other. To choose which client to use as the default, follow these steps:

1. On the Start menu, point to Settings, and click Control Panel.

2. Double-click the Network icon to display the Network dialog box.

3. From the Primary Network Logon drop-down list, choose either Client for Microsoft Networks or Microsoft Family Logon.

4. Click OK.

Installing Protocols

Your next step is to install one or more protocols that will allow your computer to communicate with other computers. There are three basic protocols used in home networks:

- **Transmission Control Protocol/Internet Protocol** (TCP/IP) is the protocol used to dial in to an Internet service, so odds are you already have it installed. However, it's not often used in smaller home networks, because it requires a few more steps to set up than the other protocols do.

- **Internet Packet Exchange** (IPX/SPX) was originally developed for an office networking system called Novell NetWare, although it can be used for any type of network.

- **NetBIOS Extended User Interface** (NetBEUI) is an easy-to-set-up network protocol for smaller networks.

Note

If you plan to extend your network to shared modems and network printers, consider using TCP/IP because it is often required for connecting devices directly to the network. See "Configuring TCP/IP," on page 122.

You can actually have all three protocols installed at the same time for compatibility with any type of network that you connect to. In fact, they may already have been installed in Windows by the manufacturer. Some NIC installation programs, such as the one from Microsoft, set up and configure all three protocols when they install the network drivers.

With all three protocols installed, your home network will probably work perfectly well by choosing the best protocol when the computers begin communicating. The IPX/SPX and NetBEUI protocols require virtually no special configuration, so once you install them and start the network, your computer should be ready to communicate with other computers on the network.

To see which protocols are already installed and to add new ones, follow these steps:

1. On the Start menu, point to Settings, and then click Control Panel.

2. In the Control Panel window, double-click the Network icon to display the Network dialog box shown in Figure 7-2. Any network protocols and services already installed are listed.

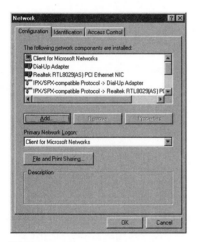

Figure 7-2.
The Network dialog box lists the protocols installed in your system.

3. Click Add.

4. In the Select Network Component Type dialog box, select Protocol and click Add to open the Select Network Protocol dialog box shown on the next page.

5. Choose Microsoft from the list of manufacturers.

6. Click a protocol in the Network Protocols list—IPX/SPX, NetBEUI, or TCP/IP.

7. Click OK to close the Select Network Protocol dialog box.

8. Click OK to close the Network dialog box.

9. Click Yes when you are asked whether to restart your computer.

Now reopen the Network dialog box again. You should see a listing for each of the protocols followed by the name of your network card in this form: TCP/IP→NETGEAR PCI Fast Ethernet, for example.

Selecting Network Services

Network services allow you to share the resources on your network—primarily files and printers—among all the computers. File sharing lets other network users access your files. If you do not allow file sharing, other users can tell that you are on the network, but they won't be able to use any of your folders or files. Because sharing files is one of the main reasons to set up a network, it makes sense to turn on this feature. You always have the option to specify which folders may be shared, and how the files in it can be accessed.

Because sharing a printer is another big advantage of networking, you'll want to turn on printer sharing as well. Before you can activate file sharing and printer sharing, however, you have to install the Windows service that allows sharing in the first place. Here's how to do this:

1. On the Start menu, point to Settings, and then click Control Panel.

2. In the Control Panel window, double-click the Network icon to open the Network dialog box.

In the list of network components that are installed, look for File And Printer Sharing For Microsoft Networks. If it is installed, you can skip the rest of these steps.

3. Click Add.

4. In the Select Network Component Type dialog box, click Service.

5. Click Add.

6. In the Select Network Service dialog box, click File And Printer Sharing For Microsoft Networks.

7. Click OK.

8. Click OK to close the Network dialog box.

9. Click Yes when you are asked whether to restart your computer.

After your computer restarts, you are ready to turn on file and printer sharing.

1. On the Start menu, point to Settings, and then click Control Panel.

2. In the Control Panel window, double-click the Network icon to display the Network dialog box.

3. In the Network dialog box, click the File And Print Sharing button.

4. Select both check boxes in the File And Print Sharing dialog box.

5. Click OK.

6. Click OK to close the Network dialog box.

This doesn't mean that your files and printer are already shared. It only means that the service that allows sharing is turned on.

Identifying Your Computer on the Network

The final step in configuring Windows for networking is to make sure that your computer has a name and that you are a member of the same workgroup as the other computers on the network.

1. On the Start menu, point to Settings, and then click Control Panel.

2. In the Control Panel window, double-click the Network icon to open the Network dialog box.

3. In the Network dialog box, click the Identification tab to see the options in Figure 7-3, on the next page.

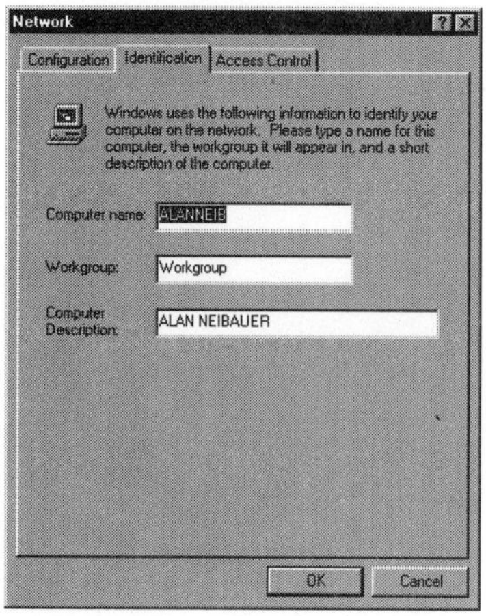

Figure 7-3.
Identify yourself and your workgroup on the Identification tab of the Network dialog box.

4. If you want, change the name for your computer.

5. Make sure the workgroup name is the same one you use for other computers on your network. Windows suggests the name Workgroup by default.

6. Enter an optional description that others who browse the network can see.

7. Click OK to close the Network dialog box.

8. Click Yes when you are asked whether to restart the computer.

Configuring TCP/IP

Once installed, the NetBEUI network protocol usually does not require any further configuration to get it working. With TCP/IP, however, you must check some settings to make sure that the computers on the network can communicate.

If you have a dial-up Internet account, then your computer is probably already using TCP/IP to connect to the Internet. In the Network dialog box, you'll see a listing for TCP/IP→Dial-Up Adapter showing that the protocol is installed.

Note

If you get a message stating that file sharing is turned on when you first connect to the Internet, turn it off and restart your computer. This will protect your files from unauthorized use by Internet hackers.

TCP/IP requires that each computer on the network have its own IP address—a string of numbers that identifies every computer linked to the Internet and every computer linked to a home TCP/IP network. No two computers on the Internet or two computers on your home network can have the same IP address. If you have a dial-up Internet account, most Internet service providers assign an IP address to your system each time you connect.

For a home network using TCP/IP, you can have Windows automatically assign an IP address to your computer every time your computer is started, or you can assign an IP address to it that will be unique on the network. For most home networks, letting Windows assign the IP address is your best bet, because it is faster and easier. The address is dynamic, meaning that it may change each time you connect to the network depending on what other computers have connected before you.

You'll only need to enter a specific IP address if you plan to use your computer with peripherals, such as a network modem or printer, that require a certain address. This is called a static address because it is the same each time you start your computer.

Avoid TCP/IP if you do not need it, because there are some possible conflicts. Some computers, with older versions of Windows 95, have difficulties when TCP/IP is used on two devices at the same time, such as your network card and over the Internet—one or the other may stop working. There are also communications programs, such as some versions of CompuServe software, that may not be able to connect to the ISP when TCP/IP is being used as a network protocol. The easiest way to resolve these conflicts is to use NetBEUI as your network protocol instead.

To set the IP address of a computer on the network, follow these steps:

1. On the Start menu, point to Settings, and then click Control Panel.

2. In the Control Panel window, double-click the Network icon to open the Network dialog box.

3. In the list of network components, click the TCP/IP setting for your network card, and click Properties to see the options in Figure 7-4, on the next page.

4. Make sure Obtain An IP Address Automatically is selected if you want Windows to assign an IP address to your computer whenever it's started, and then click OK.

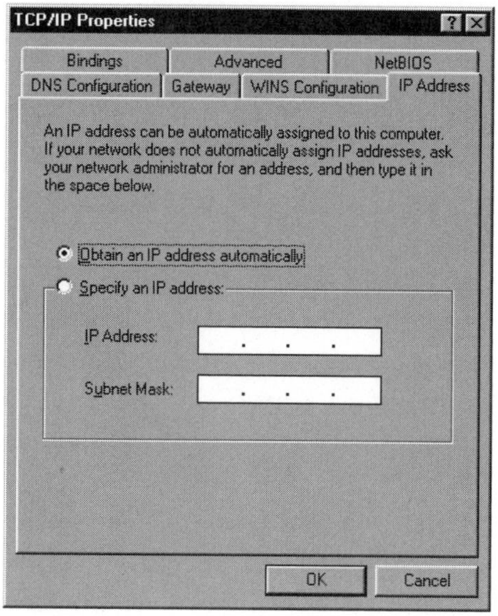

Figure 7-4.

The TCP/IP Properties dialog box displays two TCP/IP addresses: IP Address and Subnet Mask.

If you want to assign your own IP address, use these steps:

5. Click Specify An IP Address in the TCP/IP Properties dialog box.

6. Enter an IP address in the text box.

Notice that the text box next to IP Address is divided into four sections. Each of these sections can hold up to three digits. You must enter an IP address that will not duplicate an address already assigned to another computer on the Internet. Fortunately, there are special numbers you can use to assign IP addresses to computers on a home network when your computer will be connected to the Internet. For a home network, you can use IP addresses starting with 192.168.0.1 and just increment the last number for each computer. To set up the second computer in your network, for example, you'd enter *192.168.0.2* as the IP address. Press the period key between each number to separate the numbers into the four sections.

Note

Add 1 to the IP address for every other computer on your network: 192.168.0.1, 192.168.0.2, 192.168.0.3, and so on.

7. Enter *255.255.255.0* as the Subnet Mask in this and every other computer on the network.

 Because the number of IP addresses available to computer users is limited, another set of numbers, called the subnet mask, is used to further define the specific IP address of a computer. All the computers on your network must be in the same group of IP addresses, so each must have the same numbers in the Subnet Mask field.

8. Click OK to close the Network dialog box.

9. Click Yes when you are asked whether you want to restart your computer.

Welcome to the Neighborhood!

With all your hardware and software properly installed, your network is now complete. All the computers on the network are ready to communicate, and they should be able to "see" each other.

 To make sure your network is ready, double-click the Network Neighborhood icon on your Windows desktop. You should see icons for each of the computers on the network, as well as one labeled Entire Network, as shown in Figure 7-5.

Figure 7-5.
Network Neighborhood displays icons for each of the computers on the network.

Note

It may take your computer a few minutes to "see" the other computers on the network. If no other computers appear in Network Neighborhood, close the Network Neighborhood window and try again in a few minutes.

To access one of the computers on the network, double-click its icon in Network Neighborhood. You should see listed all the resources on that computer that can be shared. Don't worry if nothing appears when you try this now—you'll learn how to share resources in Chapter 9.

If you double-click the Entire Network icon in Network Neighborhood, you'll see an icon representing the workgroup. Open that icon to display the computers in your workgroup.

Network Neighborhood will appear in Windows Explorer and the File Open and File Save boxes of Windows applications. If you're using Microsoft Word, for example, you can open or save a file on a connected computer by choosing Network Neighborhood in the Look In list that appears in the Open or Save dialog box, as shown here.

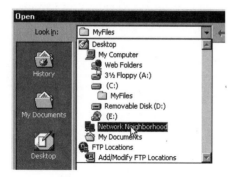

Another way to access a computer on the network is by using the Find command. Here's how:

1. On the Start menu, point to Find, and then click Computer.

2. Enter the name of the computer in the Find: Computer dialog box, and click Find Now.

Troubleshooting

Theoretically, every part of your network should be humming along now. But sometimes, even with the best planning, things can go wrong. If you cannot access the other computers on your network, you'll have to take some time and check out each aspect of the installation.

Finding a Computer

First, give your computers a few minutes to recognize each other before opening Network Neighborhood. It often takes a minute or so (sometimes longer) for the networking software to find the other computers. If no computers appear, or if you get an error message saying that the network cannot be browsed, wait a few minutes and try again.

If you know the name of another computer, try locating it using Find Computer on the Start menu. You can often access a computer this way before it shows up in Network Neighborhood.

If that fails, check all the cable connections at the computers and at the hub. Make sure the hub is plugged in and turned on and that all of the cables are securely connected.

If you still can't access the network, the problem may be the configuration of the NICs.

Checking Network Settings

The next place to troubleshoot the network is in the Network dialog box.

Make sure you are using the same workgroup name for each computer, with the same spelling and the same combination of uppercase and lowercase characters. If any computer is using a different workgroup name, change it to match the others, restart the computer, and try Network Neighborhood again.

Next, make sure you have all three protocols installed and that the Network dialog box displays a listing for each protocol. The same protocols should be installed on every computer in the network.

If you're using TCP/IP, make sure either that you're assigning IP addresses automatically or that each machine has a different address. Check that the subnet mask is the same for every machine.

Note

If all else fails, remove all the protocols except NetBEUI from all of the computers and try again. NetBEUI is the easiest protocol to get started with because it requires no special configuration.

Diagnosing Hardware Conflicts

Finally, if your network still doesn't work, check for conflicts between the NIC and other hardware on your computers. Follow the steps on page 115 of this chapter to troubleshoot for hardware conflicts.

Another way to check for conflicts is with the Windows 98 System Information program:

1. On the Start menu, point to Programs, Accessories, and System Tools, and then click System Information.

2. In the Microsoft System Information window, click the plus sign next to Hardware Resources.

3. Under Hardware Resources, click Conflicts/Sharing and see if any conflicts are listed in the right pane of the window or if your network card is using the same IRQ as another device.

4. Click Forced Hardware. This will show devices that you set up manually using settings other than those chosen by plug-and-play.

5. Click I/O and look for addresses that are shared by two devices.

6. Click IRQs and scan the list for any possible conflicts.

7. Click the plus sign next to Components.

8. Under Components, click Network.

9. Scroll through the list on the right to confirm that your network card, TCP/IP, and network clients are all listed. If they're not listed, go back to the start of this chapter and reinstall the network drivers, protocols, and clients.

Depending on your NIC, setting up your hardware can be either a breeze or a windstorm. Fortunately, almost all network cards that you get these days are plug-and-play or they include software that guides you through the process.

In the next chapter, you'll learn how to create profiles to personalize your computer if you share it with other members of your household.

Chapter 8

Creating Profiles

Even if you have more than one computer in the house, it's likely that each computer is used by more than one person. With Microsoft Windows, individual users can have their own personal settings that go into effect whenever they log on to the network. These settings personalize their screen displays, such as their screen saver and desktop theme, and they maintain other preferences, such as which folders and files to share with other users.

These personal settings are stored in a feature called a *profile*. Each user creates a profile, which is associated with a user name. When each person enters a user name upon starting Windows, the correct profile is used automatically. One set of default settings is reserved for users who do not have profiles of their own.

To use profiles, you have to turn them on and create a user name for each person who will be using your computer.

What's in a Profile?

In addition to the user name and password, a personal profile may include the following items:

- Display settings such as the screen saver, desktop theme, and the Windows color scheme
- Icons and other items on the desktop
- Internet cookies and downloaded files
- The files contained in the My Documents folder

- Recently used files in the Documents menu

- Programs on the Start menu

- Favorites in the Favorites folder (if Microsoft Internet Explorer is your Web browser)

- E-mail shown in certain e-mail programs, such as Microsoft Outlook Express

You can probably see just from this list how useful the profiles feature can be. For example, when you have your own user profile, your Web browser saves all of your Internet cookies in a file reserved just for you. A *cookie* is a small file that a site on the Internet saves on your hard disk. When you later revisit that site, it reads the information in the cookie file to identify you and any settings or options that you selected on your last visit. Your own personalized settings will show up when you return to many Web sites because your browser retrieves your cookies rather than the cookies stored for other users. Sites that sell books, such as Amazon.com, save your book-buying preferences in a cookie. When you log on to the site, you may see a list of books that match your interests. If every user of your computer used the same profile, you'd see books of interest to them, as well.

On the desktop, the My Documents folder and Documents list shows only your files, so you can quickly open files that you've worked on, instead of having to see a multitude of files from other users.

If you share your computer with another avid game player, your profile lets you avoid seeing a long list of somebody else's games in the Start menu. Those games appear only when the other player logs on with a different user name and password.

A personal Favorites list means that only the Web sites you want to visit are listed on the Favorites menu—both on the Start menu and in Internet Explorer. You won't need to scroll through a long list of favorites chosen by other users.

The same applies to e-mail messages in programs like Outlook Express. Each user sees only his or her messages in the Inbox and Sent Items folders; every other user's mail is kept private.

Turning on Profiles

In order to use the profile feature, you have to specify that you want other users to have their own settings. Otherwise, Windows displays the same desktop and uses the same settings for everyone who uses your computer.

Here's how to turn on the profiles feature:

1. On the Start menu, point to Settings, and then click Control Panel.

2. In the Control Panel window, double-click the Passwords icon to open the Passwords Properties dialog box, shown in Figure 8-1.

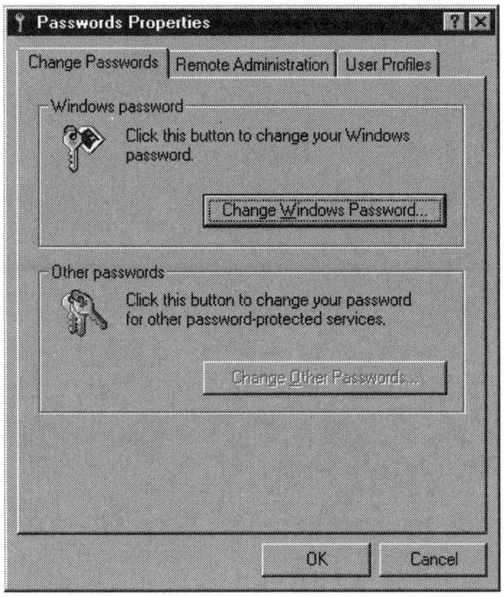

Figure 8-1.
The Passwords Properties dialog box lets you change your Windows password and set up user profiles.

3. Click the User Profiles tab.

4. Click Users Can Customize Their Preferences And Desktop Settings.

5. Click to select the two check boxes in the User Profile Settings section on the User Profiles tab.

    These settings allow individual users to add icons to the desktop and programs to the Start menu that appear only when they select their profile.

6. Click OK to close the Passwords Properties dialog box.

7. Click Yes when you are asked whether you want to restart your computer.

8. After Windows restarts, enter your user name and password, and then click OK.

9. Click Yes when you are asked if you want to retain the current settings in your profile.

You now have your own profile, containing all the settings you created when you were the computer's only user.

Adding Users

The next step is to specify who the users of your computer will be, so that each can have a personal profile. You can add as many users as you like, whenever you like, or users can create their own profiles in order to keep the password confidential.

There are two ways to add a new user. You can simply enter a new name and password when you start Windows, or you can go to Control Panel and select user options.

Note
***

Adding a new user through the Control Panel is possible only if you have Microsoft Internet Explorer, version 4 or later, on your computer.

Adding Users When You Log on

It's easy to add a new user when you start Windows, but then you'll have to go to Control Panel to select options. Here's how to do it:

1. When you start Windows or use the Log Off option from the Start menu to log on as another user, enter a new name and type a new password in the Enter Network Password dialog box, and then click OK.

   Note
   ***

   A password is optional. If you don't want to use one, just leave the Password text box blank.

   Because you've entered a new user name, the Set Windows Password dialog box appears, asking you to retype your password to confirm it.

2. Enter a password, and then click OK.

3. When a message appears asking if you want to save your own Desktop settings, click Yes.

Adding Users Through the Control Panel

If you have Microsoft Internet Explorer, version 4 or later, you can add users and select certain profile settings with the Control Panel. The first time you add a user this way, Windows runs the Add User Wizard, which takes you through the process step by step.

1. On the Start menu, point to Settings, and then click Control Panel.

2. In the Control Panel, double-click the Users icon to open the User Settings dialog box, shown in Figure 8-2.

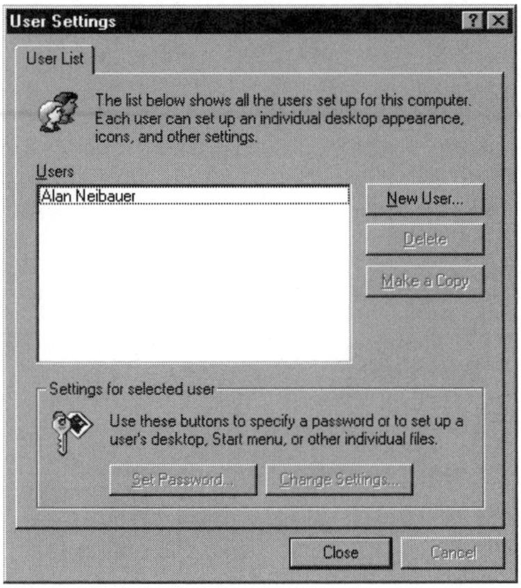

Figure 8-2.
Start the Add User Wizard in the User Settings dialog box.

3. Click New User to start the Add User Wizard.

4. Read the explanation shown on the first page, and then click Next.

5. On the Add User page, enter a new user name, and then click Next.

6. On the Enter New Password page, enter the password in both the Password and Confirm Password text boxes, and then click Next.

7. On the Personalized Items Settings page, shown in Figure 8-3, on the next page, click to select each of the check boxes for the items that you want in your personal profile. If you leave a check box cleared, you won't have a custom copy of that item.

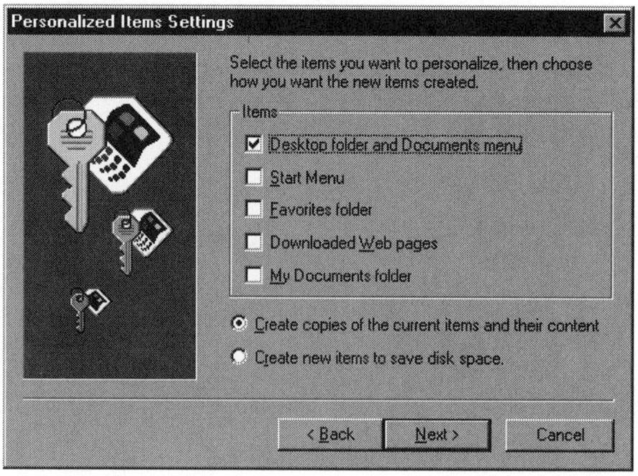

Figure 8-3.

The Personalized Items Settings page allows you to choose the contents of your profile.

8. Select one of the two option buttons near the bottom of the page to determine how you want your personal profile set up.

    If you select the first option button, Windows will make a copy of all of the items in the profile currently being used as the basis for your personal profile. If you choose the second option button, you'll have to create all of the items yourself from scratch.

9. Click Next, and then click Finish.

    Windows creates your personal desktop and displays the User Settings dialog box.

10. Click Close in the User Settings dialog box.

If you prefer to use the desktop settings of another user, it's possible to copy those settings to a new personal profile that you can use. Follow these steps to start a new profile using someone else's settings:

1. Double-click the Users icon in the Control Panel.

2. Click the user's name whose settings you want to copy.

3. Click Make A Copy to start the Add User Wizard.

4. Follow the steps of the wizard, selecting just the items you want to copy on the Personalized Items Settings page of the wizard. For example, you can clear the My Documents Folder check box if you do not want to see the other user's documents displayed in your My Documents folder.

5. Click Finish on the last page of the wizard.

Changing User Settings

Changing your password and profile settings is as easy as adding a new user.

1. Double-click the Users icon in the Control Panel.

2. In the User Settings dialog box, click your user name.

3. Click Set Password to change your password. You'll have to enter your current password, and then enter and confirm the new one.

4. Click Change Settings to open the Personalized Items Settings dialog box, and then change your settings.

    Note

    If you're not using Microsoft Internet Explorer, version 4 or later, see "Changing Passwords," on page 138, to learn how to change your password.

You can also delete a user profile. This eliminates not only the user name and password, but also all folders associated with the user name, such as the My Documents and Favorites folders. If you don't want to delete the contents of these folders, be sure to copy the files or favorites you want to save to another location before deleting the user. Then click the user name in the User Settings dialog box and click Delete.

Note

You cannot delete a user who is currently logged on.

Logging On as a Different User

You can start Windows on any computer by logging on with your own user name. If you forget your password, you can bypass the logon process and use the default desktop—the desktop that existed when the profile feature was originally enabled.

To log on to any computer, start the computer and enter your user name and password in the Enter Network Password dialog box. Leave the Password text box blank if you did not enter a password when you created your profile.

If you want to log on using the default desktop, just click Cancel in the Enter Network Password dialog box or press the Esc key. Windows will start using the settings of the default profile. Any files that were in the My Documents and Favorites folders of your personal profile won't be available on the default desktop.

If your computer is already started and you want to switch to another user profile, you have to log off and then log on again using the other profile. You might want to do this if you bypassed the logon when you first started and now want to access your personal profile files. To switch profiles in Windows 98, follow these steps:

1. On the Start menu, click Log Off.

2. Click Yes when asked whether you are sure you want to log off.
   The Enter Network Password box appears.

3. Enter the user name and password you want to log on with, and then click OK. You can also click Cancel or press Esc to log on using the default profile.

   If you're using Windows 95, the procedure for switching profiles is a little different.

1. On the Start menu, select Shut Down.

2. In the Shut Down dialog box, click Close All Programs And Log On As A Different User. Windows will restart so that you can enter another user name and password.

The Microsoft Family Logon

If a number of family members are using your computer, you can save them—and yourself—the trouble of typing in user names by choosing the Microsoft Family Logon feature. In Chapter 7, you learned how to install Microsoft Family Logon as a network client when setting up Windows for your network.

When a family member starts a computer on the network, a dialog box lists the profile names of all users. The family member can choose a user name from the list, enter a password, and then click OK to log on using the correct profile.

If you installed Microsoft Family Logon and want to use it, follow these steps to select it as the default logon option:

1. On the Start menu, point to Settings, and then click Control Panel.

2. In the Control Panel window, double-click the Network icon to open the Network dialog box.

3. In the Primary Network Logon drop-down list, select Microsoft Family Logon, and then click OK.

Note

If you no longer want to use the Microsoft Family Logon feature, select Client for Microsoft Networks instead.

Locating Your Folders

The profiles that are set up on a computer are stored in folders in the Profiles folder, which is in the Windows folder. To locate a profile folder, use either My Computer or Windows Explorer to navigate to the Profiles folder. In the Profiles folder, you'll see folders with profile names.

Double-click the profile name you're looking for to display all of the folders in that user's profile.

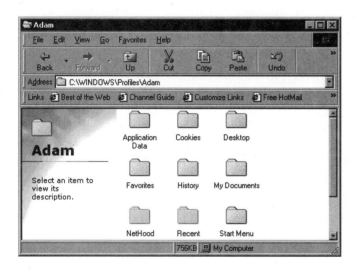

Changing Passwords

If you're using Microsoft Internet Explorer, version 4 or later, you can set and change your password in the Users dialog box. But no matter what version of Internet Explorer you're using, you can always change passwords with the Password program in the Control Panel. Here's how:

1. In the Control Panel, double-click the Passwords icon to display the Password Properties dialog box.

2. Click the Change Passwords tab.

3. Click Change Windows Password.

4. In the text boxes, enter your current password, and type and confirm your new password.

Note

The Change Other Passwords option, which is not available on all systems, lets you change the passwords you use to log on to a network server. On a family network, you don't need to worry about it.

You'll learn how to password protect individual folders and files in Chapter 9, "Learning to Share."

Surviving Password Forgetfulness

What happens if you forget your password? What you *don't* want to do is log on as a different user and delete your entire profile. This will delete settings and files that you probably want to retain.

After the initial panic wears off, you can easily delete your password and start over. Passwords are stored in files with a .pwl extension. To locate your password file, follow these steps:

1. On the Start menu, point to Find, and then click Files Or Folders.

2. In the Find: All Files dialog box, type *.pwl* in the Named text box and click Find Now.
   You'll see a list of files with the .pwl extension.

3. Click the file that has your user name, press Delete, and click Yes to confirm the deletion.

Note

After you delete your password file, you'll have to reenter your ISP password when you next log on to the Internet or check your e-mail.

You can now log on using your own user name and no password. You can also create a new password—one that you might not forget so easily. Either enter a new password in the Enter Network Password dialog box or create the new password in the Users or Passwords dialog box from the Control Panel.

Deleting All Profiles

If you ever decide that you no longer want to share your computer, you can delete all user profiles from Windows. To do so, however, you need to use the Windows Registry Editor, and this can be tricky. Because the registry is where Windows stores all of its settings, you must be extremely careful not to change a setting you don't want to change. If you do decide to delete all your profiles, follow these steps carefully:

1. Restart your computer and click Cancel when the Enter Network Password dialog box appears.

2. Double-click the Password icon in the Control Panel.

3. On the User Profiles tab, click All Users Of This PC Use the Same Preferences And Desktop Settings.

4. Click OK and restart your computer.

When the computer restarts, follow these steps:

1. On the Start menu, click Run.

2. In the Run dialog box, type *regedit*, and then click OK.
The Registry Editor starts, as shown in Figure 8-4, on the next page.

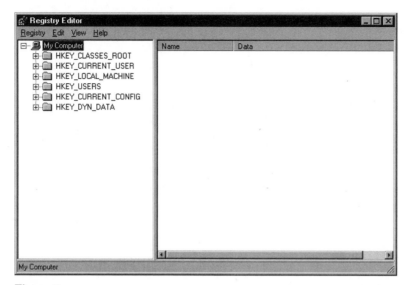

Figure 8-4.
The Registry Editor lets you change settings in the Windows registry.

3. Click the plus sign in front of HKEY_LOCAL_MACHINE to expand this section.

4. Click the plus sign in front of Software.

5. Click the plus sign in front of Microsoft.

6. Click the plus sign in front of Windows.

7. Click the plus sign in front of Current Version.

8. Click ProfileList.

   The status bar at the bottom of the Registry Editor should look like this.

   My Computer\HKEY_LOCAL_MACHINE\Software\Microsoft\Windows\CurrentVersion\ProfileList

9. Press Delete, and then press Enter if you are asked to confirm the deletion.

10. From the Registry menu, choose Exit.

    Now that you've edited the registry, follow these steps:

1. Double-click My Computer on the desktop.

2. Double-click the icon for your hard disk.

3. Open the Windows folder and click Show Files to display the contents of the folder.

4. Click the Profiles folder.

5. Press Delete to delete the folder.

6. Click Yes to confirm that you want to move the folder to the Recycle Bin.

User profiles are important when you share a computer with others. Profiles allow individual users to personalize their desktops and have a sense of ownership without changing the settings of other users. In the next chapter, you'll learn how to share files and folders across the network.

Chapter 9

Learning to Share

One of the main advantages of setting up a home network is that it gives you the ability to share files. But sharing doesn't come automatically. You not only have to turn on the file sharing service when you configure your network, but you also have to specify which resources you want to share with other users. In this chapter, you'll learn how to share disks, folders, and files.

Turning On File Sharing

Before you can activate file sharing, you must install the Microsoft Windows service that allows sharing. You probably installed this service along with your network drivers and software, as described in Chapter 7, but just in case you didn't, here's how to do it:

1. On the Start menu, point to Settings, and click Control Panel.

2. Double-click the Network icon to open the Network dialog box.

    In the list of network components that are installed, look for File And Printer Sharing For Microsoft Networks. If it's already listed, you can skip the rest of these steps. If the service is not installed, continue with these steps.

3. In the Network dialog box, click Add.

4. In the Select Network Component Type dialog box, click Service.

5. Click Add.

6. In the Select Network Service dialog box, click File And Printer Sharing For Microsoft Networks.

7. Click OK.

8. Click OK again to close the Network dialog box.

9. When you are asked whether you want to restart your computer, click Yes.

   Now that the service is installed, you are ready to turn on file and printer sharing.

1. On the Start menu, point to Settings, and click Control Panel.

2. Double-click the Network icon to open the Network dialog box.

3. Click the File And Printer Sharing button to open the File And Print Sharing dialog box.

4. Select both check boxes to allow access to your files and access to your printers.

5. Click OK.

6. Click OK again to close the Network dialog box.

Sharing and Accessing Network Resources

Installing the hardware and configuring Windows for sharing doesn't make the information on your computer instantly available to everyone. Before someone else can access a folder on your hard disk, you must first specify that the folder is shared.

Note

Resources that can be shared are called *shares*.

Windows organizes disks, folders and files in a hierarchical manner:

- Disks contain folders.

- Folders contain subfolders (and some files as well).

- Subfolders contain files.

   When you specify what can be shared on a network, everything within it is also shared. For example, if you allow a disk to be shared, all folders and files on that disk are shared as well. If you allow only a folder to be shared rather than the whole disk, all subfolders and files within that folder can be shared, but not other folders on that disk. So if you do want everything on your hard disk to be available on the network, turn on sharing for your hard disk. Once you share the disk, you don't have to turn on sharing for any of the individual folders within that disk—they are automatically shared across the network. You can also share a floppy disk, a CD-ROM, or a Zip disk. When you share a disk, an icon for its drive appears in the Network Neighborhood window for all users to see when they double-click the Network Neighborhood icon on their desktops.

Even though a folder on a shared disk is automatically available to network users, it won't appear as a separate icon in Network Neighborhood unless you specifically share that particular folder, and not just the disk on which the folder resides. If you want the folder to be seen on Network Neighborhood so that it can be easily accessed by network users, turn on sharing for the folder even if you've already turned on sharing for the disk. It's usually a good idea, for example, to share the Desktop subfolder within the Windows folder, so that any user can easily copy files to your Windows desktop.

In addition to turning on sharing, you can also specify how you want the disk or folder to be shared. There are three levels of sharing:

- **Read-Only** sharing means that users can open files in the shared folders and copy them to their own computers, but they cannot change, delete, or add files.

- **Full** sharing means that other users can do anything to shared disks or folders that you can do.

- **Depends On Password** sharing means that the password a user enters determines the level of sharing—full or read-only—granted to the user.

If you specify Read-Only access or Full access to a disk or folder, a password is optional. You can do without one and allow all members of your family to access a resource on your computer at whatever level of sharing you've specified for that resource. Or you can create a password and limit access—again, at the level of sharing you've specified— to family members to whom you've given the password.

With the Depends On Password option, you can selectively grant read-only or full access to members of your family. You create two passwords: a read-only password and a full password. Users to whom you give the read-only password can read and copy your files, but they can't change or delete them or add new ones. Users with the full password can do anything they want to your files.

Sharing Drives

To turn on sharing for an entire drive and give only certain people access to it, follow these steps:

1. Double-click My Computer on the Windows desktop.

2. Right-click the drive that you want to share.

3. Select Sharing from the shortcut menu to open the Properties dialog box shown in Figure 9-1.

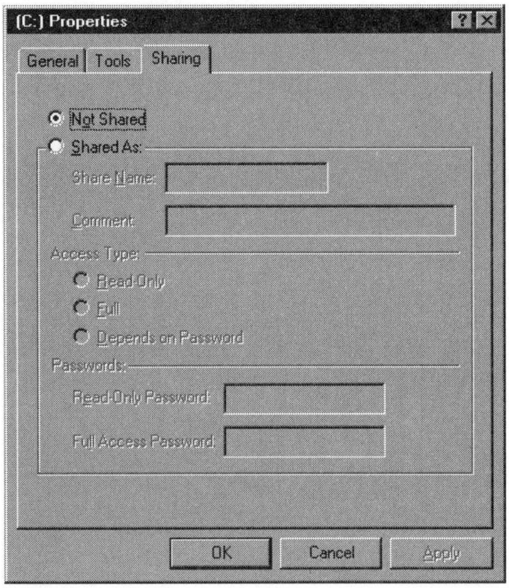

Figure 9-1.
The Properties dialog box allows you to turn on sharing for a resource and limit access to it by password.

4. Click Shared As.

    Windows places a default name in the Share Name text box, usually the same letter as the drive.

5. Leave the Share Name as it is, or change it to better identify the drive, as in *Alan's Zip disk*.

    The Share Name is what appears when network users access your computer.

6. In the Comment text box, you can enter an optional description.

7. Click one of the three access types—Read-Only, Full, or Depends On Password.

8. Enter an optional password: Read-Only, Full Access, or enter both if you want the level of access to be determined by the password that the person enters.

9. Click OK.

10. If you specified one or two passwords, reenter each in the Confirm Passwords dialog box, and then click OK.

The icon for the drive will now show, with a cradling hand, that the drive is shared.

[C:]

When another member of your family is connected to your computer and double-clicks the Network Neighborhood icon on the Windows desktop, an icon for your disk appears in the Network Neighborhood window the family member sees. If you've granted full access without a password, that family member can access your disk just as if it were a local hard disk rather than a disk in your computer.

If you turn on sharing for a floppy disk or a removable disk, such as a Zip disk, it's the drive that's actually shared rather than a particular disk. Turning on sharing for a floppy disk, for example, means that any floppy in the drive is shared. You may want to think twice about sharing removable drives if some of your disks contain sensitive information.

More on Passwords

If you want to make a shared drive or folder available to everyone on a network, you can leave the password for the resource blank. If you do enter a password, however, make sure you remember it. Let's say you're at a computer other than your own and you want to access your own files across the network. Your system won't know that it's you at the computer and will require the same password it does from the computer's primary user.

If you do forget the password that you've assigned to a shared resource, you can easily change it as long as you log on to your own computer. Unlike some passwords, a sharing password can be changed without your knowing the current one. To change a password, right-click the shared disk or folder, and choose Properties from the shortcut menu. Type the new password in place of the old one and click OK. You'll have to reenter the password to confirm it.

Note

To erase a password so that a shared disk or folder is no longer password-protected, just delete the asterisks in the password text boxes.

Sharing Folders

If you don't want to allow complete access to your disk, you can turn on sharing for only certain folders and not for the entire disk.

To turn on sharing for a folder, follow these steps:

1. Double-click My Computer on the Windows desktop.

2. Double-click the disk containing the folder you want to share.

3. Right-click the folder that you want to share.

    You may have to navigate through folders to display the subfolder you want to share.

4. Select Sharing from the shortcut menu to open the Properties dialog box.

5. Click Shared As.

6. Accept the default share name or enter a new one.

7. Enter an optional comment.

8. Choose an access type.

9. Enter an optional password—Read-Only, Full Access, or both.

10. Click OK.

11. If you specified one or two passwords, reenter each to confirm it in the Confirm Passwords dialog box, and then click OK.

You can also turn on sharing from any window that displays the folder, such as Windows Explorer, the Find dialog box, or a File Save or File Open dialog box in an application such as Microsoft Word. To turn on sharing, right-click the folder icon, select Sharing from the shortcut menu, and follow the rest of the steps in the procedure above.

Note

You cannot turn on sharing for the My Documents folder from the Windows desktop. If you want to set sharing for that folder, in My Computer, double-click the disk on which you've installed Windows, right-click the My Documents folder, and choose Sharing from the shortcut menu.

Accessing Shared Disks and Folders

Once disks and folders are shared, network users can access them in much the same way as they access disks and folders on their own computers. The trick is for them to locate the disk or folder on the remote computer.

Note

A remote computer is a computer on the network other than the one you're using.

You can always access remote computers using Network Neighborhood, so let's start from there.

1. Double-click Network Neighborhood on your Windows desktop.

    Remember, it may take a few minutes after you turn on your computer for it to recognize the remote computers on the network. You'll see icons representing all the computers on your network, as well as an icon for the Entire Network, such as the one shown in Figure 9-2.

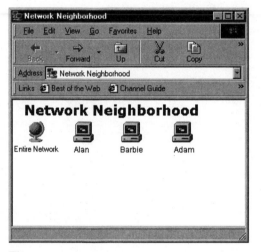

Figure 9-2.
Network Neighborhood displays icons for each computer connected to the network and an icon for the Entire Network.

Note

Clicking the Entire Network icon lets you access other workgroups that may be connected to your network.

2. Double-click the icon for the computer you want to access.

    You'll see icons representing shared drives and printers as well as folders that you've shared.

3. Double-click the disk or folder you want to access.

    If you see no individual folders at this point, the entire drive is shared.

Another way to access shared disks is from Windows Explorer or any Windows file management dialog box, such as the File Open dialog box in Microsoft Word. Let's look at Windows Explorer.

1. On the Start menu, point to Programs, and click Windows Explorer.

2. Click the plus sign next to Network Neighborhood in the list of folders.

3. Click the plus sign next to the remote computer you want to access.

4. If the disk in the computer is shared, click the plus sign next to the disk to display its contents. You can then access any of the files as if they were on your computer.

Note

The Network Neighborhood icon appears in the Open and Save dialog boxes of most Windows applications that let you access disks and folders. You can always use it to access remote computers.

Once you access a shared folder in a remote computer, you can use the files in that folder just as if you were on that computer, but only at the level of sharing you've been granted. If you have read-only access, you'll only be able to open or copy files from the shared folder. You won't be able to change or delete files or add new files to the folder. If you attempt to do so, you'll see the following dialog box.

Accessing Resources with the Run and Find Commands

While Network Neighborhood and Windows Explorer are the most common ways to access a remote computer, Windows offers two other options: the Run and Find commands on the Start menu.

If you know the name of the remote computer, you can access a shared resource on it by choosing the Run command from the Start menu. This opens the Run dialog box.

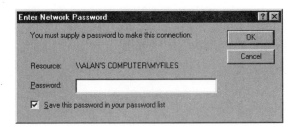

To use a resource on a remote computer, you must enter the path to the resource by typing the *universal naming convention* (UNC). You start the UNC with two backslashes (\\) followed by the name of the computer, as in *Joe*. Press Enter or click OK to open a window showing the shared resources on that computer. If you know the name of the specific disk and folder you're looking for on the remote computer, you can open it directly by adding its resource name to the UNC, as in *Joe\C\Budget*.

It's also possible to search for a computer on the network using the Find command from the Start menu. Just follow these steps:

1. On the Start menu, point to Find, and click Computer.

2. In the Find: Computer dialog box, enter the remote computer's name, and press Enter or click Find Now.

3. When the computer is located and listed in the Find dialog box, double-click its icon to access its shared resources.

Accessing Resources with Passwords

When a resource requires a password in order to be shared, you must enter the password before you can open the disk or folder—or at least you must enter it the first time you try to access the resource. As you'll see, there's a way to save the password so that you don't have to enter it each time you open a password-protected disk or folder.

When you first try to access a resource, you'll see the Enter Network Password dialog box.

Before you enter the password and click OK, you can select the check box labeled Save This Password In Your Password List. Windows maintains this password list in a file whose name is your user name plus the extension .pwl, as in alan.pwl. If you select this check box, the name of the shared resource and the password will be saved in your .pwl file. The next time you access the same disk or folder, Windows automatically locates the password so that you don't have to enter it again.

Note

Do not select the check box if you want to prevent other network users from accessing shared resources with your password.

When the Enter Network Password dialog box opens, type in your password, and then click OK. If the password you've typed is incorrect, a message appears telling you so. Click OK to clear the message, and then reenter the correct password.

Making Sharing Easier

Navigating through Network Neighborhood to locate a folder or file can be time-consuming. Fortunately Windows offers a number of ways to make network life easier.

Creating a Desktop Shortcut

The easiest way to access a remote disk, folder, or file is to add an icon for it to your Windows desktop.

1. Use Network Neighborhood to locate the disk, folder, or file on the remote computer.

2. Click the disk, folder, or file with the right mouse button, and then hold down the button while you drag the icon to your desktop.

Note

To create a shortcut to the remote computer itself, drag the remote computer icon to your desktop.

3. Release the mouse button and select Create Shortcut(s) Here from the shortcut menu.

Windows 98 also allows you to drag the shortcut icon you placed on your desktop to the taskbar so that you can access it with a single click.

Adding Shared Resources to Favorites

If you are using Windows 98 (or Windows 95 with version 4 or later of Microsoft Internet Explorer), you can store frequently used folders and files in a Favorites folder, which is quickly accessible from the Start menu.

You'll also find a Favorites menu item in Windows Explorer, My Computer, Network Neighborhood, and other dialog boxes in Windows that let you manage files. After you've added a shortcut to a folder or file to your Favorites list, you can open Favorites and click the shortcut to open the folder or file.

To add a resource to the Favorites list, follow these steps:

1. Double-click the Network Neighborhood icon on the desktop and locate the folder or file in the Network Neighborhood window.

2. Double-click the folder or file so that its path appears in the Address field in the Address toolbar.

3. From the Favorites menu, choose Add To Favorites to open the Add Favorite dialog box.

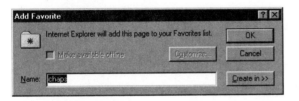

4. Click OK. You can also click the Create In button if you want to add the item to a folder within Favorites or to create a new subfolder of Favorites.

Mapping Network Drives and Folders

Another way to gain easy access to a disk on a remote computer is to assign it a drive letter on your own machine. This is called *mapping* the disk.

For example, suppose you have the following disks in your computer:

- A floppy disk drive, designated as A

- The hard disk, designated as C

- A CD-ROM or DVD disk drive, designated as D

If you frequently access a hard drive, CD-ROM, or other drive on a remote computer, you can map it so that it appears as drive E or F on your computer. Even better, you can map to a specific folder on a remote computer, giving it a drive letter, as long as the folder has been enabled for sharing. Let's say you often access a folder named Budget on a remote computer. You can map to the folder so that it shows up in My Computer as drive F on your computer.

Myfiles on
'Alan's
computer' (F:)

To map a disk or folder, follow these steps:

1. Double-click the Network Neighborhood icon on the desktop and double-click the icon for the remote computer in the Network Neighborhood window.

You'll see icons for each of the disks and folders on the remote computer that have been shared.

2. Right-click the icon for the resource you want to map to, and then choose Map Network Drive from the shortcut menu to see the Map Network Drive dialog box.

Map Network Drive	? X
Drive: F:	OK
Path: \\Alan's computer\myfiles	Cancel
☐ Reconnect at logon	

3. In the Map Network Drive dialog box, select the Reconnect At Logon check box if you want Windows to map to this resource every time you start your computer.

4. Click OK.

A window opens showing the contents of the drive or folder; the address box in the Address toolbar shows that the resource is now mapped to a drive on your computer.

If you close the window and open My Computer, you'll see the shared resource listed as a drive. Just double-click the icon as you would any actual disk drive to access its contents on the remote computer.

When you turn on Reconnect At Logon, Windows browses the network looking for the mapped disk or folder each time you start your computer. If the remote computer is not turned on, Windows starts normally but does not map to the shared resource. You'll have to remap to it after the remote computer joins the network.

If you do not select Reconnect At Logon, the drive you mapped to is disconnected when you turn off your computer or restart Windows. You'll have to repeat the procedure above to map to the drive again.

Browsing for mapped resources takes some time, and it will slow down the logon process, so if you don't need to map to the resource every time you use your computer, do not select the Reconnect At Logon option.

To speed up the process of mapping resources, an alternative is to tell Windows not to browse the network automatically when your computer starts. With the Quick Logon feature, Windows displays the icons for mapped resources in Network Neighborhood, My Computer, and Windows Explorer without checking to see whether the resource is really available. Windows waits until you first try to use the resource before actually connecting to it. To turn on the Quick Logon feature, follow these steps:

1. On the Start menu, point to Settings, and click Control Panel.

2. In the Control Panel window, double-click the Network icon to open the Network dialog box.

3. In the list of installed network components, select Client For Microsoft Networks.

4. Click Properties to open the Client For Microsoft Networks Properties dialog box shown in Figure 9-3.

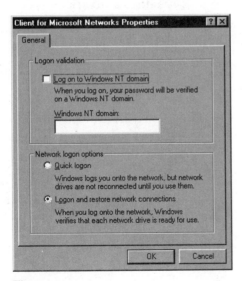

Figure 9-3.
You can change logon options in the Client For Microsoft Networks Properties dialog box.

5. Click Quick Logon.

    The other option, Logon And Restore Network Connections, maps and connects to shared resources you've mapped every time Windows starts.

6. Click OK to close the Client for Microsoft Networks Properties dialog box.

7. Click OK to close the Network dialog box.

Working with Remote Files

After you've accessed a disk or folder on a remote computer, you can start working with its files in Network Neighborhood, My Computer, or Windows Explorer. Here's how to access a file with Network Neighborhood or My Computer:

1. Double-click the Network Neighborhood on the desktop, or double-click My Computer if the disk on the remote computer has been mapped.

2. Double-click the icon for the computer you want to access.

3. Double-click the disk or folder you want to open.

4. Select the file so you can work with it.

    To access the file with Windows Explorer, follow these steps:

1. On the Start menu, point to Programs, and click Windows Explorer.

2. Click the plus sign next to Network Neighborhood in the Folders list on the left.

3. Click the plus sign next to the remote computer you want to access.

4. Click the plus sign next to the disk you want to open on the remote computer.

5. Click the folder containing the file you are looking for. If the folder contains subfolders, click the plus sign next to the folder to display its contents, and then select the subfolder containing the file.

    After you've accessed a file, you can do anything with it that your level of sharing allows. If you have read-only access to the folder, you can open the file or copy it to another location, but you can't do anything else to it. If you have full access, you can also change, delete, or move the file.

    Let's take a closer look at how to work with files on remote computers.

Opening Remote Files from Within Applications

On the network, you can open a file on a remote computer just as you would open it on your own computer. In Windows 95, you can locate the file in My Computer, Network Neighborhood, or Windows Explorer, and open it by double-clicking its icon.

You can also open files from within Windows applications, such as the programs in Microsoft Office. Because Network Neighborhood is an integrated part of the Windows file system, it shows up in all the lists you see whenever you try to access files. This means that you can treat a remote computer as you would any disk drive—locate it in the application's Open dialog box, choose the drive, the folder, and then choose the document you want to access.

For example, suppose you are working in Microsoft Word and need to open a file in the My Documents folder of a remote computer. Here's how you'd do it:

1. From the File menu, choose Open to display the Open dialog box.

2. In the Look In drop-down list, select Network Neighborhood.

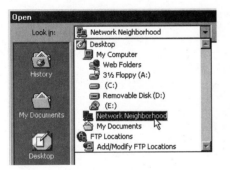

A list of computers on the network appears in the Open dialog box.

3. Double-click the icon for the computer whose disk contains the file you want.
   A list of shared resources on the remote computer appears in the Open dialog box.

4. Double-click the hard disk that contains Windows on the remote computer. It's usually the C drive.

5. Double-click My Documents.

6. Double-click the file you want to open.

Saving Remote Files from within Applications

Saving a remote file from within a Windows application is even easier than opening it, as long as you have full access privileges. If you've made changes to an existing remote file, you save it just as you would any other document, by clicking the Save button on the application's Standard toolbar or by choosing Save from the application's File menu.

You can also use the Save As command on the application's File menu to save the document to another location or with a new file name. When the Save As dialog box opens, it shows the folder from which you opened the document. Choose another location from the Save In list in the Save As dialog box, a folder either on your own computer or on any other computer on the network.

If you are working on a new document and want to save it on a remote computer, use the Save In list in the Save As dialog box to select Network Neighborhood, choose the remote computer, and then select the destination folder.

Saving a Read-Only File

If you've made changes to a file that you opened from a read-only folder, you cannot save it to the same location. If you try to do so, you'll see a warning message.

This is not to say that you can't make changes to the file; you just can't replace the existing version in the shared folder with your edited version. (Remember that when a folder has been designated as read-only, you can't change its contents.) To save your changes, you must use the Save As command and save the file as a new document in a folder to which you have full access. The folder can be on your own hard disk or on a disk in a remote computer.

To save a file to a remote computer, navigate to the computer using Network Neighborhood in the application's Save As dialog box, using these steps:

1. From the File menu of the application, choose Save As to display the Save As dialog box.

Note

In some Windows programs, clicking Save when a file is read-only automatically opens the Save As dialog box.

2. In the Save In drop-down list, choose Network Neighborhood.
   A list of computers on the network appears in the Save As dialog box.

3. Double-click the icon for the remote computer to which you want to save the file to see a list of its shared resources.

4. Double-click the disk drive.

5. Double-click the folder in which you want to save the file.

6. Click Save.

Avoiding Double Trouble

It doesn't make sense for two people to try to work on the same file at the same time. The result can be lost work and confusion.

Suppose, for example, that you and your spouse want to work on the family budget using two different computers. Here's what might happen:

1. You and your spouse both open the document and see that Entertainment is set at $100 per month.

2. You change Entertainment to $200.

3. Your spouse changes it to $50.

4. You save the document.
   The $200 amount for Entertainment is recorded on the disk.

5. Your spouse saves the document after you do. The $50 figure is recorded on the disk, and your changes to the budget are lost!

If your spouse had saved the document before you did, your $200 choice would have prevailed.

To avoid such situations, only one person at a time should work on a document in a folder to which full access has been granted. What happens, however, when one person opens a document that's already being used by another person depends on the version of Windows and the application you are both using.

For example, you may receive a message that the document you are trying to open is already in use and you may get the option to open it in read-only mode. Although this will allow you to make changes to the document, you won't be able to save it back to the same location, using the same name.

Note

There are exceptions to the one-person-at-a-time rule. With a program such as Microsoft NetMeeting, two people can collaborate on a document at the same time and see each other's changes as they are made. You'll learn more about this type of simultaneous file sharing in Chapter 11.

Some applications provide safeguards against opening a document in use. Microsoft Word 2000, for example, displays this message if you try to open a file that's being used.

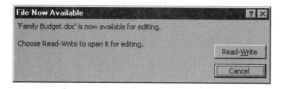

In the File In Use message box, click Read-Only to open the document in read-only mode. Clicking Notify also opens the document in read-only mode, but you'll also see a message like this when the other user closes the file.

Click Read-Write to reopen the latest version of the document with the other user's changes. If you made any changes to the document, you'll see a message that tells you so.

- Click Discard to ignore your changes and to reopen the latest version of the document.
- Click Save As to save your document under a new name and to open the latest version of the original file.

Copying and Moving Remote Files

You move or copy a file between computers on a network the same way you move or copy a file between folders on your own hard disk.

When you copy a file, you leave the original in its location and place a duplicate on another computer. Copying a file is a good idea when you want to make changes to a document without deleting the original version. Just remember that if someone changes one of the copies, there will be two different versions of the same file on the network

When you move a file, you delete the original from its location and place it on another computer. If you move a file that someone else might want to work with, let the other user know where you're placing it. You cannot move a file from a read-only folder because moving it would be the same as deleting it from that folder, and read-only access does not permit deletion of files. If you try to move such a file, you'll get an error message.

You can move and copy files between a remote computer and your own, using either Windows Explorer or Network Neighborhood.

Copying Files Between Computers

Whether you're copying a file between your folders on your own hard disk or between computers on the network, you can use two basic methods. You can drag the file from one location to another, or you can use the copy and paste method.

Dragging Files   To copy a file by dragging it, you need to have open both the folder that contains the file and the folder to which you want to copy it. This process is easiest with Windows Explorer, so let's start there.

Let's assume that you want to copy a file from a remote computer to your own computer.

1. On the Start menu, point to Programs, and click Windows Explorer.

2. In the Folders list on the left, locate the folder in which you want to place the file.
   For example, if you want to place the file in the My Documents folder, make sure you see the folder in the list. If necessary, click the plus sign next to the C drive.

3. To locate the file you want to copy, click the plus sign next to Network Neighborhood in the list on the left.

4. Click the plus sign next to the remote computer you want to access.

5. Click the plus sign next to the disk drive on the remote computer that contains the file.

6. Click the folder containing the file you are looking for.

If the folder contains subfolders, click the plus sign next to the folder to display its contents, and then select the subfolder containing the file. You should see the file you want to copy in the list on the right.

7. Now scroll through the list on the left until you see the folder to which you want to copy the file, *but do not click it*.

    Being able to see the icon for the folder is enough for now. You should still see the file you want to copy on the right.

8. Drag the icon of the file you want to copy from the list at the right to the destination folder in the Folders list on the left.

    As you drag, a small plus sign appears next to the mouse pointer indicating that you are copying, rather than moving, the file.

In Figure 9-4, the file named Budget from the Microsoft Excel book folder on a remote computer is being copied to the My Files folder on the local computer.

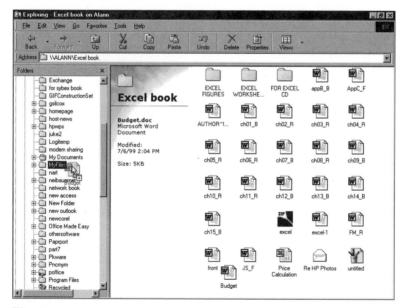

Figure 9-4.

To copy a remote file, drag it from its current location to the proper folder in the Folders list.

Note

It's also possible to drag a file by holding down the *right* mouse button as you drag rather than the left. This causes a shortcut menu to appear, from which you can choose Copy Here when you release the mouse button.

You can also copy a file using a combination of My Computer and Network Neighborhood. With this approach, you drag the file to be copied between two windows on your screen: one that shows the file's original location, and another that shows its destination. This time, you'll copy a file from your computer to a remote one.

1. Double-click My Computer on the desktop and double-click the drive containing the file.

2. Double-click the folder containing the file.

3. If the folder window fills the screen, click the Restore button to make the window smaller.

4. Drag the window to the left side of the screen.

5. Double-click Network Neighborhood on the Windows desktop.

   Network Neighborhood appears in a new window. If the two windows overlap, drag the Network Neighborhood window to the right.

6. In the Network Neighborhood window, double-click the icon for the computer you want to access.

7. In the Network Neighborhood window, double-click the disk, and then double-click the folder in which you want to place the file. The screen should look similar to the one shown in Figure 9-5.

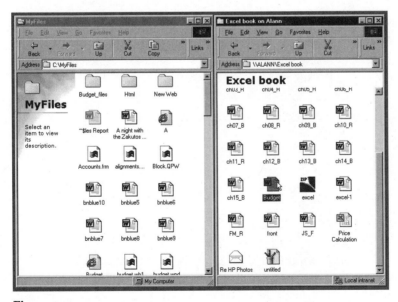

Figure 9-5.
Copy a file by dragging it between the My Computer and Network Neighborhood windows.

8. Drag the file from the Network Neighborhood window on the left to the My Computer window on the right.

Copying and Pasting   If copying a file by dragging seems too time-consuming, you can always do it the old-fashioned Windows way, by using the Copy and Paste commands. You'll still need to open both a window showing the file in its original location and a window showing the new location, but you don't need to have both open at the same time.

You can copy and paste using Windows Explorer, Network Neighborhood, or My Computer. Here's how:

1. Open the folder containing the file you want to copy and select the file.

2. Right-click the file and choose Copy from the Shortcut menu. You can also click Copy on the Windows Explorer toolbar.

3. Open the folder to which you want to copy the file.

4. Right-click and choose Paste from the Shortcut menu. You can also choose Paste from the Edit menu or from the toolbar.

Note

If you periodically access a file on a remote computer, you can create a shortcut to it on your machine by dragging it to your desktop while holding down the right mouse button and choosing Create Shortcut(s) Here from the shortcut menu that appears.

Sending Files to Remote Drives   One very handy feature of Windows is the Send To list. If you need to save a file on a floppy disk, for example, you can right-click its icon on the desktop or in any folder, and then point to Send To to see a list of possible destinations. Click 3½ Floppy (A) at the top of the list to copy the file to the floppy disk drive, for example.

It's possible to add your own destinations to the Send To list so that you can copy files quickly to a remote computer of your choice. To do this, you first have to create a desktop shortcut to the disk or shared folder on the remote computer that you want to add to the Send To list (*see "Creating a Desktop Shortcut," on page 152*). Next, right-click the shortcut you've created to the remote computer and choose Rename from the shortcut menu. Type a name that you'd want to see in the Send To list and press Enter. Finally, drag the icon to the C:\Windows\Send To folder.

Now, whenever you want to copy a file to the remote location, right-click the file, point to Send To and click the listing for the remote location.

Moving Remote Files

You move a file between computers in almost exactly the same way you copy a file. To move a file by dragging, follow the steps for copying, but hold down the Shift key when you release the mouse button. While you hold down the Shift key, the small plus sign next to the pointer disappears, indicating that you're moving, rather than copying, the file. You don't have to hold down the Shift key while you're dragging the mouse, only when you release it.

If you prefer not to move a file by dragging it, you can move the file using the Cut and Paste, rather than the Copy and Paste, method. Right-click the file and choose Cut from the shortcut menu instead of Copy. Open the folder to which you want to move the file, right-click again, and choose Paste from the shortcut menu. When you paste the file into its new location, it is removed from its original folder.

Note

As with copying, it's also possible to drag the file by holding down the *right* mouse button instead of the left. In this case, choose Move Here from the shortcut menu that appears when you release the mouse.

Deleting Remote Files

When you have full access to a remote folder, it's possible to delete it or delete the files within it. But before you delete anything, you should be aware that the Recycle Bin does not work across the network.

The Recycle Bin, on the Windows desktop, is a holding tank for files or folders that you delete from your hard disk. If you change your mind about deleting an item, you can open the Recycle Bin, select the deleted file or folder in the Recycle Bin window, and choose Restore from the File menu. If you're sure you don't need the files in the Recycle Bin any-more, you can open the Recycle Bin and choose Empty Recycle Bin from the File menu.

When you delete a file that's on another computer on the network, however, it is immediately deleted from the disk without making a protective stop at the Recycle Bin of either computer. Even dragging the file to the Recycle Bin of your computer erases it automatically.

Note

The Recycle Bin also does not work for files and folders deleted from floppy disks or removable drive disks, such as Zip disks.

With this in mind, if you're sure you want to delete a remote file, just locate the file using Network Neighborhood, Windows Explorer, or any other method. Select the file and press the Delete key, or right-click the file and choose Delete from the shortcut menu. When you are asked whether you really want to delete the file, click Yes if you do or click No if you've changed your mind.

Note

You can delete an entire folder from a remote computer with this same procedure.

Sharing Programs

So far, we've been looking rather generically at sharing files, primarily documents, graphics, sounds, and other files that are not programs. Sharing a program on a network is a slightly different matter.

What Can Be Shared?

Sharing programs on a network may have legal ramifications.

- It is not always legal to purchase one copy of a program and install it on each of the computers on your network.

- It is not always legal to purchase one copy of a program, install it on one computer, and then let more than one person on the network run the program at the same time.

Remember that software is usually licensed, and many software companies prohibit program sharing as part of their licensing agreement. This means that all you are really purchasing is a license to use the software and, according to the rules, you do not own the software itself. By opening and using a piece of software, you are agreeing to abide by the terms of your software license agreement.

Many licensing agreements require you to acquire a separate copy or license for every computer you want to run the software on, even if you're using the software on just one computer at a time.

There are also programs that can't be shared at all. Many older versions of programs, particularly those that run on MS-DOS rather than Windows, can only be run on the computer on which they are installed. These programs are designed to access additional files within the same computer. When you try to run such programs remotely, they can't find the files they need and either display an error message or don't work at all.

Running a Program Remotely

Running a program on a remote computer is essentially the same as opening it on your own computer. You locate the program file, and then open it by double-clicking it. When you run a program that's on a remote computer, the program runs in your computer, but its files remain on the remote computer.

See Also

In Chapter 13, you'll learn how to share and play games across a network.

Because some programs frequently draw information from the disk as they run, you may find that running a remote program uses up quite a bit of your network resources. You may also encounter problems with programs that won't run properly across a network. If you get error messages when you start the program or while you're using it, you won't be able to run it remotely. You'll have to either install the program on your computer (if the licensing agreement allows), or go to the computer on which it is installed and run it from there.

Sharing a Data File

Sometimes you must share access to certain files, such as calendars and databases, on other computers. The shared data file may be a calendar, for example, that each member of the family accesses to check for appointments and special events. You want only one copy of this calendar on the network so that everyone sees the same information and changes made to it are available to everyone.

You can open a data file by simply navigating to it and opening it, as you've learned in this chapter, or you can set up your application program to access the file on a remote computer automatically.

Storing Shared Documents and Data Files on the Network

If you want to share a document or data file with other network users, give some thought to the best location in which to keep the file. For example, storing it on the computer that is turned on most often increases the odds that the file will be available when someone needs to access it.

Security is another issue to consider. If you want to use a password to limit access to a file, you'll need to store the file in a folder that is password-protected, which may limit your placement options. The computer in your child's room may be on almost all of the time, for example, for game playing, doing homework, and online chatting, but you wouldn't want to store a personal or parent-only file there. The trade-off for security might be to store the file on a computer that is used less frequently, but mainly by adults.

Another factor is that many programs expect to see files in specific places. They're set up to look in a default folder for the files they need to open. When you need to use this type of program, you have two choices: place the files where the program expects to see them, or tell the program where you've chosen to keep the files.

Microsoft Money, for example, which lets you keep track of your bank accounts and even transfer funds and pay bills on line, uses a data file named Mymoney.mny. The program stores this file in a folder that it reserves for it on the hard disk.

To change where Microsoft Money should look for Mymoney.mny, just copy the file to wherever you want to store it, and then double-click Mymoney.mny to start the program. Because Microsoft Money always uses the last data file you opened, the new data file in its new location becomes the default.

You can share a Microsoft Money file between computers on the network, so that anyone who runs the program can have access to the most current bank accounts. Just copy the Mymoney.mny file to the computer where you want the shared file to be located and then have all network users start their copy of Microsoft Money by navigating to the remote computer and opening the Mymoney.mny file.

Other applications let you set the default location for documents in a dialog box, such as Microsoft Word's Options dialog box, shown in Figure 9-6.

If you want Word to automatically look for new documents on a remote computer or to save new documents to a remote computer, enter the UNC path as the Document's location. Here's how to do it:

1. Start Word and, from the Tools menu, choose Options.

2. In the Options dialog box, click the File Locations tab.

3. Click Documents in the File types list, and then click Modify.

4. In the Modify Location dialog box, type the full path for the folder on the remote computer, such as *\\Barbara\C\Myfiles*.

    You can also browse for the location by choosing Network Neighborhood in the dialog box's Look In list.

5. Click OK to close the Modify Location dialog box.

6. Click OK to close the Options dialog box.

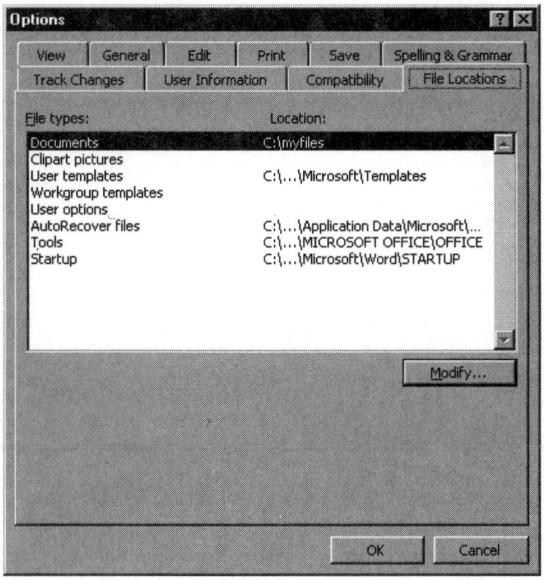

Figure 9-6.
In Microsoft Word, the default location for documents is set in the Options dialog box.

Backing Up Important Files

When it comes to backing up, the best rule of thumb is: "Back up what you don't want to lose." Unfortunately, backing up is one of those things we all know we should do but too often don't.

Backing up means making a copy of important files in some location other than your hard disk. That way, if your hard disk decides it's had enough of your interference and departs to never-never-land, your important files are safe and sound somewhere else. Sounds logical, only many of us forget to back up important files or we just get too lazy to do it.

When you're sharing files on a network, backing up is even more important for two reasons:

- The more people who access your disk, the greater the chance an important file will be deleted or corrupted. This is especially true if you allow full access to your network's resources.

- More people are dependent on being able to use a given file and will be affected by its loss. It's not just you anymore.

It's really up to all network users to take some precautions to safeguard important files that would be difficult or impossible to re-create. Backing up programs is not as critical because you can always reinstall them from their original disks. But your documents, database files, spreadsheets, banking files, and other data files might be unique and not easy to replace.

Some programs, such as MECA's Managing Your Money and Microsoft Money, automatically create a backup file each time you exit them. While the setup procedure varies, in most cases the backup option is available as a menu choice or in a dialog box that opens when you choose to exit the program. You can usually specify the backup location, including a disk on a remote computer.

Using Removable Disks

The best choice for quick and easy backups of files and folders is a Zip, Jazz, or other type of removable disk anywhere on your network. Removable disks hold at least 100 MB of information, the equivalent of about 70 floppy disks. That's not as much storage as you have on a hard disk or tape drive, but it can certainly accommodate a lot of files. Because the disk is removable, you can use multiple disks to store as much information as you like.

If the drive is attached to your computer, it will appear as a drive icon in My Computer. Just drag the files or folders you want to back up to this icon. If your computer has a built-in removable disk or tape drive, it may appear automatically in your Send To list. If it doesn't, create a shortcut to the drive on the desktop and add it to the Send To folder yourself. *See "Sending Files to Remote Drives," on page 164.*

When the drive is attached to a remote computer, consider mapping to the drive, so that you can access it from My Computer, or creating a shortcut to it in the SendTo folder.

Storing Files Remotely

Another option worth considering is backing up your files to the hard disk of a remote computer. One of the computers on the network might be newer and have a much larger hard disk than the disk in your own computer. Or it may not be used quite as much as other computers in the house, so it has extra hard disk space that can be shared among the family.

Create a folder on that computer with your name so you can easily identify it. Create a shortcut to the folder on your desktop, and then add the shortcut to the Send To folder. You'll now be able to back up folders and files to that remote disk quickly and easily.

Using Microsoft Backup

As an alternative to backing up individual files and folders, you can automate the backup process with Microsoft Backup. The program comes with Windows, so you can't beat the price, and it works with floppy disks, tape backup drives, and most removable disks. It's great for a network because you can use it to back up files from your own or any other computer on the network, and store the backup on a remote computer.

Backup is not usually installed in Windows, so you'll have to do it yourself. But don't worry, it's easy. Just follow these steps:

1. Insert your Windows CD in the CD-ROM drive.
2. On the Start menu, point to Settings, and click Control Panel.
3. In the Control Panel window, double-click Add/Remove Programs.
4. In the Add/Remove Programs Properties dialog box, click the Windows Setup tab. After a moment or two you'll see a list of Windows components.
5. Scroll through the list and click System Tools. Make sure you do not remove the check mark from the check box to the left.
6. Click Details to see a list of items in the System Tools category.
7. In the System Tools dialog box, click the Backup check box to enable it.
8. Click OK to close the System Tools dialog box.
9. Click OK again to close the Add/Remove Programs Properties dialog box.
10. Click Yes when you are asked whether you want to restart your computer.

After your computer restarts, you are ready to configure and run Microsoft Backup. The process varies slightly, depending on the type of drive you're using for backup—tape, removable disk, or floppy disk.

Note

If you don't have a tape backup drive or another device automatically recognized by Backup as a backup device, you may be asked the first time you run the program whether you want it to search for a backup device. Select No.

Microsoft Backup lets you create a *backup job* that defines which files you want to back up and where you want them stored. It's possible to have any number of backup jobs defined, and you can easily repeat a backup to save updated files.

To start the program, follow these steps:

1. On the Start menu, point to Programs, point to Accessories, point to System Tools, and then click Backup.

   You'll see the Microsoft Backup dialog box shown in Figure 9-7.

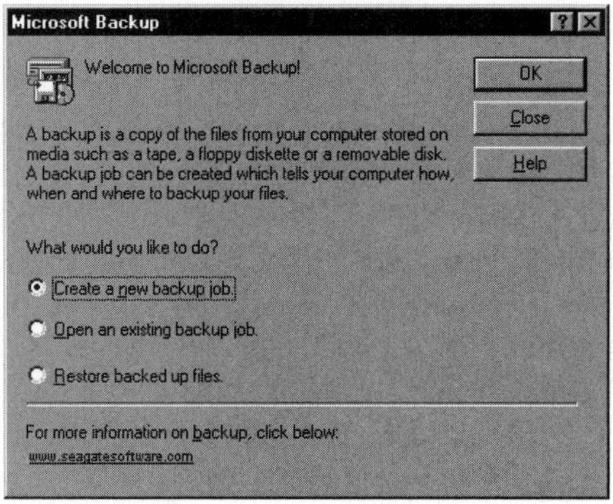

Figure 9-7.
The Microsoft Backup dialog box prompts you to create a new backup job, which starts the Backup Wizard.

2. Choose Create a New Backup Job to define a backup job, and then click OK to start the Backup Wizard.

The wizard takes you step by step through the process of defining a backup job and performing the backup itself. You can choose options such as

- The name of the backup job
- Whether to back up your entire computer or only selected files
- The storage location for backup files
- Whether backups and originals are compared to verify their accuracy
- Whether backup files are compressed to save space

The Backup Wizard isn't the only way to define a backup job. You can also use the main Backup window, shown in Figure 9-8. This window allows you to specify what to back up, where to store it, and how to save it. Then you just click the Start button. To back up important files from a remote computer, for example, you just scroll through the What To Back Up list and click the plus sign next to Networks to access remote computers.

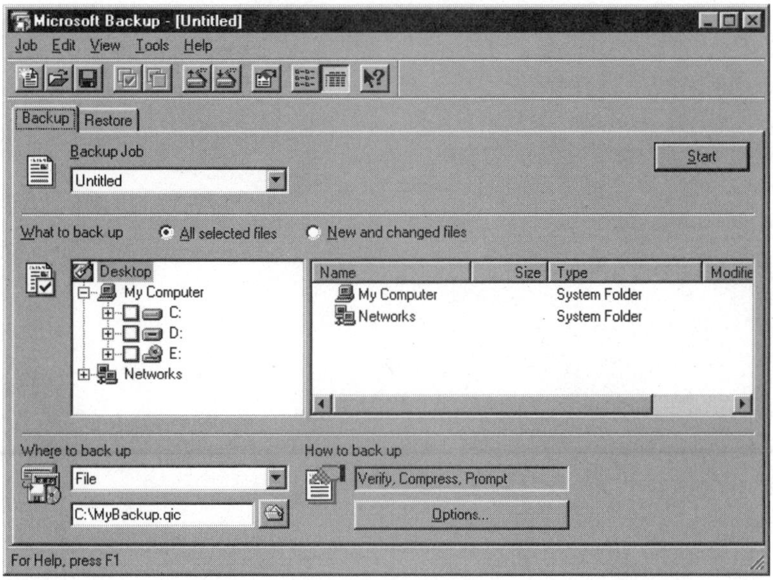

Figure 9-8.

Using the controls in the Microsoft Backup window is an alternative to using the Backup Wizard.

Microsoft Backup doesn't store files individually. Instead, it combines them in one large file or a series of large files spread over several disks. For this reason, you can't use standard Windows or MS-DOS techniques to access individual files in a backup. If you want to retrieve files from the backup, you have to perform a *restore* operation.

To restore files, choose the Restore Backed Up Files option when you start Microsoft Backup. This opens the Restore Wizard. You can also click Close on the Microsoft Backup dialog box after you start Microsoft Backup and use the controls on the Restore tab to specify restore options. If you choose to restore selected files, you'll see a list of the individual files in the backup from which you can choose.

In this chapter, you've learned to share disks, folders, files, and programs among computers on the network so everyone can use them. You've also learned how to back up important files to a different computer. In the next chapter, you will learn how to share another important resource on a network, the printers connected to the computers.

Part 4

Running the Network

Chapter 10

Printing Across the Network

Sharing files and folders is one great advantage of connecting computers in a network; sharing printers is another. When you share printers, everyone on the network can access them. You may need to walk to the printer in another room to retrieve your printed copies, but the pages will be there, ready and waiting for you.

You should share printers if

- You don't have a printer for each computer

- You want to use a feature of a printer that is connected to a remote computer

Let's say you purchased printers for some but not all of the computers in the home. If your computers are not connected to a network, you'll need to do one of two things to get a printout from a computer that doesn't have a printer:

- Save your documents on a disk and take the disk to a computer that is connected to a printer.

- Disconnect the printer from one computer and hook it up to the computer you want to print from.

If you've set up a home network, it doesn't matter whether all your computers have printers. You can send a document to printers connected to other computers on the network.

Even if you do have a printer for each computer, the printers may not all be of the same type. For example, you might have a laser printer connected to your computer for printing business documents, while your children have a color printer for school reports and kids' stuff. If your computers are connected in a network, you can get to your kids' color printer whenever you want, and the kids will be able to print with your laser printer.

See Also

Chapter 2 covered ways to share printers without a network.

There are two basic ways to link a printer to a network. The cheaper and easier method is simply to connect the printer to the parallel or USB port of one of the computers in the network. The other way is to connect the printer directly to the network. Although this second option is more expensive, connecting a printer directly has many advantages, as you'll learn later in "Connecting Printers Directly to the Network," on page 187.

Sharing Printers

When you print to a printer connected to a remote computer, your print job travels over the network, through the remote computer, and then to the printer attached to it. It's the remote computer, rather than your own, that causes the printer to print.

Let the Printer Beware!

Sharing printers attached to computers connected in a network is a great time-saver, but there's one big gotcha: both the printer and the computer it's attached to must be turned on, and the printer must be on line, stocked with paper, and ready to go. Otherwise, it's no go!

This means that before you print to a printer on the network, you have to check to make sure it's ready. If no one is using the computer that is attached to the printer, you may have to go to the computer, turn on both the computer and the printer, and set up the printer for printing.

Even if the computer and printer are turned on and ready, they may be busy with someone else's print job. When the printer completes the job, it will start printing your document and others that are waiting on a FIFO basis, which is old accounting talk for "First In, First Out," meaning the first in line gets printed first. Another problem can occur if the person using the computer attached to the printer shuts the computer down before the printer starts printing your work. A little coordination among the family is clearly needed here.

You might suggest to everyone on the network that anyone who wants to print to someone else's shared printer should first send a short message to make sure the printer is on and ready. In Chapter 11, you learn how to send messages to other people on your network. You could also try yelling from room to room, but that's not always the best approach.

Setting Up Printer Sharing

Before you can share the printer connected to your computer on the network, you must have installed the File and Printer Sharing for Microsoft Networks service. Chances are, you already did this when you set up file sharing (*see "Turning on File Sharing," on page 143*). But to make sure that you've enabled the printer sharing part of the service, follow these steps:

1. On the Start menu, point to Settings, and then click Control Panel.

2. In the Control Panel, double-click the Network icon to open the Network dialog box.

3. Click the File And Print Sharing button to open the File And Print Sharing dialog box.

4. Make sure the I Want To Be Able To Allow Others To Print To My Printer(s) check box is selected.

5. Click OK to close the File And Print Sharing dialog box.

6. Click OK to close the Network dialog box.

Installing a Printer

The next step in setting up a printer is to check that the printer is actually installed on your computer and working properly. If you can't use the printer directly attached to your computer, no one else will be able to use it over the network.

To make sure that your printer is installed in Microsoft Windows, point to Settings on the Start menu, and then click Printers. If you see a listing for your printer, it's already installed and you can close the Printers window. If your printer isn't listed in the Printers window, you'll have to add the printer now.

If your printer came with a floppy disk or CD, it may have its own special printer drivers and installation program. Take a quick look at the documentation that came with the printer, and if the printer came with a CD, take a look at the CD too—sometimes you'll see instructions printed right on the CD.

Depending on the type of printer, running its special installation program can be as simple as inserting the CD in the computer and waiting for the installation program to start by itself. If nothing happens when you insert the CD, go to My Computer and double-click the icon for the CD. If that doesn't start the installation program, you might have to run the Setup or Install program on the CD. When the installation program starts, just follow the instructions that appear on the screen.

In many cases, however, setting up your printer does not require running a special installation program. Instead, you can set up the printer using the Add Printer Wizard in Windows. Here's how:

1. Insert your Windows CD in the CD-ROM drive.

    This may not be necessary depending on how your computer was set up, but it can't hurt.

2. On the Start menu, point to Settings, and then click Printers.

3. Double-click the Add Printer icon to start the Add Printer Wizard.

4. Click Next.

Now the Add Printer Wizard will take you through the steps of installing the printer. At this next step of the wizard, you'll be asked whether you want to install a local printer or a network printer.

1. Because you are installing a printer that's directly connected to your computer, click Local Printer, and then click Next.

    You'll now see the dialog box shown in Figure 10-1, which contains lists of printer manufacturers and printer models.

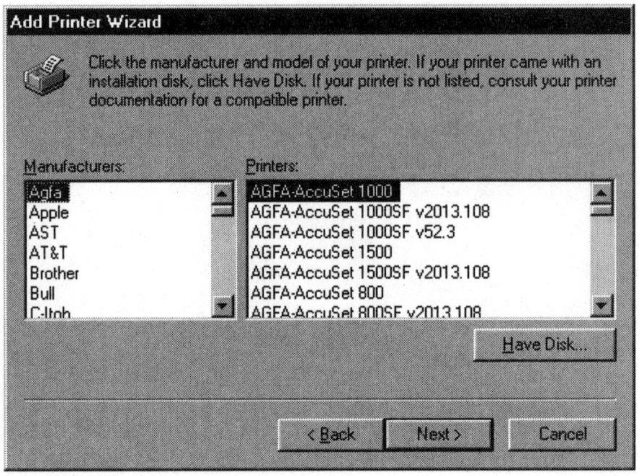

Figure 10-1.
Select your printer's make and model in the Add Printer Wizard.

Note

If your model printer is not listed, see "Handling Problem Printers," on the next page.

2. Click the manufacturer of the printer on the left, click the model of the printer on the right, and click Next.

   You'll now be asked to select the port to which the printer is attached. In most cases, your printer is attached to the LPT1 port, the standard parallel printing port on most PCs. If your computer has more than one printer port, the ports will be labeled LPT1, LPT2, and so on. If you have a USB or serial printer, it may be connected to the USB or a serial (COM) port instead.

3. Click the port that your printer is attached to, and click Next.

4. Type in a new name for the printer if you want, such as *Dad's laser printer*, or leave the default name.

5. Click Yes if you want the printer to be the default printer in all Windows programs. Click No if you want to leave another printer as the default. You can still select the printer when you're ready to print (*see "Selecting a Different Printer on the Network," on page 186*).

6. Click Next.

The Printer Wizard will now test your printer and finish up its business. If the printer does not work properly, the wizard will start the Print Troubleshooter, which may be able to help you get your printer going.

1. Make sure your printer is turned on and loaded with paper, and then click Yes.

   Printing a test page isn't really necessary, but it's a good idea to confirm that everything is working properly rather than waiting until you have an important document to print.

2. Click Finish.

   Windows loads the appropriate printer drivers and prints the test page. A dialog box opens to ask whether the page printed correctly.

3. Click Yes if the page printed without a problem. If the page did not print correctly, click No to start the Print Troubleshooter. Follow the dialog boxes that appear, selecting the answers that best explain the problem you are having.

Handling Problem Printers

If you run the Add Printer Wizard and your printer's model does not appear on the list, don't give up hope. Many new printer models and many very old ones may not be listed.

If your printer is new, insert the floppy disk or CD that came with it in the appropriate drive before you start the Add Printer Wizard. When you see the dialog box in the Add Printer Wizard that prompts you to select the printer's manufacturer and model, click the Have Disk button. In the dialog box that appears next, specify the location of the disk and then continue following the prompts. You may have to specify a subfolder on the disk that contains the proper drivers for your printer or browse the disk in order to locate the drivers.

If your printer is older, it may not be listed in the Add Printer Wizard, and you may no longer have its installation disk. If this is your case, try selecting the same manufacturer as your printer's and choosing one of the older models listed for that manufacturer. If that doesn't work, look for information in the printer's manual about other printers that yours can emulate. Many laser printers, for example, use the same drivers as some Hewlett-Packard (HP) printers. If you have an older laser printer with no documentation or software, try selecting the LaserJet Plus, LaserJet II, or LaserJet III models from the HP list.

If you still can't get the printer to work, hit the Web. You may able to download the drivers you need to install the printer. On the Web, look for the printer manufacturer's home page. If the manufacturer is out of business, search the Microsoft Web site, *www.microsoft.com*, for driver information or do general searches using your printer's make and model as search words. You may be able to find someone at some site to help you.

Turning On Printer Sharing

The last step you must take to share your printer is to tell Windows that the printer can be shared. This is similar to turning on sharing for a disk drive or folder.

1. On the Start menu, point to Settings, and then click Printers.

2. In the Printers window, right-click the printer you want to share.

3. Select Sharing from the shortcut menu.

4. On the Sharing tab of the Properties dialog box, click Shared As.

5. In the Share Name text box, enter a name for the printer that will identify it to other network users.

   You also have the option of entering an identifying description of the printer in the Comment text box. To make it easier for other users to select the printer, include its type, such as Canon Color InkJet or HP LaserJet Printer, in the description.

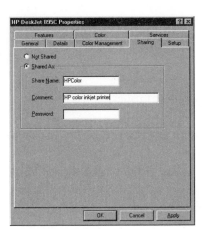

6. If you want to allow sharing only for users with a password, enter a password.

7. Click OK.

8. If you entered a password, type it again to confirm it, and then click OK.

   The printer's icon now shows that it is a shared resource.

HP LaserJet
1100

The check mark next to the printer icon in the Printers window indicates that the printer is the default in all Windows applications. To make a different printer the default, right-click its icon and choose Set As Default from the shortcut menu.

Separating Print Jobs

Once other folks start using your printer, don't be surprised if it starts churning out pages that you're not expecting. Windows will print documents in the order they are received, so if another network user starts a job before you do, you'll have to wait a bit for your document to print.

If you're not careful, you may wind up with several documents in the printer's output tray at one time. And you certainly wouldn't want to grab your quarterly report and your kid's homework and distribute both to the board members later in the morning. You also wouldn't want your document to disappear with someone else's job.

To help prevent this, you can have Windows automatically print a separator page between documents. The page prints at the start of each job and shows the name of the person who printed it.

Here's how to turn on the separator page feature:

1. On the computer to which the printer is attached, click Start, point to Settings, and then click Printers.

2. Right-click the printer that is being shared, and select Properties from the shortcut menu.

   The General tab of the printer's Properties dialog box appears, as shown in Figure 10-2.

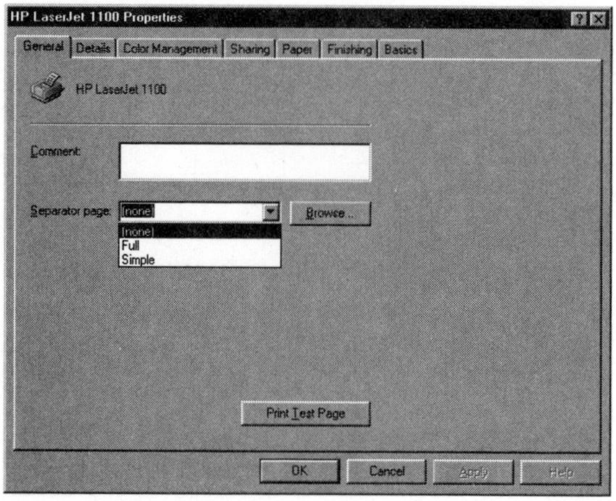

Figure 10-2.
You can turn on separator pages on the General tab of the printer's Properties dialog box.

3. Pull down the Separator Page list and select Full or Simple. Both options print the user's name, document name, and current date and time. The Full option just prints it larger.

Note

Choose None from the Separator Page list if you no longer want to print separator pages.

4. Click OK.

Accessing a Shared Printer

The printer you have set up and shared is now available to all the family members on the network. But to access it, each person must first install the printer, as a remote network printer rather than a directly connected local printer, in the Printer dialog box. The procedure for installing a network printer is similar to that for a local printer, but with a few twists along the way. And you must be sure that everyone who wants to add the network printer to a computer has access to the printer drivers.

To install a network printer, each person on the network must follow these steps:

1. Insert the Windows CD in the CD drive.

    This may not be necessary because the drivers may already be on the computer's hard disk, but it can't hurt.

2. Double-click Network Neighborhood and then double-click the computer connected to the shared printer.

3. Right-click the icon for the shared printer and choose Install to start the Add Printer Wizard.

You now have to specify whether you want MS-DOS programs, such as an older version of WordPerfect or dBase, to be able to print to the network printer. Normally, MS-DOS programs can't print to printers across the network. They can only print to local printers. But when you tell Windows to provide network printing capability to MS-DOS programs, Windows captures the information the MS-DOS program is trying to print and then channels it to the network printer.

4. If you want to be able to print from MS-DOS programs to network printers, click Yes. If you don't use MS-DOS programs or you want to print with them only to a local printer, click No.

5. Click Next.

6. If you chose to capture MS-DOS printing, you'll be asked to select a port. Click the button labeled Capture Printer Port, select LPT1, and then click OK.

7. Enter a name for the printer if you want, such as *Mom's color printer*, or leave the default name, which is usually the printer's model name.

8. Select Yes if you want the printer to be the default printer in all Windows programs. Select No if you want to leave another printer as the default. You can still select the printer when you're ready to print (*see "Selecting a Different Printer on the Network," below*).

9. Click Next.

10. When you are asked whether you want to print a test page, make sure the printer is turned on and loaded with paper, and then click Yes.

11. Click Finish.

12. When a message box appears to ask if the page printed correctly, click Yes. If the page did not print, click No to start the Print Troubleshooter. Follow the dialog boxes that appear, selecting the answers that best explain the problem you are having.

Selecting a Different Printer on the Network

Whenever you set a printer as the default, either your local printer or one of the printers on the network, all your documents are directed to that printer unless you choose a different printer. To change which printer is the Windows default, double-click the Printers icon to open the Printers window, right-click the printer you want as the default, and then choose Set As Default from the shortcut menu.

You can also choose to print a particular document at a printer other than the default printer. How you do this depends on the application you're using. In many programs, such as Microsoft Word, clicking the Print button on the toolbar automatically prints the document to the default printer. If you want to choose a different printer, you must select the printer in the Print dialog box.

For example, suppose your own laser printer is the current default, but you want to print a document in color. Your kids have a color printer that's been set up as a network printer. Here's how you'd print a document on your kids' printer:

1. Select Print from your application's File menu.

2. Click the drop-down arrow next to the Name box, which shows the default printer, and choose the printer in your kids' room from the drop-down list.

3. Click OK.

4. Go and get your document before the kids turn it in as homework!

Using Printer Shortcuts

Normally, you start an application and then print a document. But with Windows, you can use several shortcuts for printing documents.

In My Computer or Windows Explorer, you can right-click a document's icon and choose Print from the shortcut menu. Windows opens the application used to create the document, sends the document to the printer, and then closes the application.

You can also drag a document onto a printer icon that you've placed on the Windows desktop. To place a printer icon on the desktop, follow these steps:

1. On the Start menu, point to Settings, and then click Printers.

2. In the Printers window, right-click a printer and choose Create Shortcut from the shortcut menu.

3. When a message tells you that you can't place a shortcut in the Printers folder, and asks whether you want to place the shortcut on the desktop instead, click Yes.

Connecting Printers Directly to the Network

Because a printer that's connected to a computer on the network only works when the computer is on, you may want to use an alternative: connecting the printer directly to the network.

Connecting a printer directly to the network also frees up a computer's printer port so that you can hook up an external Zip drive, scanner, or other parallel device without conflict.

In a twisted pair network, you use twisted pair cable to connect a printer to the hub. In a Thin Ethernet network, you use coaxial cable to connect the printer to the NIC of the nearest networked device. Because the printer is not connected to the printer port of a computer, anyone on the network can access it directly, as long as the printer is turned on.

The disadvantage to connecting printers directly to the network is expense. Most printers are designed for standard parallel connections only. To connect them directly to the network, you'll need to purchase either a network-ready printer or a device, called a *print server*, that makes your printer network ready.

Network-ready printers have a NIC built in. They cost more than standard printers and can be a little harder to find. An alternative is to purchase a print server, which is equipped with an Ethernet connection on one side and a parallel connection on the other.

The least expensive printer servers are called *pocket servers*. About the size of a pack of cigarettes, a pocket server plugs directly into a printer's parallel port. The twisted pair cable from the network hub or the coaxial cable from another networked device plugs into the other end of the server.

Another type of print server connects to a printer with a cable. These external servers are usually more expensive than pocket servers, but they may include additional features. Some models, for example, have more than one parallel port, allowing them to connect several printers to the network at the same time.

Note

For some Hewlett-Packard LaserJet printers, you can purchase an internal print server that fits inside the printer, much the way some NICs fit inside a computer.

When selecting a print server, make sure it matches your cable type—either twisted pair or coaxial. Some print servers, but not all, can accommodate both types.

The print server must also support the protocol you're using on your network. Some print servers support only IPX/SPX; others require either TPC/IP or NetBEUI.

Finally, while most printers have a standard-sized parallel port, called a *Centronics* port, some models, like the LaserJet 1100, have a smaller mini-Centronics port. The standard-sized connection on a pocket print server will not fit a mini-Centronics port. If you're using such a printer, you'll need an adapter for the print server.

Note

To install an external print server, just connect the cable that came with the printer to the server's parallel connection. Connect the network cable to the server's network connection.

Setting Up a Pocket Print Server

There are many different models of pocket print servers. While they all operate in about the same way, their setup procedures vary. Most servers are sold with software that helps them connect to the network, but the process really depends on the type of protocol the server supports.

TCP/IP servers need to be assigned an IP address. With a Windows peer-to-peer network, you'll probably have to assign the server a static IP address that is not used by any computer on the network. Check the literature that came with your server for step-by-step directions for assigning it an IP address.

Most manufacturers provide programs to help you through the process. The Microplex Ethernet Pocket Print Server, for example, offers three programs for configuring the print server—IPAssign, NPWIN Configure, and Waldo. The IPAssign program, whose main dialog box is shown in Figure 10-3, accesses the print server through the Ethernet address and assigns it an IP address of your choosing.

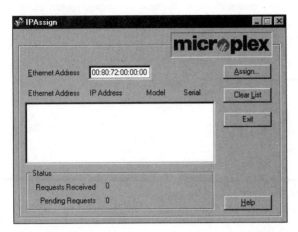

Figure 10-3.
The IPAssign program for a Microplex print server assigns an IP address to the server.

Once you assign an IP address to your server, you configure Windows to communicate with the printer, as you learned in "Installing a Printer" on page 179.

Microplex certainly isn't the only maker of pocket print servers. Table 10-1, on page 191, lists other print server makes and models. One example, the Lantronix Micro Print Servers consist of a series of pocket print servers, similar to the Microplex line, that also support TCP/IP, IPX, and other protocols. Lantronix includes its own program, EZWebCon, to assign the server an IP address.

Setting Up an External Print Server

External print servers, an alternative to pocket print servers, connect to a printer by cable rather than plug directly into the printer itself. External servers work in the same way and are set up the same way as pocket print servers, although they are more expensive than pocket print servers. Many models also come with two or more parallel connections that allow you to place multiple printers on the network so you can use different printers for different documents.

Hewlett-Packard's JetDirect print servers, for example, work with virtually any printer equipped with a parallel port—not just HP's own brand. The line includes two models that have three parallel connections and a one-printer model, the 170X, that is more suitable for home networks.

Setting up an HP print server is easy. After you connect the server both to the printer and to your network hub, you press a small button on the back of the server to print out a page of configuration information, including the electronic hardware address that is built into the device.

You then install the JetAdmin program supplied with the server and use the HP JetDirect Printer Wizard to configure the device. Figure 10-4 shows the wizard page in which you select a protocol and enter the unit's hardware address.

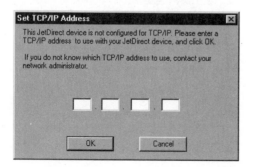

Figure 10-4.
The HP JetDirect Printer Wizard prompts you to select a protocol and enter the server's hardware address.

Using the address, JetAdmin locates the printer and displays a dialog box in which you can specify an IP address if you're using the TCP/IP protocol. After a few additional steps, JetAdmin starts the Add Printer Wizard in Windows, which opens a dialog box that prompts you to assign an IP address.

After the JetAdmin setup, you can send documents to the printer from your computer, and other network users can select the printer as their network printer and print documents even when your computer is not on.

There are many manufacturers of print servers, so you have plenty of choice. Table 10-1 lists print server makes and models and each manufacturer's Web address.

Table 10-1. Print Server Manufacturers and Models

Manufacturer	Models	Web site
Axis Communications	Pocket, and one- and two-port models, some with both parallel and serial ports	*http://www.axis.com/*
NETGEAR	One- and two-port models, some with built-in four-port hub	*http://netgear.baynetworks.com/*
Emulex	Pocket, and two- and three-port models	*http://www.emulex.com/*
Extended Systems	One- and two-port models, some with both parallel and serial ports	*http://www.extendedsystems.com/*
Hewlett-Packard JetDirect	One- and three-port models, external and internal	*http://www.hp.com/*
Intel NetPort Express	One- and three-port models	*http://www.intel.com/*
Lantronix	Pocket and external print servers, up to six-port models (four parallel and two serial)	*http://www.lantronix.com/*
Linksys EtherFast	Pocket, one- and three-port models	*http://www.linksys.com/*
MicroPlex	Pocket, and a four-port model (two parallel and two serial)	*http://www.microplex.com/*

Sharing printers on a network can be a great time-saver and step-saver. You'll no longer need to carry a disk to another computer to print a document or carry a printer to another computer. With Windows, you don't have to purchase any additional software or hardware, unless you want to connect your printer directly to the network.

Sharing files and printers is not the only benefit of connecting computers in a network, however. You'll learn in the next chapter that you can use your network to create a family e-mail system for sending and receiving messages between family members.

Chapter 11

Communicating Over the Network

You've seen how a home network is great for sharing files and printers, but it's also a convenient way to communicate with other members of your family. Why yell across the house or leave scribbled notes, when you can transmit messages over your network?

In this chapter, you'll learn three ways to communicate via the network, ranging from the easiest to the most advanced. You'll learn how to

- Send and receive short messages that pop up on the recipient's screen

- Send and receive e-mail messages just as you can over the Internet

- Set up Microsoft Outlook to communicate over your network

Note

You can also communicate over the network with the program Microsoft NetMeeting, which is described in Chapter 15. You can use NetMeeting like an intercom system to speak with other family members and even see them, if your computers are equipped with cameras.

Sending and Receiving Pop-up Messages

The easiest and least formal way to communicate over the network is to send and receive pop-up messages. You can send a message to a specific family member or "broadcast" it to everyone on the network.

With a program called WinPopup, which comes with Microsoft Windows 95, Microsoft Windows 98, and Microsoft Windows 98 Second Edition, you can announce that dinner is ready, tell your daughter that the phone call is for her, or send out a quick reminder or word of wisdom to your loved ones. Your message simply pops up in a window on the recipient's screen.

Note

WinPopup does not save your messages after it is closed or your computer is turned off.

Starting WinPopup

WinPopup is usually installed when you set up Windows, but it's not listed with other programs on the Start menu. If you plan to use WinPopup regularly, you can add it to the Start menu, to your desktop, or to your Windows taskbar.

To locate WinPopup and add it as a shortcut on your Windows desktop, follow these steps:

1. On the Start menu, point to Find, and click Files Or Folders.

2. In the Named text box, type *winpopup* and click Find Now.

    Windows searches your disk and locates the WinPopup program. *If Windows does not locate the program, see "Installing WinPopup," on the next page.*

3. In the list of files in the Find dialog box, right-click Winpopup and choose Create Shortcut from the shortcut menu.

4. Click Yes when a message appears reporting that you cannot add the shortcut to the current location and asking if you want to add the shortcut to your desktop.

5. Close the Find window.
   You now have a shortcut to the program on your desktop.

If you are using Windows 98, you can add the shortcut to your Quick Launch toolbar on the taskbar so that you can access it from within any application. To do this, drag the shortcut icon to the Quick Launch toolbar, which is just to the right of the Start button. You can now delete the shortcut from the desktop, if you want, by right-clicking it and choosing Delete from the shortcut menu.

Note

If the Quick Launch toolbar is now too narrow to fit all the icons it needs to display, you can bring them all back into view by dragging the vertical line to the right of the last icon further to the right.

Because WinPopup must be running for someone to send or receive messages, you should have everyone on the network copy the WinPopup shortcut to the Startup folder located at C:\Windows\Start Menu\Programs\StartUp. When the shortcut is in that folder, it automatically starts whenever Windows is started.

Installing WinPopup

If the WinPopup program is not already installed on your computer, you'll have to install it yourself. Insert the Windows CD in your CD-ROM drive, and then follow these steps:

1. On the Start menu, point to Settings, and click Control Panel.

Note

If you do not have a Windows CD, the installation program may already be on your hard disk.

2. In the Control Panel window, double-click Add/Remove Programs.

3. In the Add/Remove Programs Properties dialog box, click the Windows Setup tab.

4. In the list of components, click System Tools, but be careful not to remove the check mark in the check box to its left.

5. Click Details.

6. In the System Tools dialog box, scroll through the components list and select the check box next to WinPopup.

7. Click OK to close the System Tools dialog box.

8. Click OK again to close the Add/Remove Programs Properties dialog box.

At this point, you might need the Windows CD. On some computers, the files that Windows needs are already stored on the hard disk. If that's the case, WinPopup will be installed and you're ready for the next stage. If the programs are not on your hard disk, you'll be asked to insert the CD in the drive and click OK.

Using WinPopup

WinPopup must be running in order for you to send or receive a message. If the WinPopup shortcut is not in the Startup folder on your machine, which starts WinPopup automatically when you start Windows, you must run WinPopup by double-clicking the icon you placed on the desktop.

When WinPopup starts, you see the dialog box shown in Figure 11-1. If you're not ready to send a message, just minimize the window so that WinPopup appears on the taskbar.

Figure 11-1.

The WinPopup dialog box allows you to send or receive messages on the network.

Here's how to send a message:

1. Click the WinPopup button on the taskbar to open the WinPopup window.

2. Click the Send button on the toolbar, which shows a picture of an envelope, or choose Send from the Messages menu to open the Send Message dialog box.

3. To send a message to everyone on the network, click Workgroup. To send a message to a specific person on the network, click User Or Computer.

4. If you want to send a message to everyone and the workgroup name does not appear automatically, enter the name of the workgroup in the text box in the To area of the Send Message dialog box. If you want to send a message to one person, enter that person's user name or computer name.

5. Type the message (up to 128 characters) in the Message box, and then click OK. A complete message might look like this.

Note

To paste text into the message from the clipboard, right-click the message text box and choose Paste from the shortcut menu.

6. A message box reports that the message was sent successfully.

7. Click OK.

When you receive a message from another computer on the network, you'll hear a beep. If the WinPopup window is open, the message appears in the window, as shown in Figure 11-2.

If the window is minimized, click its button on the taskbar to display the message. The WinPopup icon in the taskbar, by the way, indicates whether or not you have pop-up messages to read. When you have no messages, the icon looks like this.

As you receive messages, the icon indicates how many you have. Here's what the icon looks like when you've received a message.

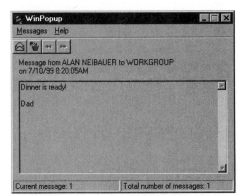

Figure 11-2.

A received message appears in the WinPopup window.

If you want the WinPopup window to open automatically when a message arrives, choose Options from the Messages menu and select the check box for Pop Up Dialog On Message Receipt. Other options allow you to turn off the beep that sounds when a message arrives and to keep the WinPopup window in the foreground above other program windows.

When you have more than one message, click the Previous and Next buttons in the WinPopup toolbar to switch from one message to the next. Click the Delete button in the toolbar to delete a displayed message.

When you close the WinPopup window, a message reminds you that you can't send or receive any more messages. If you still have undeleted messages, the message box also reminds you that all of them will be discarded when you close WinPopup, because the program does not save messages from session to session. Click OK to close the WinPopup window.

Creating Your Own Post Office

While WinPopup is free (with Windows), quick, and convenient, it does have its limitations. A pop-up message can be no longer than 128 characters and it's available only while WinPopup is open. When you exit WinPopup, all messages you've received are erased. It certainly would be better if you could send and receive e-mail over the network, just as you can over the Internet. Well, as it happens, Windows allows you to do just that.

In order to send and receive e-mail on your network, you must set up a network mail server. The mail server lets you create mailboxes in which messages are stored until they are read by the recipient.

Windows includes a mail server program called Microsoft Post Office. You can also find shareware mail server programs that you can download from the Internet. We'll look at both Microsoft Post Office and a shareware server program, VPOP3, in this chapter.

Mail Servers and E-Mail Clients

To understand how e-mail works, you should understand the different roles played by the mail server and an e-mail program, such as Microsoft Outlook Express.

A mail server, like the mail server at your ISP, or the mail server you set up on your network, receives incoming e-mail, transmits outgoing messages, and organizes and stores in mailboxes messages that have been received. Your ISP's mail server, for example, maintains a mailbox for each member, and stores incoming messages until you retrieve them. Similarly, programs for creating a post office on your network let you create a mailbox for each user and they handle the transfer of messages between the sender and the recipient.

An e-mail program, called the *e-mail client*, on the other hand, is the software that you run on your computer to read and write messages. It also transfers the messages you send to the mail server, and picks up from the mail server messages that are waiting for you.

Most ISP mail servers on the Internet use the Post Office Protocol (POP). This means that you can communicate with them using any e-mail program that can handle POP e-mail. Outlook Express, Outlook, Eudora, and Netscape Messenger are all POP e-mail programs.

Note

Some mail servers, such as the one used by America Online (AOL), are designed to communicate only with the e-mail programs built into their own software.

When you install Microsoft Post Office to add e-mail capabilities to your network, an e-mail program called Windows Messaging is installed at the same time. Windows Messaging works with Microsoft Post Office, but it doesn't work with Internet mail servers because it's not POP-compatible. That means you can't use it to send and receive e-mail over the Internet.

Note

The abbreviation POP3 that you'll often see indicates version 3 of the Post Office Protocol.

Outlook Express, the e-mail program that comes with Internet Explorer version 4 and 5, and with Windows 98, is POP-compatible, so it can work with Internet e-mail servers, but it doesn't work with Microsoft Mail Postoffice. So if you want to use Microsoft Post Office for network e-mail, you've have to use Windows Messaging for your network e-mail and Outlook Express for Internet e-mail.

Fortunately, there are some better alternatives.

You can use Microsoft Outlook as your e-mail program, because it can communicate both with Internet POP e-mail servers and Microsoft Post Office. Microsoft Outlook has more features than Windows Messaging but you must purchase it separately as it does not come free with Windows. *See "Communicating with Microsoft Outlook," on page 212, if you want to use Outlook for your network e-mail.*

Another alternative, covered later in this chapter on page 223, is to set up a POP mail server on your network rather than Microsoft Post Office. The shareware program VPOP3, for example, lets you handle e-mail both over the Internet and on your network using a regular e-mail program such as Outlook Express.

Using Microsoft Post Office

Just like an Internet e-mail server, your network post office can handle messages of any length, including attachments. Messages you send are stored in your own Sent Items folder, so you can keep a record of your communications. Messages you receive are stored in an Inbox until you decide to delete them. You can reply to messages and forward them to others on the network with a single click.

You do all this by creating a post office on one of the computers on the network. The post office acts as a central station for channeling mail from senders to receivers. If you send a message to someone whose computer is not turned on and ready to receive the message, the post office stores it until it can be received.

The person who sets up the post office has to specify who will be using it. Each user gets a post office mailbox in which messages are stored, and a password for accessing the messages.

In order to work with the post office, each computer on the network must have Microsoft Post Office installed.

If you create a message and the post office is closed—the computer storing the post office is turned off or disconnected from the network—your message is held in the Outbox on your own computer until it can be sent. To ensure that messages won't sit in a sender's Outbox for too long, it's a good idea to set up the post office on the computer that's turned on most often.

Installing Microsoft Mail Postoffice

The first step in creating your postal system is to make sure the Microsoft Mail Postoffice program that comes with Windows is installed on each computer on the network. To install the program, open each computer's Control Panel and look for two icons, labeled Mail and Microsoft Mail Postoffice, on each computer.

Mail

Microsoft Mail
Postoffice

If you are running the original version of Windows 95, Microsoft Mail Postoffice was installed automatically with the program Microsoft Exchange. If your computer came with one of the updates to Windows 95, the Microsoft Mail Postoffice was installed along with Windows Messaging.

Windows Messaging Service

Fixing Office 2000

If you have Microsoft Office 2000 installed at the time you install Microsoft Mail Postoffice, the WMS program may replace some Office 2000 files on the hard disk, making Office 2000 unstable or unusable. If you run WMS after installing Microsoft Office 2000, you should then repair the Office installation by following these steps:

1. Insert the Office CD in your CD-ROM drive.

2. Double-click My Computer.

3. In the My Computer window, double-click the Control Panel icon.

4. In the Control Panel window, double-click the Add/Remove Programs icon.

5. In the list of installed software, click Microsoft Office 2000, and then Click Add/Remove.

6. In the Microsoft Office 2000 Maintenance Mode window, click the large Repair Office button.

7. In the Reinstall/Repair Microsoft Office 2000 window, choose Repair Errors In My Office Installation.

8. Click Finish, and then wait until the process is completed. This may take some time. Repairing Microsoft Office will not cause any harm to the files installed by WMS.

If you don't see the Microsoft Mail Postoffice icon in the Control Panel, use the Add/Remove Programs option in Control Panel to install either Exchange or Windows Messaging. When you look in the list of components that you can install, one or the other will be available.

Setting up Windows 98 or Windows 98 Second Edition does not install Microsoft Mail Postoffice. If you installed either version of Windows 98 over Windows 95, Windows 98 will leave the existing version of Microsoft Mail Postoffice on your computer, though.

To install Microsoft Mail Postoffice in either version of Windows 98, run the WMS program, which you'll find on your Windows CD in the \tools\oldwin95\message\us folder. If you have an international installation, choose the \intl directory instead of \us.

Restart your computer after running the program, even if you are not prompted to do so.

Creating the Post Office

Now that each computer on the network has Microsoft Mail Postoffice installed, you're ready to create the post office itself on one of them. Be sure to pick a computer that will be on frequently and then create and share a folder on that computer's hard disk, in which you will store the post office files. Here's how it's done:

1. On the Windows desktop, double-click My Computer.

2. Double-click the C: drive icon.

3. Right-click in the C: window, point to New, and click Folder.
   The new folder is created and its default name is highlighted.

4. Type *POFFICE* to replace the default name of the folder and press Enter.

5. Right-click the POFFICE folder and choose Sharing from the shortcut menu.

6. In the Properties dialog box, click Shared As.

7. Click Full.

8. Click OK.

   You now have to create the post office itself, along with your own mailbox.

1. In the Control Panel window, double-click the Microsoft Mail Postoffice icon.

2. In the Microsoft Workgroup Postoffice Admin window, click Create A New WorkGroup Postoffice, and then click Next to see the dialog box shown in Figure 11-3, on the next page.

3. Type the path of the folder you created to store the post office (*c:\poffice*), and then click Next.

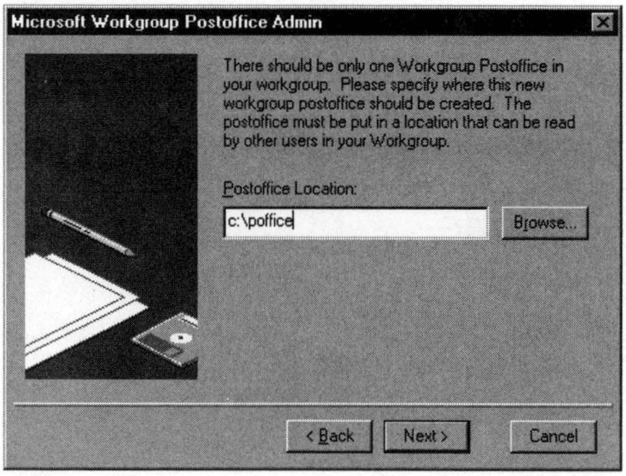

Figure 11-3.

Type the path in the Microsoft Workgroup Postoffice Admin dialog box.

4. The Microsoft Mail Postoffice program creates a folder within the C:\poffice folder named Wgpo0000 that contains numerous files and subfolders and it asks you to confirm its location.

5. Click Next.

6. In the Enter Your Administrator Account Details dialog box, type your name in the Name text box.

7. Make a note of the Mailbox name in the Mailbox text box. You'll need to know it later.

8. Press Tab twice and type a replacement password in the Password text box.

9. Click OK.

10. Click OK in the Mail dialog box.

Adding Postoffice Users

When you set up Microsoft Mail Postoffice, a mailbox is created for you. For other post office users, you'll need to create additional mailboxes. To add a user and automatically create a mailbox, follow these steps:

1. In the Control Panel window, double-click the Microsoft Mail Postoffice icon.

2. In the Microsoft Workgroup Postoffice Admin dialog box, click Administer An Existing Workgroup Postoffice, and then click Next.

3. Click Next to accept the path to your post office.

4. Enter your mailbox name as the post office administrator.

5. Enter the password you entered earlier.

6. Click Next to open the Postoffice Manager dialog box, which lists all current users.

7. Click Add User to see the dialog box shown in Figure 11-4.

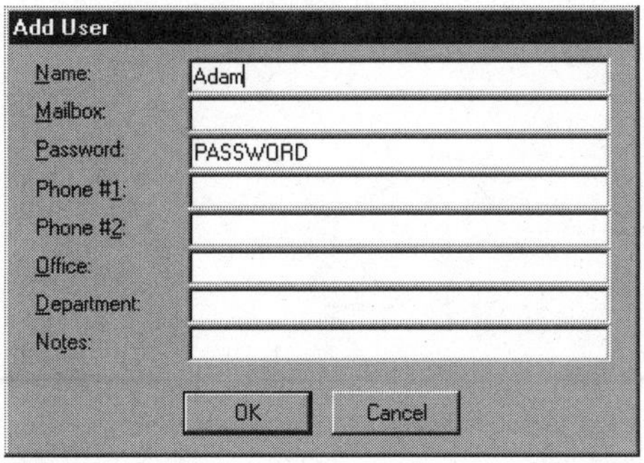

Figure 11-4.
The Add User dialog box allows you to add new users to your post office.

8. Enter the user's name.

9. Enter the name for the user's mailbox.

10. Click OK.

11. Give to the user the path and name of the post office, the name of the mailbox, and the password.

12. Repeat steps 7 through 11 for each additional user, and then click Close.

Setting Up Windows Messaging

Each user must set up an e-mail program in order to be able to send and receive files through the Microsoft Mail Postoffice. All users should now have an Inbox icon on their desktops. Double-clicking this icon starts an e-mail program called Windows Messaging or Exchange, depending on the version of Windows you use, through which you can send and receive information over the network. You can also use Microsoft Outlook to send and receive mail through the network. Because Windows Messaging is included with Windows, we'll look at this program in some detail. You'll learn how to set up Microsoft Outlook for network e-mail later in this chapter.

The first time you open the Inbox, you must create a *profile*. A profile lists the mail services that Windows Messaging can use. To create a profile, follow these steps:

1. Double-click the Inbox icon on the desktop to see the Inbox Setup Wizard dialog box shown in Figure 11-5.

Figure 11-5.
In the Inbox Setup Wizard dialog box, you can select the information services that you want to use with Windows Messaging.

Fixing Windows 98 Second Edition

If you have Windows 98 Second Edition, you may get the following error message when starting Windows Messaging:

MAPISP32 caused an invalid page fault in module KERNEL32.DLL

If this happens to you, you'll need to take a few extra steps to get Windows Messaging working. Here's how to fix the problem:

1. Restart your computer.

2. Locate the file mapi32.dll file in your Windows\System directory.

3. Rename the file to mapi32.lld.

4. Reinstall Windows Messaging from your Windows 98 Second Edition CD.

5. Restart your computer.

2. Make sure the Use The Following Information Services button is selected and the Microsoft Mail check box is selected, and then click Next.
You'll be asked to provide the path to the post office folder.

3. Click Browse to open the Browse For Postoffice dialog box.

4. Double-click Network Neighborhood and locate the post office folder you created earlier.

5. Click OK to return to the Inbox Setup Wizard, and then click Next.
The wizard displays a list of mailboxes in the post office.

6. Click your mailbox, and then click Next.

7. In the box that appears, enter your mailbox password, and then click Next.
The wizard now shows you the default location of your personal address book. This is where you can store e-mail addresses.

8. Click Next to accept the default location.

9. The wizard now shows you the default location of your personal folder, in which your messages are stored.

10. Click Next to accept the default location and to see a summary of your profile.

11. Click Finish.

If you are already using Windows Messaging or Exchange for your Internet e-mail, you can add Microsoft Mail to your profile to send and receive mail over the network. Here's how:

1. In the Control Panel window, double-click Mail.

2. If the profile to which you want to add Microsoft Mail is not displayed, click the Show Profiles button to display the Mail dialog box, select the profile you want to change, and then click Properties.

3. In the Properties dialog box, click Add to display a list of services that can be installed in Windows Messaging.

4. Click Microsoft Mail in the list of information services.

5. Click Properties.

6. On the Connection tab of the Microsoft Mail dialog box, shown in Figure 11-6 on the next page, enter the name of the post office folder or browse for it. The name contains the path to the computer on the network. If the post office is on your com-

puter, it might appear as C:\poffice\wgpo0000. If the post office is on another network computer, the path may be something like \\JoesComputer\C\poffice\ wpgo0000.

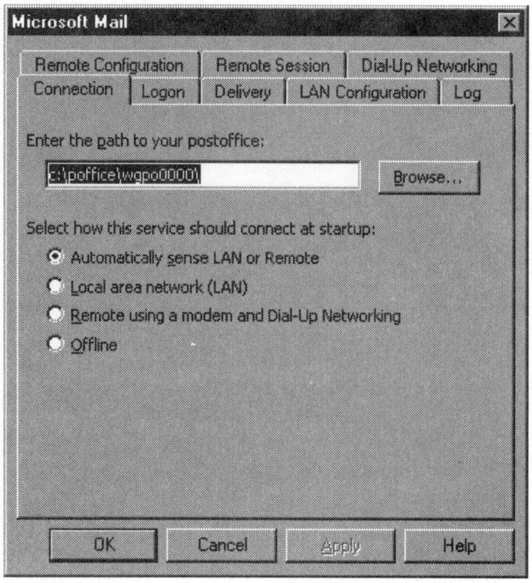

Figure 11-6.
Enter the path to your post office in the Microsoft Mail dialog box.

7. On the Log On page, enter your mailbox name and password.

8. Click OK.

Sending and Receiving E-Mail

After you create a profile, opening the Inbox opens the Windows Messaging window shown in Figure 11-7. The window shows the Inbox, which displays the messages you've received. An initial welcoming message from Microsoft appears in the Inbox the first time you use Windows Messaging.

Creating and Addressing a Message

To create a message, click the New Message button in the toolbar. A new message window opens, as shown in Figure 11-8. Click the To box to view a list of post office mailboxes. In the list of mailboxes, click each person to whom you want to send a message, and then click the To button. When you've selected all the intended recipients, click OK.

Figure 11-7.

The Windows Messaging Inbox displays your incoming messages.

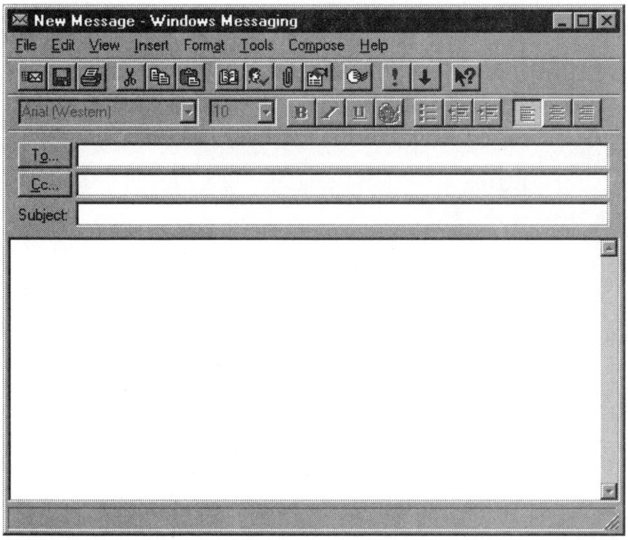

Figure 11-8.

A new message window opens when you click the New Message button on the toolbar.

Instead of clicking the To button to select recipients' names, for example, you can just type a recipient's user name in the To text box rather than look up the recipient in the address book. But if you type a name, click the Check Names button on the toolbar before you send the message. This feature makes sure that each name you've entered belongs to a person who actually has a mailbox in the post office and warns you if that's not the case.

Next, enter the subject of the message and press Tab to move the cursor to the main message area, in which you type the message.

Attaching a File

To send a file along with your message, click the Attach button, select the file you want to send, and then click OK. The file becomes an attachment that is transmitted along with the message.

Special Message Options

If you click the Read Receipt button before sending a message, Microsoft Mail Postoffice will send you an e-mail message when the recipient opens the message. This confirms that the message was at least opened, if not necessarily read.

The two Importance buttons allow you to assign a level of importance to your message. By clicking either button, the message will be flagged in the recipient's Inbox with an icon indicating its level of importance—*High* or *Low*.

Clicking the Properties button on the toolbar displays information about the selected message and offers you additional delivery options, as shown in Figure 11-9. It also allows you to assign your message one of four sensitivity levels—*Normal*, *Personal*, *Private*, or *Confidential*. When you designate a message as Private, for example, the recipient can't modify it when replying or when forwarding it to someone else. The other options merely display an icon next to the message in the Inbox showing the message's sensitivity level.

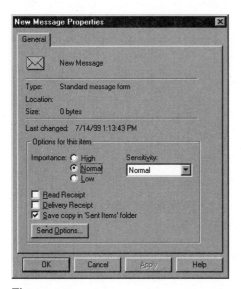

Figure 11-9.

Message properties include several useful delivery options.

Note

Using the Columns command on the View menu, you can add a column to the Inbox that shows the sensitivity level of a message.

In addition to a read receipt, you can also request a delivery receipt—an e-mail message that Windows Messaging sends you when your message is delivered. To request a delivery receipt, select the check box for The Item Has Been Delivered in the Send tab of the Options dialog box.

Sending the Message

When your message is ready to go, click the Send button on the toolbar to move the message to the Outbox, where it is temporarily stored until it is sent to the post office. To make sure that all of your messages are actually sent to and received from the post office, choose Deliver Now from the Tools menu, which sends and also collects all e-mail.

Reading Messages from Others

When you receive mail through the post office, its header appears in your Inbox. The header shows the sender, subject, and the date and time the message was received. Double-click a message header to read the message.

If the message has an attachment, you'll see a paper clip icon to the left of its header. Open the message and then double-click the icon representing the attachment that appears in the body of the message. Depending on the format of the attachment, its contents may appear immediately or you may be prompted to save the attachment to your hard disk.

After you read a message, you can close it and do nothing (to leave it in your Inbox) or delete it. The headers of messages you haven't read appear in bold text. To reply to a message, click the Reply To Sender button. You'll see a message window addressed to the sender and containing the text of the original message. If the sender sent the message to more than one person, you can click Reply To All to send your reply to all recipients of the original message.

Click the Forward button to send a copy of the message on to someone else, without responding to the original sender.

Filing Messages in Folders

In addition to an Inbox, Windows Messaging has an Outbox, a Sent Items folder, and a Deleted Items folder. To display the entire list of folders when you have one of the folders open, click the Up One Level button.

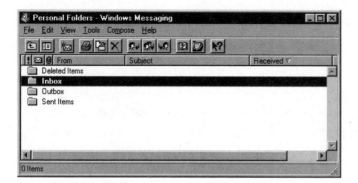

Double-click the folder you want to open. You can also display the list of folders by clicking the Folder List button in the toolbar. Click a folder in the folder list to display its contents.

The Deleted Items folder stores the messages that you delete from the other folders, just in case you change your mind. By default, these messages are permanently deleted when you exit Windows Messaging. To keep the messages in the Deleted Items folder, choose Options from the Tools menu, and clear the Empty The Deleted Items Folder Upon Exiting option. Then if you really want to erase the messages, you can always open the Deleted Items folder and delete the messages you find there.

Communicating with Microsoft Outlook

Microsoft Outlook is an e-mail program that is a component of Microsoft Office. If you are using Microsoft Office and Outlook is installed on your computer, you can use Outlook to send and receive mail through your network as well as through the Internet.

Note

Outlook Express, which comes with Internet Explorer version 4 or later, is designed for Internet e-mail. Only Outlook is also capable of sending and receiving e-mail over a network.

To use Microsoft Outlook for your network e-mail, you have to install the Microsoft Mail Postoffice program, as described earlier in this chapter. You can then install Outlook in its Corporate/Workgroup configuration and create or choose a profile. A profile tells Outlook how to connect to your e-mail server, your network, or the Internet.

Selecting the Mail Service

When you first start Outlook, you'll be given three options: Corporate Or Workgroup, Internet Only, and No E-Mail. Choose Corporate Or Workgroup to send and receive e-mail messages either through the network or over the Internet. The other two options are:

- **Internet Only** This option lets you exchange e-mail only through the Internet. When you choose Internet Only, you will not be able to use Outlook on a network to send and receive e-mail. But you will be able to send and receive e-mail, check schedules, assign tasks, and perform other Outlook functions through the Internet.

- **No E-Mail** This option lets you use Outlook's record-keeping and time-management tools but not its communications capabilities. You won't be able to use Outlook to send or receive e-mail through your network or the Internet.

If you've already set up a profile, such as a profile that was set up for a previous version of Outlook, Outlook will use that profile. If you haven't yet set up a profile when you choose the Corporate/Workgroup installation, Outlook begins the Inbox Setup Wizard that guides you through the process. You set up Outlook to use your Microsoft Mail Postoffice for network e-mail by using the Inbox Setup Wizard as described in "Setting Up Windows Messaging," on page 205. If you already have a profile, you can add your PostOffice to your Outlook Profile, as described in "Modifying a Profile," on the next page.

Note

If you have already installed Outlook in its Internet Only or No E-Mail configuration, you can change it to Corporate Or Workgroup without reinstalling the entire program. Start Outlook, choose Options from the Tools menu, and click the Mail Delivery tab. Click the Reconfigure Mail Support button and choose the Corporate Or Workgroup option in the dialog box that appears.

Working with Profiles

After you create a profile, it's not too late to create a new profile, or to add, remove, or modify the properties of the services within a profile. If you use your computer at more than one location, for example, you may need a separate profile for each location. You might also want a separate profile to send faxes from your computer over a telephone line that you also use for connecting to an Internet e-mail server. Just be cautious when you make changes. An incorrect profile could prevent Outlook from starting or connecting to your network or ISP, or you could potentially lose the information you have stored in Outlook.

Creating a Profile

You can set up, change, and remove a profile with the Mail option in the Control Panel. After you've set up Outlook, you can add services to a profile or remove them from within Outlook.

To create a new profile, follow these steps:

1. Double-click the Mail icon in the Control Panel window.

2. If one or more profiles have been set up, click the Show Profiles button in the Properties dialog box for the currently active profile. This displays the Mail dialog box. If no profiles have been set up on your system, the Mail dialog box opens automatically.

3. Click the Add button in the Mail dialog box to start creating a new profile using the Inbox Setup Wizard.

4. After completing all the steps of the wizard, click Finish to return to the Mail dialog box.

5. In the Mail dialog box, you can choose a default profile in the box labeled When Starting Microsoft Outlook, Use This Profile.

6. Click Close.

You can use the Inbox Setup Wizard to create profiles specific to each location from which you use Outlook: office, home, and on the road.

Modifying a Profile

Suppose you signed up for a new online service. At the same time, you also bailed out of an online service that wasn't giving you what you wanted. Your profile is now out of date, so you want to update the online service information. Here's how you do it.

1. Double-click the Mail icon in the Control Panel window to open the Properties dialog box.

2. If the profile you want to change is not displayed, click the Show Profiles button to display the Mail dialog box, select the profile you want to change, and then click Properties.

    The Services tab of the Properties dialog box lists all of the services in the profile you've selected.

3. On the Services tab of the Properties dialog box, you can

    - Click Add to install a new service to the current profile. Fill in the text boxes in the dialog boxes that appear to help you configure the service.

- Click Copy to copy the selected service to another profile.

- Select a service and click Properties to view or edit its settings.

- Select a service and click Remove to delete the service from the profile.

Click OK when you're finished modifying the profile. If you want to make changes to another profile, click Show Profiles and repeat the process. Click the Close button in the Mail dialog box when you've finished.

Using a Different Profile

If you have more than one profile set up, you can select which profile to use when you start Outlook.

1. Double-click the Mail icon in the Control Panel window.

2. Click Show Profiles, and then open the list labeled When Starting Microsoft Outlook, Use This Profile.

3. Choose the profile you want to use by default, and then click Close.

You can set Outlook to always use a particular profile or to let you choose a profile each time you start the program.

To use the same profile every time, do this:

1. In Outlook, choose Options from the Tools menu, and then click the Mail Services tab, if it isn't already displayed.

2. Enable the Always Use This Profile option, and then select the profile you want to use from the drop-down list.

3. Click OK.

If you prefer, you can choose a profile at the start of each Outlook session. For this option, follow these steps:

1. In Outlook, choose Options from the Tools menu, and then click the Mail Services tab, if it isn't already displayed.

2. Click the Prompt For A Profile To Be Used option.

3. Click OK.

Once the Prompt For A Profile To Be Used option is selected, you'll need to select a profile in the Choose Profile dialog box each time you start Outlook.

Removing a Profile

Now suppose that your situation changes and you no longer need all the profiles that you created. Perhaps you no longer have access to a corporate network and you want to delete the profile that includes the Exchange service. To simplify your Outlook life, you can remove the unwanted or unnecessary profiles.

To remove a profile from the Control Panel, follow these steps:

1. Double-click the Mail icon in the Control Panel window.

2. In the Properties dialog box, click the Show Profiles button.

3. Select the profile you want to remove.

4. Click the Remove button, and then click Yes when asked whether you want to remove this profile.

5. Click the Close button.

The Outlook Address Book

Outlook maintains its own address book, separate from addresses you might have in Windows Messaging, Microsoft Outlook Express, and other mail programs.

Network users will have more than one address list within the address book. On a peer-to-peer network using Microsoft Mail Postoffice, you have the post office address list of other network users. You'll also have a personal address book for e-mail addresses of people not on the network, and maybe an offline address book so you can address messages when you are not connected to the network. You'll also probably have an Outlook address book, which is created automatically from entries in your Contacts folder. And finally, you can have separate address lists for each online service you use to send and receive e-mail.

When you open the Outlook Address Book, you have to select the address list that contains the names to which you want to send your e-mail.

Opening the Address Book

To open the Address Book, choose Address Book from the Tools menu or click the Address Book button on the Standard toolbar—the button is displayed when the Inbox, Outbox, Outlook Today, Sent Items, Drafts, or other mail folder is open. If you are creating an e-mail message, click To in the new e-mail message. The Address Book opens and displays the names from the address list that is set up as the default, as shown in Figure 11-10.

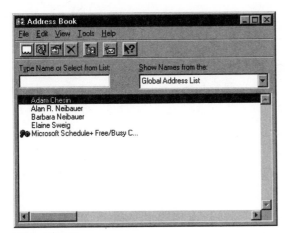

Figure 11-10.

Choose a name from the Outlook Address Book.

Note

You can change the default address list using the Services dialog box. To open this dialog box, choose Services from the Tools menu. Click the Addressing tab and select the list you want to see first from the Show This Address List First list.

If the list of names in the Address Book that appears is not the one with the information you need, do the following:

1. Click the arrow next to the Show Names From The drop-down list to display the available address lists.

2. Select the list you want to open, such as Postoffice Address List for addresses on your peer-to-peer network.

Adding a Personal Address Book to Your Profile

You cannot add names to the Postoffice Address list of the Address Book. The names in this list are taken directly from the Postoffice mailbox names that you've set up as the Postoffice administrator.

If you want to use the address book for Internet e-mail as well, you can add a personal address list to the address book by adding it to your profile. To add a personal address list, follow these steps:

1. Start Outlook and choose Services from the Tools menu.

2. On the Services tab, click the Add button.

3. In the Add Service To Profile dialog box, select Personal Address Book, and then click OK.

4. In the Personal Address Book dialog box, enter a name for the personal address book in the Name box.

5. In the Path text box, enter the path of the personal address book file, or click the Browse button to locate a personal address book file that already exists. Personal address books are maintained in files with a .pab extension.

6. Click OK in the Personal Address Book dialog box, and then click OK again in the message box that appears.

7. Click OK in the Services dialog box, and then exit and restart Outlook.

To add a personal address book to a profile other than the one you are currently using, double-click the Mail icon in the Windows Control Panel. On the Services tab, click Show Profiles. On the General tab, click the profile you want in the Profile box, click Properties, and then follow steps 2 through 7 above.

To add a name and address to your personal address book, do the following:

1. Choose Address Book from the Tools menu, or click the Address Book button on the Standard toolbar.

2. Click the New Entry button on the Address Book toolbar to open the New Entry dialog box, shown in Figure 11-11.

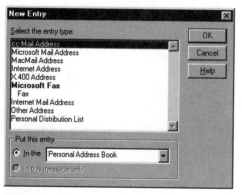

Figure 11-11.
You can choose a new entry type and destination in the New Entry dialog box.

3. Click the arrow next to the Put This Entry In The drop-down list and choose Personal Address Book in the list.

4. In the Select The Entry Type list, select the type of address you want to enter and click OK.

    The next dialog box you see varies according to the type of entry you've selected. For most new entries, you'll enter information to display in the address book and the e-mail address. The example in Figure 11-12 is based on selecting Other Address in the Entry Type list.

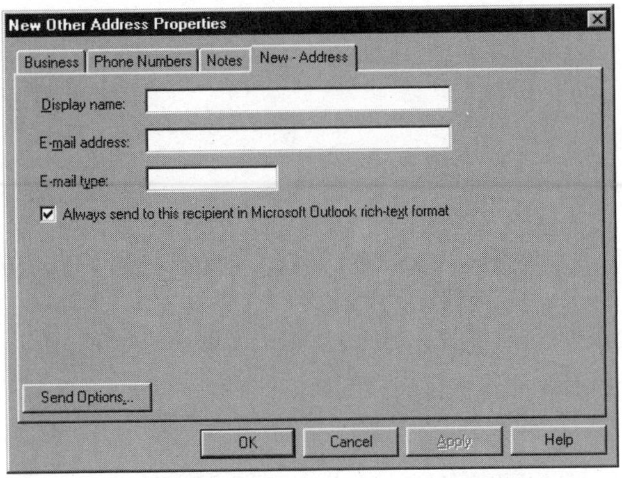

Figure 11-12.
You enter contact information in the New Other Address Properties dialog box.

5. In the Display Name text box, type the name as you want it to appear in the address book.

6. In the E-mail Address text box, type the e-mail address, such as *alan@neibauer.net*.

7. In the E-mail Type text box, enter the designation for the recipient's e-mail system, such as *SMTP*, a common format for Internet e-mail.

8. Select the check box labeled Always Send To This Recipient In Microsoft Outlook Rich-Text Format if you want to send meeting and tasks requests to other Outlook users.

9. Fill in the text boxes on the other tabs with as much information as you want. For example, the Business tab provides text boxes for a mailing address and phone number. The Phone Numbers tab contains text boxes for multiple phone numbers, including a text box for a fax number. If you will want to send a fax to this person, be sure to enter the fax telephone number.

When you add a name and address, Outlook requires only that you fill in the text boxes on the New Address tab. You can leave the other tabs blank and fill them in later by double-clicking the name in the Address Book window or by using the Properties button on the Address Book toolbar.

10. Click OK.

Note

If you communicate with other Outlook users over the Internet, make sure you select the Always Send To This Recipient In Microsoft Outlook Rich-Text Format check box. Then you can send Outlook items, such as meeting and tasks requests, which will be properly formatted when opened by others in their Calendar or Tasks folders.

Sending a Message

The fastest and easiest way to send a message is simply to type the text and click Send. To send a simple message from a mail folder, do the following:

1. Click the New Mail Message button at the left end of the Standard toolbar to open a message window, as shown in Figure 11-13. Depending on how you set up Outlook, the window might look a little different on your screen.

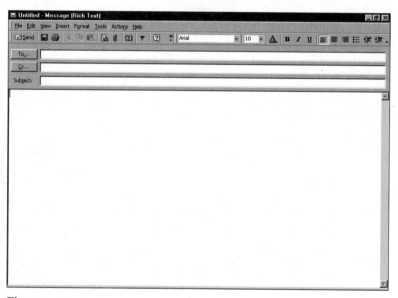

Figure 11-13.

Enter a new e-mail message in a new message window.

Note

You can create a new message from any folder in Outlook. From the Inbox, Outbox, or Drafts folder, click the New Mail Message button. From another folder, click the down arrow on the Standard toolbar's New button and select Mail Message.

2. In the new message window, click the To button to display the Select Names dialog box, as shown in Figure 11-14.

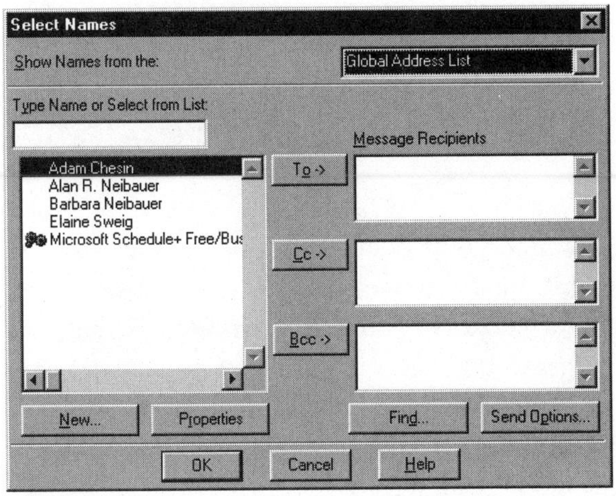

Figure 11-14.
Choose addressees in the Select Names dialog box.

3. Select the address book you want to use from the Show Names From The list box.

4. In the Type Name Or Select From List text box, type part of the name of a recipient, type the full name, or select a name from the list below.

When you type the beginning of a name in the Type Name Or Select From List box, Outlook scrolls through the list of addresses to the first name that matches the letters you've typed. You can then scroll further, if you need to, to find the name you want.

You can also select a distribution list from either the personal address book or from the Contacts list to send the message to a group of people. To select more than one addressee, hold down the Ctrl key and click each name.

5. Click the To button to enter the main addressees, and click the Cc or Bcc box to send copies to others.

The name or names you've selected appear in the boxes to the right of each button.

6. Click OK when you've chosen all the addressees.

7. In the message window, click in the Subject box and type a brief description of the subject of your message.

8. Click the message area or press the Tab key to move to the message text area, and then type your message.

9. When your message is ready to send, click the Send button.

Note

If you do not complete your message and are not ready to send it, choose Save from the File menu. Outlook stores the message in the Drafts folder. To complete the message, open the Drafts folder, and then double-click the message in the message list. Click Send when you are ready to send the message.

What happens when you click the Send button depends on how your system is set up and to whom the mail is addressed. E-mail messages that you've sent to recipients on your network (those people who have mailboxes in your Microsoft Mail Postoffice) are transmitted immediately. E-mail messages to Internet recipients, however, are stored in the Outbox until you are ready to dial in and connect. To actually send the messages, click the Send And Receive button on the Standard toolbar. Outlook sends any messages in the Outbox and checks for new messages waiting for you.

When you send a message, Outlook automatically saves a copy of it in the Sent Items folder. To check your sent messages, click the Sent Items folder.

Reading a Message

When e-mail arrives in your Inbox, you can read it, respond to it, and forward it to others. You can read a message in the preview pane or in a separate window. The preview pane is an area at the lower right of the Inbox that displays the contents of the selected message. If the preview pane is not displayed, choose Preview Pane from the View menu.

To quickly read e-mail text when the preview pane is displayed, click the message in the Inbox message list. If part of a long message falls below the bottom of the preview pane, scroll through the message window to read the rest of the message. To see the first three lines of messages directly in the message list, choose AutoPreview from the View menu.

To read the message in its own window, simply double-click the message line in your Inbox's message list. If you want to add the sender's name to your address book, right-click the person's name in the open message, and then choose Add To Personal Address

Book. Choose Properties from the shortcut menu if you just want to see the sender's e-mail address.

Note

Once you've opened a message in its own window, you can use the Previous Item and Next Item buttons on the Standard toolbar in the message window to move from message to message (the buttons with the large up and down arrows). Next to each of these buttons is a small down arrow that you can click to see a list of commands that let you move more quickly to the messages you want to read. For example, you can move to the next or previous message from the same sender or to the next or previous unread message.

See Also

For more information on using Microsoft Outlook for network and Internet e-mail, see *Running Microsoft Outlook 2000*, from Microsoft Press.

Using a Shareware Mail Server

While using Microsoft Outlook for all your e-mail needs is a good solution, you may want to use Outlook Express or some other e-mail program for both Internet e-mail and e-mail on your home network. If so, you'll need a mail server other than Microsoft Post Office.

The shareware program VPOP3 (for Virtual POP3 server) is one example of such a mail server. You can download an evaluation version of the program at this address: *http://www.pscs.co.uk/software/vpop3.html.*

VPOP3 installs a mail server that monitors incoming and outgoing mail. It collects mail coming from your ISP and channels it to your e-mail program. It also sets up its own network post office for collecting mail to and from network users. You can then use an Internet e-mail program, such as Outlook Express to send e-mail to other family members on the network. This e-mail is stored in a mailbox until the recipient checks the VPOP3 server for mail with an e-mail program.

VPOP3 is a robust mail program with a great many features. I'll just summarize here how the program works.

You only need to install and run VPOP3 on the computer you plan to use as your mail server. When you first run the program, the VPOP3 Configuration Wizard lets you specify how it should connect to your Internet mail server. You can select from several popular ISPs, or if your ISP is not listed, specify how to connect as shown in Figure 11-15, on the next page.

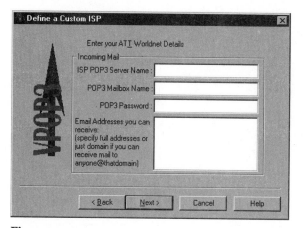

Figure 11-15.

Configuring VPOP3 for your ISP.

When you start VPOP3 for the first time, you'll be asked to designate yourself as the post office administrator so you can create and manage mailboxes.

You can then log on as the administrator when you start VPOP3.

You create mailboxes by adding users, and make other changes to VPOP3 settings using the VPOP3 Settings dialog box, shown in Figure 11-16, which appears when you start the program and log on. On the Users tab, for example, you can create a VPOP3 mailbox by clicking Add User, and then entering a user name and password, as shown in Figure 11-17.

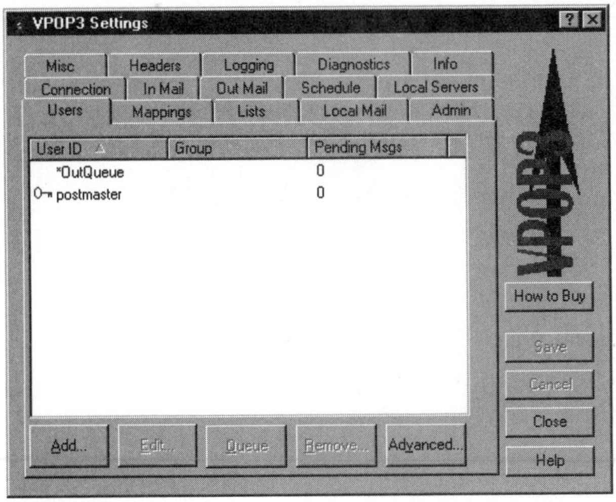

Figure 11-16.
VPOP3 settings.

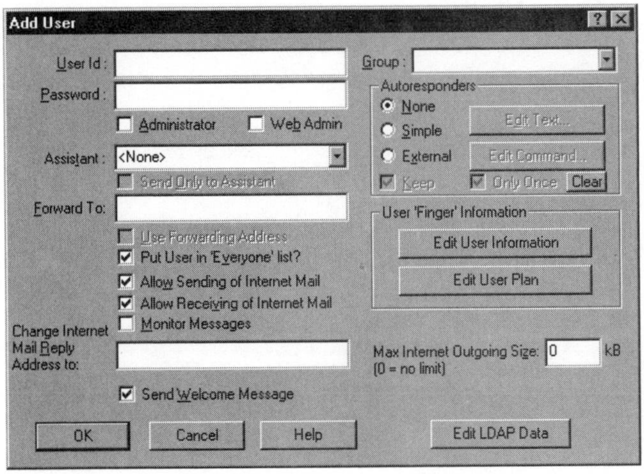

Figure 11-17.
Adding a VPOP3 user.

On the Local Mail tab of the VPOP3 Settings dialog box, you enter the local do-main of your network users. The local domain is actually the part of your Internet e-mail address after the @ symbol. If you access the Internet and get e-mail through AT&T Worldnet, for example, your local domain is att.net. After you set up your e-mail program to work with VPOP3, you can send mail to someone with that domain. For example, if you create a VPOP3 post office for a user named Barb, you can then use Outlook Express to send mail to barb@att.net through VPOP3 to the user on the network.

Once you configure VPOP3 and add users, however, you must adjust your e-mail program to send and receive mail locally through the network. As an example of this, here are the steps you'd follow in Outlook Express to create an account for a VPOP3 post office user. Outlook Express allows you to create and use more than one mail account so you can use it to check for e-mail sent to more than one member of the family over your ISP, or to check multiple ISPs or free Web-based e-mail services.

Before you start, however, you'll need to get the IP address of the computer on which VPOP3 is installed. Outlook Express uses the IP address to connect to the VPOP3 server through the network. Once you have the server's IP address, just follow these steps.

1. Start Outlook Express.

2. Select Accounts from the Tools menu.

3. Click Add and then click Mail to start the Internet Connection Wizard.

4. Type your name and then click Next.

5. Enter your e-mail address, consisting of your VPOP3 user name and the default domain, and then click Next.
   You can now enter the server names.

6. In both the Incoming Mail Server and Outgoing Mail Server text boxes, enter the IP address of the VPOP3 server, as shown in Figure 11-18.

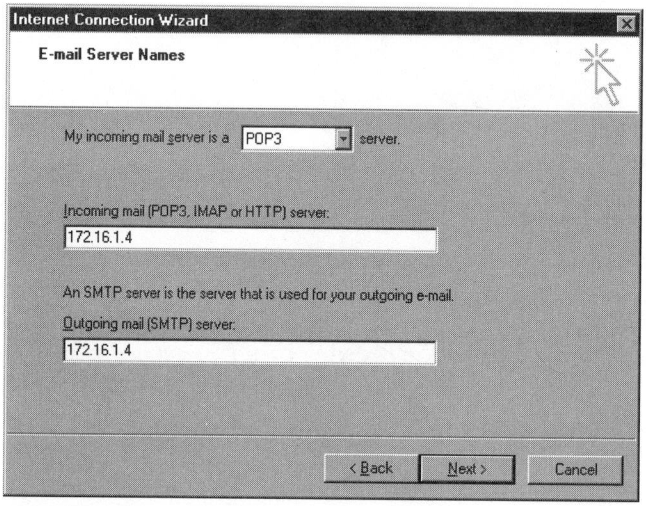

Figure 11-18.
VPOP3 server IP address.

7. Click Next, enter your VPOP3 user name and password, and then click Next again.

8. Click Finish.

    You now see the IP address listed as mail account in the Internet Accounts dialog box.

9. Click the IP address and then click Properties to open the dialog box shown in Figure 11-19. Replace the IP address in the top box of the General tab with VPOP3.

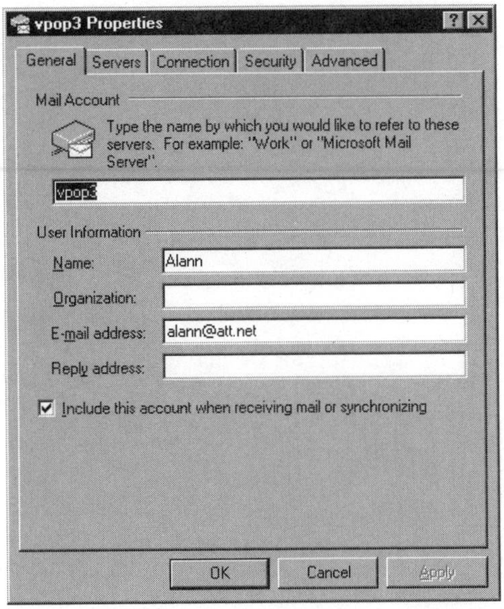

Figure 11-19.
Configuring the e-mail account.

10. Click the Connection tab.

11. Select the check box labeled Always Connect To This Account Using.

12. Click the down arrow next to the drop-down list below the check box and choose Local Area Network from the list.

13. Click OK.

    Now when you want to send an e-mail message to a network user with Outlook Express, click the New Mail button on the toolbar to open a new message window, pull down the From list, and choose your VPOP3 account from the list.

Complete the message as you would normally and click Send.

You can then click Send/Recv on the Outlook Express toolbar to send and receive mail from all of your accounts, or pull down the list associated with the Send/Recv button and choose the VPOP3 account to send and receive mail just over the network.

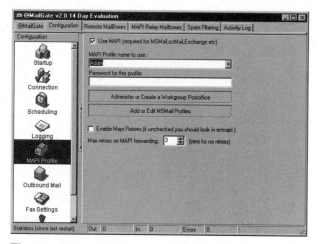

VPOP3 certainly isn't the only alternative for sending and receiving both Internet and network mail. The program @MailGate (*http://www.titansoft.com*), for example, gets mail from your ISP and channels it to your Microsoft Post Office mailbox. The @MailGate program is shown in Figure 11-20 being configured to copy Internet e-mail to Adam's Post Office mailbox.

Figure 11-20.
Configuring @MailGate.

E-mail, whether over your network or the Internet, is a great way to communicate. When the computers in your home are connected by a network, you can use Microsoft Mail Postoffice or another mail server to send messages and files and share information with all members of the family. E-mail over the Internet lets you connect to family and friends all over the world. If you only have one phone line and one Internet account, however, you may think that your family can only use the Internet one at a time. In the next chapter, you'll learn how to share Internet accounts.

Chapter 12

Going On Line
Through the Network

Chances are, if you have more than one computer in the household, you have more than one modem. But if you have only one phone line, only one family member at a time can be on line. Even if you have two phone lines at home, most ISPs won't allow more than one person at a time to access the Internet using the same account. If you try, you'll get a message telling you that the account is already in use. Most ISPs prefer that you sign up for multiple accounts.

However, another great advantage to connecting your home computers through a network is that it allows you to share one phone line and one Internet account with everyone in the household. You could look up stock quotes, for example, while someone else is downloading software or just surfing the Net for fun or profit.

See Also

See the note on the next page for important information about sharing an ISP account.

Sharing a phone line is especially useful when one computer on the network has a modem that's faster than the others, such as a 56 Kbps modem or an ultra-fast cable modem. In fact, when you're connected on a network, you don't even need a modem on more than one machine. All the computers on the network can share the high-speed modem that's connected to one computer.

When a modem is shared on a network, only one user—the first to dial in to the ISP—is actually logged on, and that user can be anyone on the network. Other users who want to access the Internet just piggyback onto the existing connection through the network. Their modems do not need to dial in because the connection has already been made by the first computer. As far as the ISP is concerned, only one person is logged on.

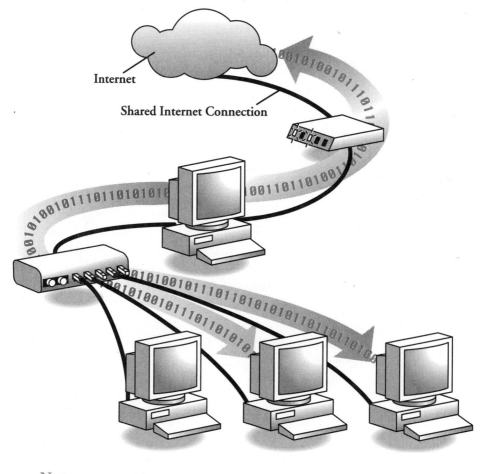

Note

With modem sharing now so easy and popular, many ISPs have fine-tuned the small print in their customer agreements to discourage simultaneous sharing of an account. You should not share an ISP account if the membership agreement forbids it.

Internet Sharing Alternatives

There are two basic ways to share a modem and an Internet account—by using software or by using hardware.

When you use software to share a modem, you have to designate one computer on the network as the *host*. That computer's modem will then be shared by the other computers on the network, called the *clients*. A modem-sharing program, like Microsoft Windows Internet Connection Sharing or one of the others described in this chapter, reconfigures the network to accept Internet requests from the client computers and channels them to the shared modem on the host computer. The host computer's modem dials the ISP directly; the client computers are reconfigured to connect to the ISP through the network rather than through their own dial-up connections and modems.

If the host computer is already on line, a client computer can go on line without dialing. If the host computer is turned on but is not on line, the client computer dials in through the modem connected to the host computer.

The shared modem can be any of the following types:

- A standard modem
- An Integrated Services Digital Network (ISDN) modem
- A digital subscriber line (DSL) modem
- A cable modem

Table 12-1, on the next page, summarizes the advantages and disadvantages of each type of shared modem.

Whatever the type of modem you have in your home, just select the one that's fastest or most reliable and designate the computer connected to it as the host.

The main disadvantage to using software to share a modem is that the host computer must be turned on for its modem to be shared. If the computer is turned off, a client computer will get an error message when it tries to connect to the Internet through the host on the network.

There are ways around this problem, however. The fastest solution is to just go to the room with the shared modem and turn on the computer. An alternative to sharing a modem with software is to buy and install special hardware, called a LAN modem, that is connected directly to the network. A LAN modem (LAN stands for local area network) is directly connected to the network in the same way a printer can be connected to a network, as you learned in Chapter 9. As long as the modem and network hub are turned on, anyone on the network can access the Internet at any time.

The downside to a LAN modem is its cost. LAN modems are more expensive than standard modems and they can be difficult to set up.

Table 12-1. Sharing Different Modem Types: Advantages and Disadvantages

Modem Type	Advantages	Disadvantages
Standard modem	Connects to a standard telephone line. Usually included with PCs or inexpensive to purchase and upgrade.	Connects at the slowest speeds, with a maximum of 56 Kbps.
ISDN	Connects at a high speed, up to 128 Kbps. Uses a dedicated connection so you can use your regular phone line at the same time.	More expensive than a standard modem and requires special telephone service that costs more than a regular phone line. Most ISPs charge more for ISDN service.
DSL	Connects at an ultra-high speed, up to 1.5 Mbps. Uses a dedicated connection so you can use your regular phone line at the same time.	More expensive than standard modems and requires special telephone service that costs more than a regular phone line. DSL service may not be available everywhere, and your ISP may not support it.
Cable	Connects at an ultra-high speed, up to 10 Mbps. Uses cable TV service instead of your phone line.	Not all cable companies offer modem service. You'll have to pay a setup and installation fee, as well as monthly ISP charges that are usually higher than regular dial-up ISP charges.

Getting Ready to Share a Modem

If you're considering using software to share an Internet connection, make sure that the modem on the host computer works and that you can use the host computer to connect to the Internet.

The network connections between computers must also be working properly. Each computer should be able to see the others in Network Neighborhood and communicate with them.

Making Sure TCP/IP Is Installed

Almost all Internet connection sharing requires that you have the TCP/IP protocol installed on each computer connected to the network. You'll need TCP/IP installed even if it's not the primary protocol you use for the network.

To determine whether TCP/IP drivers are installed on computers running Windows 95 or Windows 98, follow these steps:

1. On the Start menu, point to Settings, and then click Control Panel.

2. In the Control Panel window, double-click the Network icon.

3. On the Configuration tab of the Network dialog box, look for an entry in the installed network components list showing TCP/IP→followed by your network card.

If the listing is not present, you'll need to install the TCP/IP protocol. You'll find instructions for setting up a network protocol in "Installing Protocols," on page 118, but here's a recap of the steps:

1. In the Network dialog box, click Add.

2. In the Select Network Component Type dialog box, click Protocol, and then click Add.

3. In the Select Network Protocol dialog box, choose Microsoft from the list of manufacturers.

4. Select TCP/IP from the Network Protocols list.

5. Click OK to close the Select Network Protocol dialog box.

6. Click OK to close the Network dialog box.

7. Click Yes when you are asked whether to restart your computer.

You'll have to configure TCP/IP, but how you do it depends on the particular software you're using for sharing an Internet connection and on whether or not you're also using TCP/IP as your network protocol. For more information, see "Configuring TCP/IP" on page 122.

Using Modem-Sharing Software

Many programs let you share a modem and Internet connection (subject to the terms of your ISP agreement) over a network. One such modem-sharing program is built into Microsoft Windows 98 Second Edition. If you have that version of Windows, you don't need to download or purchase any additional modem-sharing software.

You'll also find modem-sharing software in most network starter kits, although the programs vary in the way they are set up.

Some modem-sharing programs are also available as shareware. This means that you can download them from the Internet and try them out for free during a trial period. If you like the program, you can then register it for a fee. When you register, you'll get a password or serial number that enables the program to work beyond the trial period.

Installing Windows Internet Connection Sharing

Internet Connection Sharing is a new feature that comes with Windows 98 Second Edition. But it isn't installed automatically when you install or upgrade to Windows 98 Second Edition, so you'll need to add it as an additional component to the Windows installation on the computer you plan to use as the host. Here's how to do it:

1. Make sure the Windows 98 Second Edition CD is in your CD-ROM drive.

2. On the Start menu, point to Settings, and then click Control Panel.

3. In the Control Panel window, double-click the Add/Remove Programs icon.

4. In the list of components on the Windows Setup tab, click Internet Tools to select it. Do not deselect the check box to the left of Internet Tools.

5. Click the Details button to see a list of the items in the Internet Tools category, as shown in Figure 12-1.

Figure 12-1.
Select Internet Connection Sharing from the list of components in the Internet Tools dialog box.

6. In the list of components, select the Internet Connection Sharing check box.

7. Click OK to close the Internet Tools dialog box.

8. Click OK in the Add/Remove Programs Properties dialog box.

Windows installs the Internet connection sharing feature and then displays the Internet Connection Sharing Wizard page, which starts the process of setting up connection sharing.

1. Read the information and then click Next.

2. Click Next on the next page.

    The wizard explains that it will create a floppy disk to set up the client computers for Internet sharing through the host computer.

3. Click Next.

4. Insert a formatted floppy disk that has at least 200 KB of space in your floppy disk drive, and then click OK.

5. When the wizard tells you to do so, remove the disk, and then click OK.

6. Click Finish.

7. Click Yes when you are asked whether to restart the computer.

The wizard makes some changes to the network settings in the Control Panel. It adds a binding for Internet connection sharing to each of the installed protocols, and it sets or changes the IP address and subnet mask of the network card to a special address.

If you set up your network using TCP/IP addresses that you entered yourself rather than letting the computers obtain their TCP/IP addresses automatically, you will have to configure the client computers on the network so that they get their IP addresses automatically. You don't need to make any changes to the host computer's TCP/IP settings. You'll learn how to do this in "Setting Up the Client Computers," on the next page.

After you install Internet connection sharing, you can make the following adjustments to its settings:

- Turn Internet sharing on or off.

- Place an icon for changing Internet sharing in the system tray.

- Select which connection the host will use to access the Internet, if you have more than one Internet account.

- Choose which NIC to use for the network, if you have more than one.

To change any of these Internet connection sharing settings, follow these steps:

1. On the Start menu, point to settings, and then click Control Panel.

2. In the Control Panel window, double-click the Internet Options icon.

3. In the Internet Properties dialog box, click the Connection tab.

4. Click Sharing in the Local Area Network (LAN) Settings section of the dialog box.

5. Change options in the Internet Connection Sharing dialog box, and then click OK.

If you choose to show the icon in the taskbar, you can right-click the taskbar icon to see a shortcut menu.

Choose Status to see which computers are sharing the Internet connection, or choose Options to change your connection and NIC. If you find that sharing your connection slows down Web surfing or program downloading significantly, you may want to turn off

Internet connection sharing. To turn off Internet connection sharing, you can choose the Disable Internet Connection Sharing option.

Setting Up the Client Computers

After you've installed Internet Sharing on the host computer, the next step is to configure each client computer to access the Internet through the network rather than through its own dial-up connection and modem. But first you need to set up each client computer so that its TCP/IP protocol gets an IP address automatically. Here's how to do this:

1. On the Start menu of each client computer, point to Settings, and then click Control Panel.

2. In the Control Panel window, double-click the Network icon.

3. On the Configuration tab of the Network dialog box, select the TCP/IP listing for your network card.

4. Click Properties.

5. On the IP Address tab of the TCP/IP Properties dialog box, select Obtain An IP Address Automatically.

6. Click the WINS Configuration tab, shown in Figure 12-2.

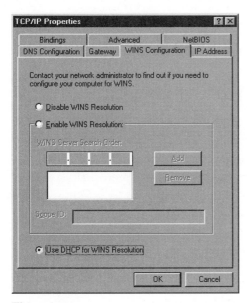

Figure 12-2.
The WINS Configuration tab of the TCP/IP Properties dialog box.

7. Make sure the Use DHCP For WINS Resolution option is selected.

8. Click the Gateway tab.

9. Make sure the Installed Gateways list is empty.
    If you see entries in the Installed Gateways list, select each entry and then click Remove.

10. Click the DNS Configuration tab.

11. Make sure the Disable DNS option is selected.

12. Click OK.

13. Click OK to close the Network dialog box.

14. Click Yes when you are asked whether to restart your computer.

Running the Browser Connection Setup Wizard

When you installed Internet connection sharing on the host computer, you created a floppy disk containing the Browser Connection Setup Wizard. You now need to use this disk to configure each of the client computers so that they access the Internet through the network.

1. Start the host computer and use it to connect to the Internet.

2. Insert the disk in the floppy drive of a client computer.

3. On the Start menu, click Run.

4. In the Run dialog box, type *A:\Icsclset.exe* and click OK.

5. Click Next until the last wizard page appears, and then click Finish.

6. Repeat the process on each client computer.

Once you've configured the client computers, you'll be able to access the Internet from any of them through the host computer's modem. If, however, you try to connect to the Internet from a client computer and receive an error message, it may be that the host computer is turned off. In this case, you can change the client computer's settings to connect through its own modem rather than through the host's. How you do this depends on your browser. With Microsoft Internet Explorer, follow these steps:

1. Right-click the Internet Explorer icon on the client's desktop and choose Properties from the shortcut menu. If there is no icon, double-click the Internet Options icon in the Control Panel.

2. Click the Connection tab.

3. With Internet Explorer 5, select Always Dial My Default Connection. You can also click Setup and use the Internet Connection Wizard to select your dial-up connection.

   With Internet Explorer version 4, select Connect To The Internet Using A Modem on the Connections tab, or click Connect to start the wizard.

The Browser Connection Setup Wizard does not change the settings of other programs that access your ISP, including e-mail programs such as Outlook Express. If you want these programs to connect through the network as well, you have to change their setup yourself. Most of these programs have a dialog box or menu option that allows you to specify a type of connection. As an example, let's run through the process for Microsoft's Outlook Express program.

Click the Outlook Express icon in the taskbar, or start the program as you would normally, and then follow these steps:

1. From the Tools menu, choose Accounts.

2. In the Internet Accounts dialog box, click your account, and then click Properties.

3. On the Connection tab of the Properties dialog box, click Always Connect To This Account Using.

4. Click the down arrow next to the drop-down list and choose Local Area Network.

5. Click OK.

6. Repeat the process for each account and then click Close to close the Internet Accounts dialog box.

Note

Versions of Outlook Express earlier than 5 have an option button on the Connection tab that you can click to connect through the network.

Connecting to the Internet through Internet Connection Sharing

When you're ready to connect to the Internet, just start your browser as you would normally. If you're on a client computer, it will connect through the network, dialing the modem on the host computer if the host is not already connected.

If you are on the host computer, do not disconnect from the Internet unless you are certain no one else is connected through the network.

To check whether anyone is on line, use the Sharing options to place the icon in the system tray, the area of the taskbar adjacent to the clock. Then right-click the Internet Connection Sharing icon in the system tray, and choose Status. A box appears reporting the number of computers using the connection. The number includes your own computer even if you are not connected, so do not disconnect if the number is greater than one. If you do, you'll disconnect the other members of your family who are connected.

If no one else is connected to the Internet, you can disconnect. If you're used to seeing a message asking if you want to disconnect when you close your browser, don't be surprised if it no longer appears. The message is turned off to avoid disconnecting when someone else is using the modem.

Other Software Solutions for Internet Connection Sharing

Other software solutions for sharing an Internet connection are similar in concept to Internet connection sharing in Windows 98 Second Edition, but they're set up differently. Table 12-2 lists some of the Internet connection sharing programs you can download from the Internet.

Table 12-2. Other Internet Connection Sharing Software

Software	Internet Address
aVirt Gateway Server	http://www.avirt.com
Internet Gate	http://www.maccasoft.com
i.Share	http://www.artisoft.com
LanBridge	http://www.virtualmotion.com
MidPoint Companion	http://www.midcore.com
PPPShar	http://www.pppindia.com
RideWay	http://www.itserv.com
ShareTheNet	http://www.sharethenet.com
SyGate	http://www.sygate.com
Wingate	http://www.wingate.com

All these programs require that the TCP/IP protocol be installed on the computers on the network and that you install their Internet sharing software on the host computer. The main difference among the programs is how the client computers are configured to access the shared modem.

With aVirt Gateway software, for example, each of the clients must be set to access the Internet through a *proxy server*. A proxy server is a computer that handles the flow of information between the Internet and other computers sharing the modem. Although you can do this manually in your browser by designating the IP address of the computer with the shared modem, aVirt provides a client wizard to set up all of the Internet applications automatically.

The RideWay program works similarly, except that you must manually enter the host computer's IP address to use as the proxy server.

With Wingate, you install the program on all of the computers on the network. The initial dialog box of the installation program asks if you are setting up a Wingate Server or a Wingate Internet Client. If you choose the client option, the program configures your computer to access the modem connected to the server.

With SyGate, you only need to install the program on the host computer and set up the browser on each client computer to access the Internet through the network. If you have Internet Explorer, for example, you can run the Internet Connection Wizard and select I Connect Through A Local Area Network (LAN), as shown in Figure 12-3.

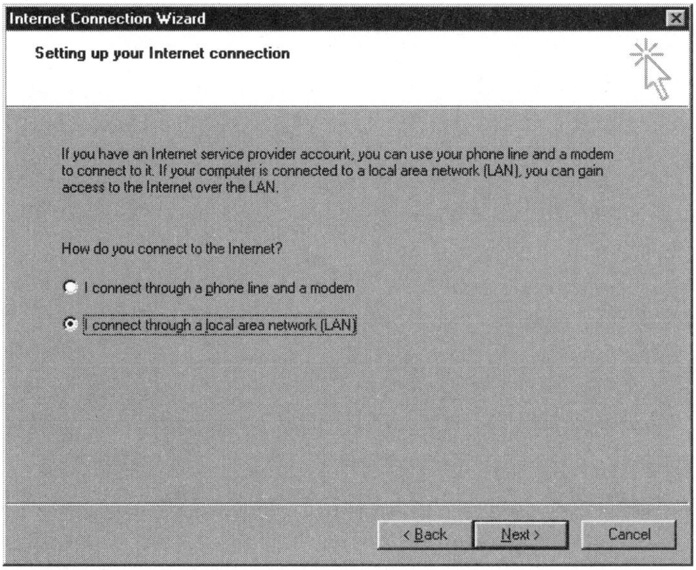

Figure 12-3.
Choose to connect to the Internet through a local area network in the Internet Connection Wizard.

Using Internet-Sharing Hardware

As an alternative to using software to share an Internet connection, you can purchase hardware that provides a modem sharing solution.

A LAN modem, for example, connects directly to your network hub. The computers on the network are set to connect to the Internet through the LAN modem. If you have a LAN modem, you should set up your hardware so that the LAN modem is turned on whenever your network hub is turned on. That way, the modem will be available to everyone on the network all the time regardless of which computers on the network are turned on.

LAN modems can be expensive, though, and difficult to set up. While you can purchase an internal 56 Kbps modem card for under $50, LAN modems cost $250 or more. They also require quite a few steps to set up, sometimes involving complex protocol configurations. Still, if you have a few extra dollars to spend and the time to set it up and configure it, a LAN modem can be a very useful addition to your home network.

The OfficeConnect LAN-modem from 3Com, for example, even includes its own four-port hub, which allows it to serve as the network's modem and hub at the same time. After connecting the device, you can set it up just by starting your browser and connecting to a configuration Web page that's stored within the modem. Use the information on the Web page to set up the modem for your ISP. At the time of this book's printing, the 56 Kbps version of the LAN modem cost under $300; the ISDN version was just under $400.

There are seven models in the WebRamp series of LAN modems, ranging from just under $400 to over $800. Some models have built-in 56 Kbps modems; others have ISDN modems with enhanced features for business users. For home users, the model 200i, available for under $400, contains a built-in 56 Kbps modem and 4-port hub, and you can connect to it another external 56 Kbps or ISDN modem.

Other companies that manufacture LAN modems include Netopia, Adtran, and Intel.

If you already have an external modem, you can purchase a device called a modem server that, in effect, turns your external modem into a LAN modem. In that setup, the server connects to the network and your modem connects to the server. A modem server does not usually have its own modem built in, but some models do give you that option.

Companies such as Atronics, Lantronix, Netgear, Perle, and others make a variety of models. A modem server, however, is more expensive than a LAN modem, and you still need to connect it to an external modem. Prices start at about $500 and go into the thousands.

By sharing a modem and Internet connection, you can save a lot of money, even if you purchase a LAN modem rather than a purely software solution. You can also avoid having to wait for the telephone line in your home to be free. With the time you save waiting, you can play some of those cool computer games with other members of your family on the network. Playing games on the network is the subject of the next chapter.

Chapter 13

Playing Games

Playing games across the network encourages communication and competition and can be a great stress-reliever—especially if you win! But even if you don't win, network game playing can be a great family experience. You can share a virtual world with your family, fighting a common foe or going head-to-head in the spirit of friendly competition.

Solo vs. Network Games

Solo games on a computer can be fun and exhilarating, but you're playing against the computer. It's the computer that represents your foe—whether it's a galactic warrior, a World War II dog fighter, or a chess player at the other end of the board.

While the computer can make all the right moves to keep a game interesting, it has no personality. When you're playing against a real person, you can try to anticipate your opponent's moves based on previous games or on what you know about his or her way of thinking. Human players provide more drama and a keener sense of competition. You can gently gloat over your win and someone else can gloat when you lose, making rematches all the more interesting.

Because many computer games allow more than two players, several members of the family can play. Usually, in fact, as many can play as there are computers on your home network. Games that require more players than you have available can sometimes create computer-generated competitors, so you can still practice your skills when other members of the family are busy.

When you don't feel competitive, you can play games that simply allow you to share experiences with other family members. With Microsoft's Flight Simulator, for example, you and another family member can soar over scenic landscapes and travel to distant lands in separate planes.

Preparing for Network Play

There are hundreds of games that you can play over a network. Windows even comes with one, a game called Hearts. If you purchased a network kit, the accompanying CD may have network games on it, too. Check the documentation that came with the kit for a list of the games or insert the CD in the drive and browse through its folders to learn what is included.

Selecting the proper games for you and your family and installing them on your network are the first steps toward network playing. But before you purchase or install any games, make sure your network is up and running.

To accommodate as many games as possible, you should make sure all three popular protocols are installed: TCP/IP, IPX/SPX, and NetBEUI. Check that all of the computers on the network show up in Network Neighborhood and that you can transfer information among them.

Selecting Games for Network Play

When choosing games, make sure that they fit your family's interests and standards and that they can be run on every computer on the network.

Many computer stores offer previews of popular games on special computers set up just for that purpose. You can play the game in the store before purchasing it to see if it meets your standards. Bring your children with you and let them preview the game as well. There are also many sites you can visit on line to read about games and download demonstration versions, such as *http://www.gamespot.com* and *http://www.gamecenter.com*.

You also need to make sure that your computers and network are capable of running the game you want. The minimum and recommended hardware requirements are usually listed right on the game's box. The minimum requirements are those that are absolutely necessary for the game to play, although its performance might not really be satisfactory. The recommended requirements are those that the game's manufacturer suggests for good game play. The box may also list optional hardware, such as advanced sound and display systems, that will provide higher quality video or audio.

Note

Network play normally requires greater resources than single-player action. For network play, your computers should meet the recommended speed and memory requirements rather than just the minimum requirements.

Some of the hardware requirements you'll need to consider:

- **Processor type and speed** Most of the sophisticated action games require at least a Pentium, or a Pentium-compatible processor, running at a certain speed or above. Older Pentiums running at 90 MHz are often too slow for the newest games. In fact, new games are designed for high-speed processors, so don't be surprised to see 300 MHz or more listed as the minimum or recommended processor speed.

- **Amount of RAM** Some games, especially those with lots of graphics, require 32 MB or more of memory.

- **Available disk space** Programs that feature sound and video require a lot of storage space. A typical game may require 40 megabytes of disk storage or more, even when you run the program from the CD rather than installing it all on your hard disk.

- **Sound card** To hear the sound effects that help make many computer games so exciting, you'll need a sound card in your computer. Most newer computer sound systems come with sound cards. Older computers may not be able to generate a game's sounds unless you add a sound card.

- **Display requirements** Look on the game's box for the minimum and recommended color and screen resolution settings. Many games require your system to be set at 256 colors or more, with a screen resolution of at least 800 by 600 pixels. In some cases, the game will start with lower settings, but the display will not be very clear. In other cases, you won't be able to start or play the game until the display is adjusted to the minimum settings. Although many games recommend advanced 3D or graphic accelerator cards, they're usually not part of the minimum requirements.

- **Joystick** For flight simulators, combat games, and other action games, a joystick or yolk is highly recommended. You can still play the game using the keyboard or mouse to control movement, but you will not experience the same sense of control.

If some of your computers don't meet a game's minimum or recommended requirements, consider playing the game on only the computers that do meet them. Or you can use the most advanced computers in the house to play the game on the network, leaving less sophisticated computers for solo action.

Most network games require that a single computer serve as the host, starting and organizing the game, and running its CD while the game is played. (The other computers on the network do not have to run the game CD during play.) For maximum performance, choose as the host the computer with the greatest memory, speed, and storage space.

Installing Games for Network Play

In most cases, you don't have to do anything special to install a game for network play. The usual setup process installs both the single and multiple player versions of the game. If you are presented with options to install the single or multiple player version, choose the multiple player version.

Install the game separately on each computer on the network. For games on CD or floppy disk, insert the CD or disk in each computer and run the installation program. If you downloaded the game from the Internet, copy the file to each of the computers in Network Neighborhood, and then run the installation program on each machine.

At installation, most games present a series of dialog boxes that prompt you to select hardware options. Make sure you choose options appropriate for the machine on which you are installing the game.

If you are not asked to select options during the installation process, you may have to do so when you first start the game. For example, you may have to select from a menu of input devices used to manipulate objects, such as a keyboard, mouse, or joystick. Be sure to start and set up the game on each computer before playing it on the network.

Playing Games on the Network

To play a network game that was supplied on a CD, you usually need to insert the CD in the host computer's drive. Once the host starts the game and sets its options, other computers on the network can join in.

The procedure for starting games varies. The installation process may either place an icon on the desktop or add a listing to the Start menu. To begin playing, double-click the icon or select the program from the Start menu.

With some older games, the Start menu listing accesses the CD directly and can be used only on the host. To start the game on the other computers, each player has to find the game program in its folder.

Once you start the game, you'll be asked to choose whether you want the computer you're playing on to be the host or whether you want to join a game that's already in progress. Again, the process varies widely. In the dialog box shown here, from the game HyperBlade, you can select the type of network you are using, choose to host a new game, or wait until a game in progress appears in the Open Games list and choose to join that game.

To give you an idea of some of the possibilities for network game playing, we'll look at two examples of network games.

Hearts

Hearts is a card game for four players that comes with Microsoft Windows. To see if Hearts and the other Windows games are installed on your computer, click Start, and point to Programs, Accessories, and then Games.

If the Windows games are not installed on your computer, follow these steps:

1. Insert the Windows CD in your CD-ROM drive.

2. On the Start menu, point to Settings, and then click Control Panel.

3. In the Control Panel window, double-click the Add/Remove Programs icon.

4. In the Add/Remove Programs Properties dialog box, click the Windows Setup tab.

5. Click Accessories. Do not select the check box to the left of Accessories or you will clear the check mark.

6. Click Details to see a list of the items in the Accessories category.

7. In the list of components, click the Games check box to enable it.

8. Click OK to close the Accessories dialog box.

9. Click OK to close the Add/Remove Programs Properties dialog box. Windows installs the games.

To start Hearts, point to Programs on the Start menu, point to Accessories and then to Games, and then click Hearts. You'll see the dialog box shown on the next page.

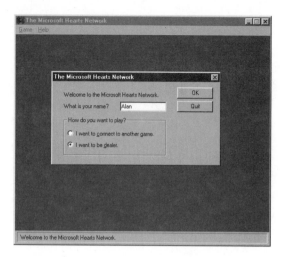

Enter your name, if it's not already shown in the What Is Your Name? text box, and choose whether you want to connect to a game in progress or be the dealer, the host, of a new game.

To start a new game, choose I Want To Be Dealer, and then click OK. The Microsoft Hearts Network window appears as shown in Figure 13-1, with your name as the dealer at the bottom of the window. As other members join the game, their names are added to the window. If you want to play against three computer-generated opponents, you can press the F2 key.

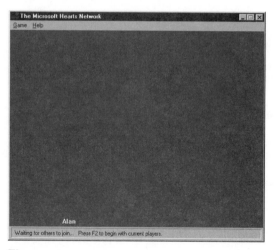

Figure 13-1.
The Microsoft Hearts Network window displays the name of the dealer when you start a new game.

To join a game that someone has already started, select I Want To Connect To Another Game, and then click OK to open the Locate Dealer dialog box. You must enter the name of the computer that the dealer is using and click OK to join the game. The Microsoft Hearts Network window appears and shows you as one of the players.

When another member joins the game, the new player's name appears in the Hearts window of all the other players. Once all the network players are signed in, the host presses the F2 key to start play. If there are fewer than four human players, the program adds its own players to bring the total up to four, as shown in Figure 13-2.

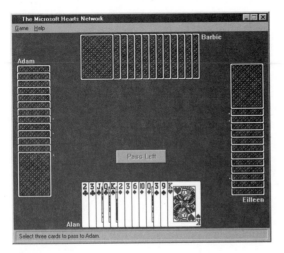

Figure 13-2.
Hearts can be played by a combination of human and computer-generated players.

To change the name of the computer-generated players for the next game, select Options from the Game menu to see the Hearts Options dialog box.

In the Hearts Options dialog box, you can also change the names of your computer opponents and, if you want, the speed at which the animation runs in the game.

Choose Sound from the Game menu to turn sound effects on or off; and choose Score to see the current score.

Microsoft Flight Simulator

Flight Simulator has long been a popular game and learning program. If you enjoy flying, or want to learn how, Flight Simulator lets you practice the skills you'd need to fly an actual airplane. Because the program so accurately depicts actual flying, many trainee pilots use Flight Simulator, and programs like it, to supplement their time in the air. With its displays of detailed scenery from hundreds of locations around the world, Flight Simulator is great fun even if you just want to enjoy the view and leave the real flying to others.

If you are on a network, you can also fly with other members of the family, each network player in his or her own plane. You can do some sightseeing or try to outmaneuver each other through the skies and around the airport.

When you start Flight Simulator 98, select the Multiplayer option and click Next in the first dialog box that appears to see the Session Setup options, shown in Figure 13-3. Enter the name you want to use as your call sign, and choose whether you want to host the session, join one that's already started, or search the Internet for a session in progress. Click Next after you've made your choice.

Figure 13-3.
Before starting a Flight Simulator session, you need to choose whether or not to host it.

If you choose to host a new session, you'll be asked to set session options such as

- The session name
- Maximum number of pilots
- Maximum number of observers
- Whether or not you want to host as an observer

Note

As an observer, you can lock into another aircraft's cockpit view to see that plane's instrument panel and view from the cockpit window.

Set the options for the session, and then click Next. In the next dialog box, you can select the type of network connection you're using from the following choices:

- IPX
- Internet TCP/IP
- Modem Connection
- Serial Connection

On a home network, choose either IPX or TCP/IP, depending on your network protocol. When you've made your choice, click the Host button. You'll now be able to see the names and planes of other network participants in the session you're hosting.

To join a flight being hosted by someone else, choose Join An Existing Session from the Session Setup options, and click Next. Choose the network protocol and click Next. When the Locate Session dialog box appears, enter the computer name or IP address of the computer hosting the session, and click OK. You can also leave the address blank to have Flight Simulator search the network for a hosted session.

When Flight Simulator finds a host, it displays the Multiplayer Connect dialog box shown in Figure 13-4. Select the session you want to join, and then click Join.

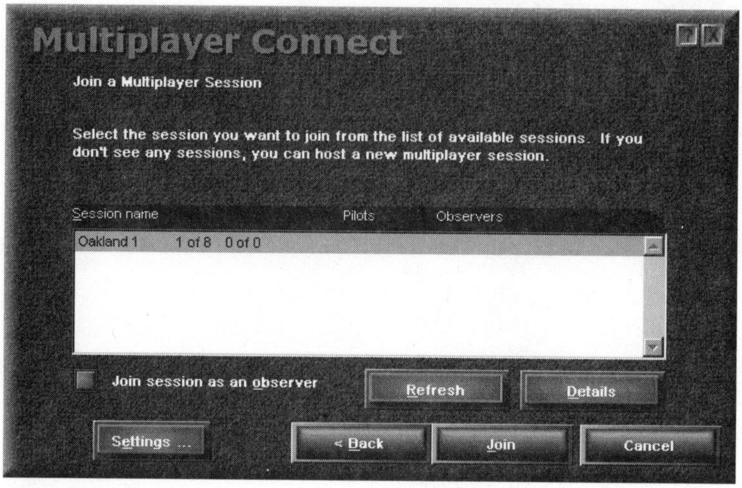

Figure 13-4.
The Multiplayer Connect dialog box allows you to pick the flight you want to join.

In addition to the Flight Simulator window, you'll see a Chat window. Use this window to send messages to other planes. Enter your message in the text box at the bottom of the Chat Window, and then press Enter or click Send.

Watching Out for Pitfalls

Because network games are played in *real time*, family members might want to practice on their own before joining a multiple-player game. They should learn the rules and be able to control movement and play. It's actually no pleasure to win too easily or to wait while a novice player stops the action to learn the rules.

Network playing requires a lot of system resources, so don't be surprised if the sound or video sometimes slows down during a game. The game may be accessing more information on the CD, or another player on the network may pause a game, which sometimes slows down the action for other players. Still, playing games on the network can be fun and challenging, and a great way to compute with the family.

In the next chapter, you'll learn another way to share with the family by setting up your own family Web using Microsoft's Personal Web Server.

Part 5

Extending the Network

Chapter 14

Setting Up a Web

Now that your home computers are connected together on a network, you can easily set up your own Web. Your Web can have a Web site for each member of the family who wants one, a guest book for collecting messages, and it can offer each family member the ability to post documents that others can view easily with a Web browser. In a very real sense, it's like having your own version of the World Wide Web, but right on your home network so you can share family news and information.

Each family member's Web site can have a custom home page that everyone else on the network can see in their Web browsers. Figure 14-1, on the next page, for example, shows how dad's home page might look on the family Web. It includes information that dad wants to share with the family, and photographs of the family's award-winning son. The home page also provides three links to other pages that make up dad's Web site. Anyone viewing dad's home page can click a link to see vacation photographs, read dad's favorite jokes, or return to dad's home page, the first page that someone sees when viewing that Web site.

Note

A private Web over a network, such as your own home Web, is called an *intranet*.

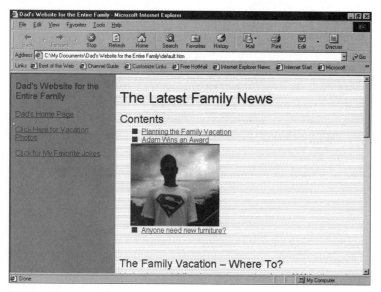
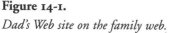

Figure 14-1.

Dad's Web site on the family web.

Of course, mom can have her own Web site on the family Web as well, as shown in Figure 14-2. On her home page, mom shares an old photograph she found when rummaging through the attic and passes on some news about other relatives.

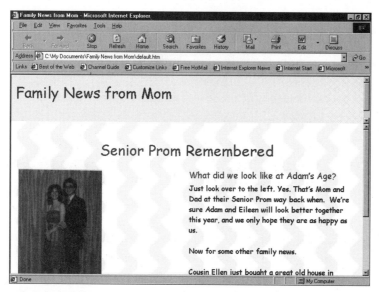

Figure 14-2.

Mom's Web site on the family Web.

Web sites are not just for adults, so Beth has her own Web site on the family Web as well, which is shown in Figure 14-3. Of course her Web site reflects her own personality, with links to her schoolwork and to news about her most recent boyfriend, and some graphics about her favorite subject, music.

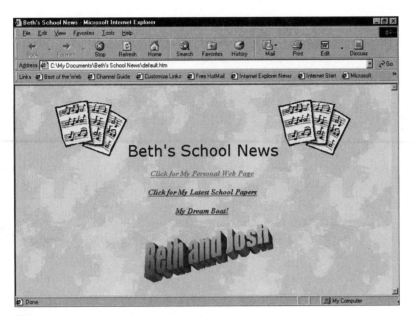

Figure 14-3.
Beth's Web site on the family Web.

What's in a Web Site?

Web sites, whether on the Internet or on your own home network, consist of one or more pages of text, specially formatted to enable Web browsers to display them on the screen. The formatting instructions for Web pages are called HTML (Hypertext Markup Language) tags. The pages are connected by hyperlinks, usually simply called links. You click a link to jump to another page of the Web site, to send e-mail, or to go another Web site on the Internet or intranet.

The first page that you encounter when you go to a Web site is called the site's home page. The other pages of the site are separate files that are retrieved and displayed on the screen when you click their associated links.

As you can see from these examples, a family Web is a great way for everyone to share information, express themselves, and get to know a little more about other family members. While it's still not as personal as a good-old family meeting, a family Web lets everyone be creative in a different way, and it serves as a terrific learning experience about the way the Web works.

If you have a personal Web site with your ISP, you can also use your home Web to fine-tune and test your Web pages before uploading them to the ISP. This way you can be sure your Web site looks right and works correctly before you expose it to the world.

Creating a Web Site with Personal Web Server

All the software you need to set up a Web server and create a home page comes with Microsoft Windows 98 and Microsoft Windows 98 Second Edition. The program, called the Microsoft Personal Web Server (PWS), lets you set up and maintain a Web site on any computer on the network. In fact, each computer on the network can host its own Web site, as long as it has the Personal Web Server program installed. If you have three computers connected on a network, for example, you can have three separate personal Web sites, any of which can be viewed by the entire family.

Family members can then access everyone's pages using their Web browsers in much the same way as they access Web pages on the Internet. Instead of dialing in to an ISP to connect to the worldwide Internet, however, a user's browser connects to a personal Web server on the network. The personal Web server delivers the Web pages to the viewer's screen. As far as that browser is concerned, it is connected to a Web server just as if it were actually on the Internet.

Installing Personal Web Server

Personal Web Server is included on your Windows 98 CD, but it is not installed as part of Windows. You have to install it yourself, directly from the CD, on the computer that you plan to use to create a Web site.

Note

If you use PWS to create a home page, it creates a file with the ASP (Active Server Pages) extension. Some computers on the network may not be able to access ASP Web pages unless you install Personal Web Server on those computers as well. If a user has trouble accessing your Web site from a computer on the network, install Personal Web Server on it.

Follow these steps to install PWS:

1. Insert the Windows CD in your computer. If the Windows installation menu appears, click its Close button.

2. On the Start menu, click Run.

3. Type *D:\add-ons\pws\setup.exe* (if your CD drive's letter is not D, use the correct drive letter instead), and then press Enter.

4. When the setup program begins, click Next.
   You'll see three setup options: Minimum, Typical, and Advanced.

5. Click Typical, which supplies all the services you'll probably need.
   The next screen, shown in Figure 14-4, lets you set the location for the WWW Service (your Web site).

6. Accept the default for the location of the WWW Service by clicking Next.

Figure 14-4.
This Personal Web Server dialog box lets you set your Web site's location.

7. Windows installs the Personal Web Server and displays a final dialog box. Click Finish.

8. Click Yes when you are asked whether to restart your computer.

Now that PWS is installed, you're ready to create a home page and make it available to other family members on your own personal Web site.

Note

When you install PWS on a home network, you can ignore any error messages you encounter during setup that report problems with Microsoft Transaction Server (MTS) or Core Components, and just click OK. These messages may appear if your Windows registry is full, and the setup program is unable to add the necessary entries for Microsoft Transaction Server in your registry. If you want to learn more about these messages, and how to correct the error, use your Web browser to visit *http://support.microsoft.com/support/ kb/articles/q214/6/44.ASP.*

Using the Personal Web Manager

When you restart your computer after installing Personal Web Server, you'll see a Publish icon on your desktop and a new icon in the system tray next to the clock. Double-clicking either of these icons opens the Personal Web Manager, which helps you create and manage your Web site. If you right-click the system tray icon, you'll see Start Service and Stop Service options on a shortcut menu; these options allow you to turn Personal Web Server on or off or to pause or continue the service.

You can also open the Personal Web Manager window by clicking Start, pointing to Programs, Accessories, Internet Tools, Personal Web Server, and then clicking Personal Web Manager.

The Tip Of The Day window appears first. You can click Close to close this window, or click Next to read another tip. You can also click to disable the Show Tips At Startup check box if you want to skip seeing tips each time you start the program. After closing the Tip of The Day, you'll see the Personal Web Manager window, shown in Figure 14-5.

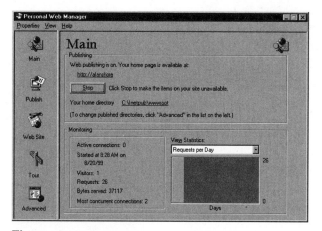

Figure 14-5.

The Personal Web Manager helps you to create and manage your home page.

Along the left side of the window is a sidebar with five icons:

- **Main** displays the initial window that you now see.

- **Publish** lets you add documents to your Web site that you want to share over the intranet.

- **Web Site** runs the Home Page Wizard, which lets you create a personal home page.

- **Tour** takes you through a PWS tutorial.

- **Advanced** lets you change the directories in which your Web site is stored and the default home page document.

In the Personal Web Manager window, you'll see your home page address, which is *http://* followed by your computer's name, and the name of the home directory in which the new Web site will be stored, such as C:\Inetpub\wwwroot. You'll also see a Stop button, which allows you to temporarily disable your Web server. Once you click the Stop button, the button changes to Start to allow you to turn the Web site back on. The number of times your Web site has been accessed over the intranet is listed at the bottom of the window along with other useful information, such as the number of people who are currently connected.

To access your Web site, just click the link to your home page. Until you create your own home page, you'll see a default home page in its place. Click the Home directory link to display the subfolders and files in that location. To go to your site from My Computer or Windows Explorer, type your home page address in the Address text box, such as *http://alanneib*, and press Enter.

Note

When it creates an http address, PWS substitutes dashes for the spaces and apostrophes in your computer's name. For example, the computer named Barb's Room becomes *http://barb-s-room*.

Creating Your Home Page

Your next step is to create a home page on your server. You can do this manually, using a Web page creation program, such as Microsoft FrontPage or FrontPage Express, or you can use the Personal Web Server's Home Page Wizard.

Although it offers only a limited number of Web site design options, the Home Page Wizard is still great for creating a family Web site because it is easy to use and it lets you add two very handy features to your site: a *guest book* and a *drop box*. A guest book displays messages from network users that all visitors to your site can view. You can use the guest book to hold family "conversations" and to leave messages for other people on the network.

A drop box contains private messages that only you can view. To read drop box messages, you have to log on to your computer with your own user name and start PWS.

To create a home page with the Home Page Wizard, follow these steps:

1. In the Personal Web Manager, click the Web Site icon to start the wizard.

2. A dialog box appears, along with a small, animated figure of a wizard.

3. Click the animated wizard or the Advance (>>) button.

On the next page of the Home Page Wizard, you can select from a list of templates, shown in Figure 14-6, to set the design of your home page.

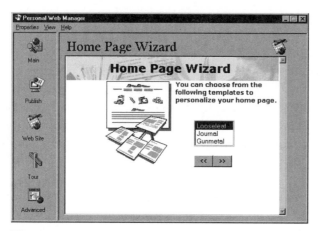

Figure 14-6.
Select a template for your home page in the Home Page Wizard.

4. Select one of the templates, and then click the Advance button to move to the next page.
   You'll now be asked whether you want a guest book for public messages.

5. Click the Advance button to accept the default response of Yes.
   You'll now be asked whether you want a drop box for private messages.

6. Again, click the Advance button to accept the default response of Yes.

A message appears in the Home Page Wizard reporting that you are ready to personalize your home page.

7. Click Advance to open the PWS Quick Setup page in Windows Explorer, as shown in Figure 14-7.

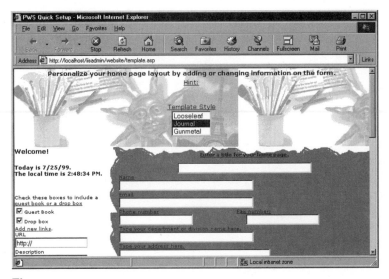

Figure 14-7.

By filling in the text boxes on the PWS Quick Setup page, you can personalize your home page.

You use the PWS Quick Setup page, which is actually a Web page in your browser, to create and edit your home page. Notice that the page contains an underlined link above each text box. To get help on the text box, click the link.

The PWS Quick Setup page shows the template you've selected and whether you've included a guest book and drop box. If you did not change these settings in the Home Page Wizard, such as choosing a guest book, you can them here. Each of the templates you can select contains the same items; only their arrangement and background graphic differs.

On the PWS Quick Setup page, you can enter the following elements for your home page:

- A page title
- Your name

- Your e-mail address

- A phone and fax number

- Your department or division name

- Address

- Four headings and a paragraph of text under each heading

You can also enter links to favorite Web sites and documents on your computer. In the URL and Description text boxes type the URL or path of a site, enter a brief description, and click Add Link.

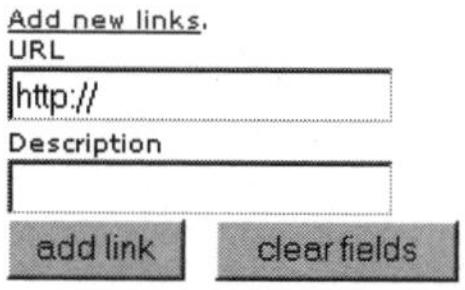

After you add your first link, it will be shown in a list box along with the Remove Link button.

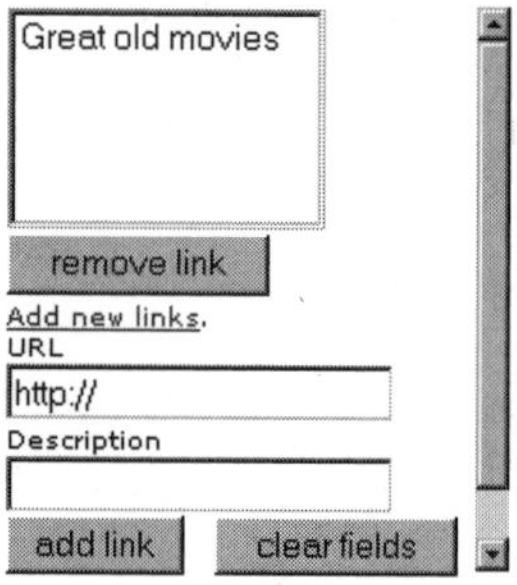

Note

If you want to change the information on your home page, click Web Site in the Personal Web Manager window, and then click Edit Your Home Page. After you make your changes, click Enter New Changes.

After you've entered information in as many text boxes as you'd like, click the Enter New Changes button near the bottom of the page. The Web page appears, as shown in Figure 14-8. Close the Browser window when you finish reviewing the page.

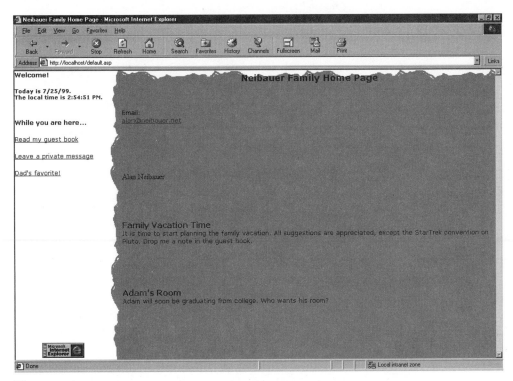

Figure 14-8.
Your completed Web page can be viewed by all network users.

Accessing Your Home Page

When you want to access your home page to see how it looks, enter its address in your Internet browser's address box or as the address in Windows Explorer. You can also choose Run from the Start menu, type your home page address (*http://your computer's name*), and then click OK.

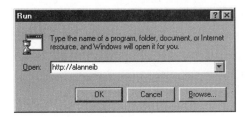

Other family members on the network can access your home page in the same ways, from either the Run box, their Web browser, or Windows Explorer. In some cases, however, a browser may try to dial in to the ISP rather than access the intranet. If this happens, the browser has to be set to access the intranet using the local area network rather than the dial-up connection. Here's how it's done with Microsoft Internet Explorer:

1. Right-click the Internet Explorer icon on your desktop and choose Properties.
   You can also double-click the Internet Options icon in the Control Panel.

2. Click the Connections tab.

3. With Internet Explorer version 5, select Dial Whenever A Network Connection Is Not Present or Never Dial A Connection. With earlier versions of Internet Explorer, select Connect Through A Local Area Network.

4. Click OK.

Using Your Guest Book and Drop Box

The guest book serves as a bulletin board on which family members can leave their names, a short message, or even a favorite link. It's a great place to post important announcements or everyday information that you or another family member wants to share with everyone else on the network. Placing a message in the guest book is like sending e-mail, except that the guest book message can be viewed by anyone who visits your site.

To leave a message in someone's guest book, go to the home page on that person's computer and click the Read My Guest Book link. The guest book appears, formatted in three columns, as shown in Figure 14-9. Click a column heading to sort the list. To read a message, click its link.

Leave a message by clicking Click Here To Sign The Guest Book. Type the information you want in the message window, as shown in Figure 14-10, and then click Send Message. To clear the message window and start again, click Clear Fields.

If you want to leave a private message that only the owner of the home page can read, click Leave A Private Message. Type the message text, and then click Send Message. The message is stored in the drop box.

Once your guest book and drop box contain messages, you can view, sort, and delete messages. Open Personal Web Manager and click Web Site to see three options: Edit Your Home Page, View Your Guest Book, and Open Your Drop Box.

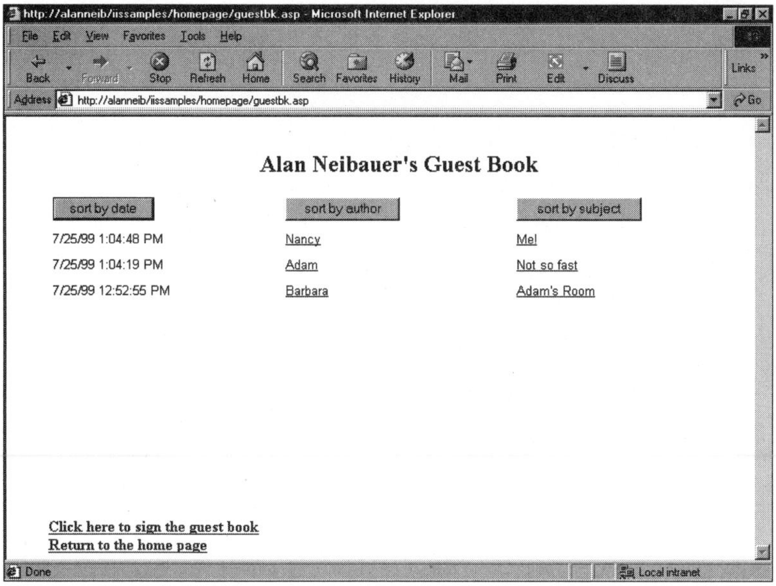

Figure 14-9.

Open a Guest Book message by clicking its link.

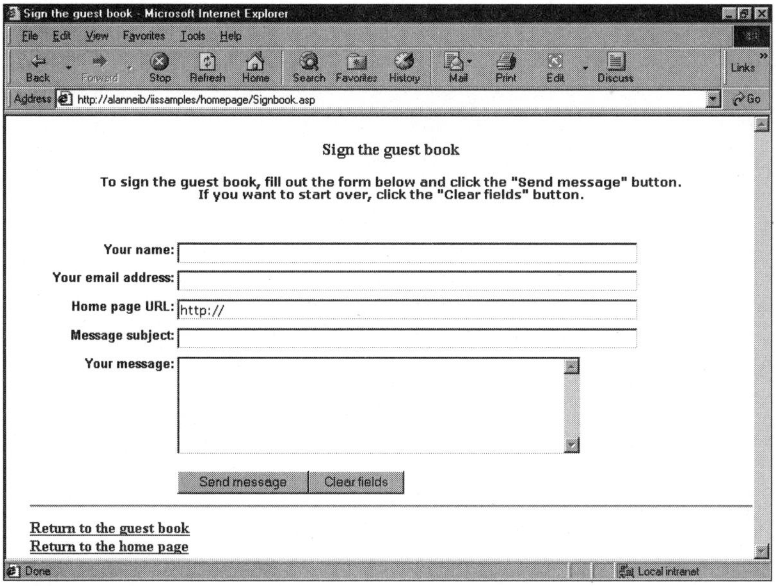

Figure 14-10.

Enter your Guest Book message in the Sign The Guest Book message window.

To read your guest book messages, click View Your Guest Book to open a window like the one shown in Figure 14-11.

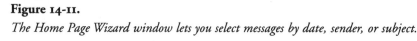

Figure 14-11.

The Home Page Wizard window lets you select messages by date, sender, or subject.

Use the options in this window to construct a query that will find certain messages to display according to the criteria you supply. You can display messages by the date they were written, the person who sent them, their subject, or any combination of these categories. By default, the search is set to display all messages written before the current date and time. To view these messages, just click the Submit Query button.

By using the drop-down lists and text boxes, however, you can fine-tune your search for specific messages. Next to the MessageDate option, you can choose Less Than, Equal To, or Greater Than, and then enter a certain date as the criterion. To display messages written after a certain date, for example, you'd choose Greater Than from the drop-down list and enter the date in the text box to its right.

With the MessageFrom option, you can choose to list messages from persons whose names begin with, contain, end with, or are equal to the text you enter in the box. The MessageSubject option works the same way, except that it searches the Subject field of messages. For example, to look for messages whose subject contains the word "vacation," select Contains from the MessageSubject drop-down list and enter the word *vacation* in the text box to its right.

When you click Submit Query, you'll see a list of messages in the Home Page Wizard that meet the criteria you've entered. You can sort the messages by date, author, or subject by clicking the appropriate column heading. To read a message, click its link. Click Delete Message to erase the message from your guest book. You can also click New Query to change the search criteria or you can click Web Site to return to the Web Site options.

Note

To update the time in a query to the current time, click the Web Site link, and then click View Your Guest Book again.

The Drop Box is similar to the Guest Book, except that it contains messages that only you can see and you do not have the opportunity to create a query. When you click Web Site in the Personal Web Manager window and then click Open Your Drop Box, all messages in your drop box appear automatically.

Publishing Documents on Your Site

In addition to adding a home page, you can place all sorts of documents on your Web site and share them with family members. You can post scanned family pictures, information about vacations, or instructions on how the family can reach you when you're away on business.

One way to place a file on your Web site is simply to copy the file to the C:\Inetpub\ Webpub folder. Or you can let the Publishing Wizard do it for you. The Publishing Wizard lets you select one or more files from any location on your hard disk to copy to the Web site folder. Here's how this wizard works:

1. Click the Publish icon on the Personal Web Manager sidebar.

    If you have not yet used the wizard to publish a file on your Web site, the animated wizard figure appears.

2. Click the wizard figure or the Advance (>>) button to see the page shown in Figure 14-12.

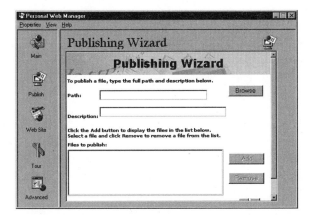

Figure 14-12.

The Publishing Wizard allows you to select files to publish on your Web site.

3. Enter the file's path and name or click Browse and locate the file using this dialog box.

4. To locate a file, click the underlined link for the folder or subfolder containing the file, and then click the file itself.

5. Enter a description of the file in the Description text box.

6. Click Add.

7. Repeat the process for other files you'd like to add.

8. When you've added all the files you want, click the Advance button.

Personal Web Manager copies the files to the C:\Inetpub\Webpub folder. Now they're available to anyone who clicks View My Published Documents on your home page. They will see a list of files, as shown in Figure 14-13.

Note

As a shortcut, you can drag the file name to the Publish icon on the Windows desktop or to the Personal Web Manager sidebar to start the Publishing Wizard. You can also right-click a file, click Send To, and then click Personal Web Server to publish a file.

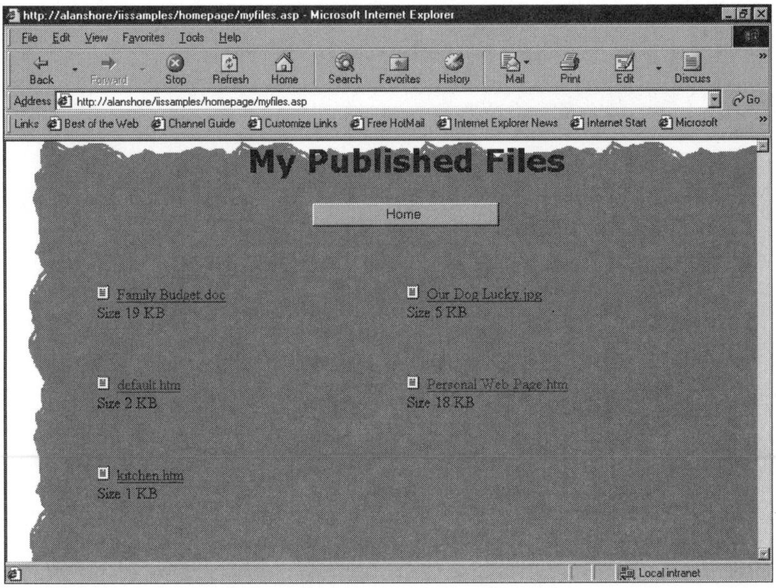

Figure 14-13.
Published files are available for anyone to open with a single click.

Once you publish the first file on your Web site, clicking Publish displays these options rather than the animated wizard.

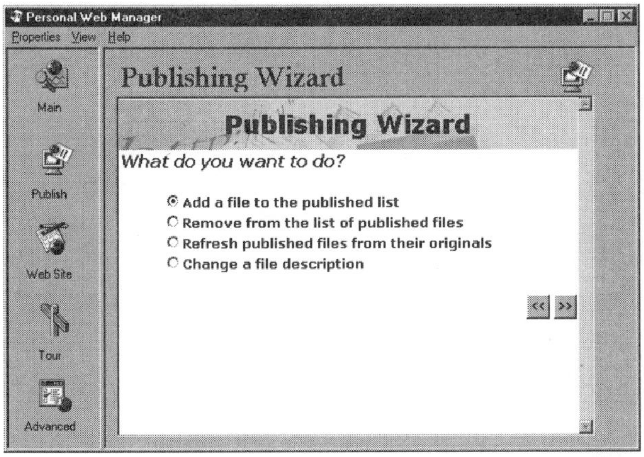

Make your selection, and then click the Advance button to add the new file or files to your published file list.

Creating Web Pages with Microsoft Word

The Home Page Wizard is fast and fun, but it generates only one type of home page, even if it does come in three designs. Whether you're dealing with the Internet or your own home intranet, what makes creating pages for a Web enjoyable is that you can let your imagination go wild and create really personalized Web sites.

When you use the Home Page Wizard to create a home page, it automatically adds the HTML tags to the information that you enter. You do not see the tags in a Web browser; you just see the finished result in the form of a formatted Web page. If you want to, you can learn how to write the HTML tags yourself and create a Web page with even the simplest of text editors, such as Windows Notepad.

To create more personalized Web pages, however, you really don't have to rush out and take a course on writing HTML code. You can use any of the dozens of programs that write the tags for you as you design web pages. Programs such as Microsoft FrontPage and FrontPage Express are specifically designed to create Web pages and manage all the pages that make up a Web site. But you can also create Web pages with most of today's major applications, such as those that come with Microsoft Office 2000. Using programs included in Office, you can write documents, create spreadsheets and databases, and design slide shows. The programs then convert the formats in your document, spreadsheet, or slideshow into HTML tags so that you can publish them on the Internet or to your home network web.

Microsoft Word offers you two ways to create a Web page. You can use Word's Web Page Wizard to design a Web page in much the same way you use the Home Page Wizard in Personal Web Server to design a Web page. You follow a series of pages to select the format and enter the content of the page. Word then displays the resulting Web page so that you can further personalize it. You can also write and format a document using all of Word's formatting features and then have Word convert the document into a Web page for you. Word will convert the formatting you've set up, such as boldfaced headings, into the HTML tags that your Web browser can understand.

Using the Web Page Wizard

The Web Page Wizard creates a small Web site of one or more Web pages with links that you can click to navigate between the pages.

One of the first things you'll have to do with the Web Page Wizard is to decide where you want the Web page to be stored. If you choose to save it in C:\Inetpub\Webpub, network users can then access the Web page, and any other files you have stored in that folder, by selecting View My Published Documents on your home page. You do not have to use the Publish command in Personal Web Manager.

If you want to use your Word Web page as the Personal Web Server home page, the page that people see when they enter the address of your computer into their browsers, you can delete all the files in the C:\Inetpub\Webroot folder and select that folder as the location of your Word home page. This will also delete, however, your guest book and drop box, and your PWS home page will have only the features you've added in Word.

Now let's go through the process of creating a Web page in Word using the Web Page Wizard to see how it is done. You'll go step by step through creating your own Web page and placing it in the C:\Inetpub\Webpub folder to publish it.

Here are the generic steps to using the Web Page Wizard to create a Web site.

1. From the File menu in Word, choose New.

2. In the New dialog box, click the Web Pages tab, shown in Figure 14-14.

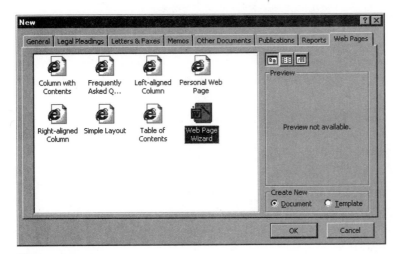

Figure 14-14.
Click the Web Pages tab to start the Web Page Wizard.

3. On the Web Pages tab, double-click the Web Page Wizard icon to begin a series of wizard pages.

4. Read the information on the first page of the wizard, and then click Next to see the page shown in Figure 14-15.

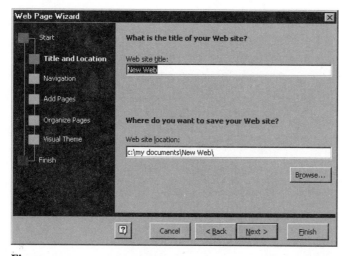

Figure 14-15.
This Web Page Wizard allows you to set the title and location of your Web site.

5. Enter the title for the Web page and specify the location where you want it stored—usually C:\Inetpub\Webpub.

6. Click Next to see the options shown in Figure 14-16.

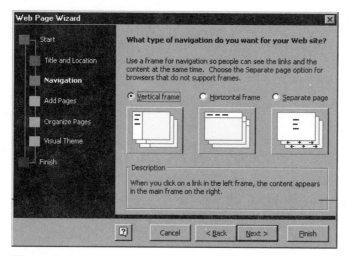

Figure 14-16.
Select the layout of your Web page from the options in this window.

You can select one of three navigation methods for your home page and the other pages you add to the Web site. The page can have hyperlinks in a vertical or horizontal frame, or it can have navigation buttons that link to other pages you add.

7. Select a navigation method and click Next.

You can now add more pages to the Web site, as shown in Figure 14-17.

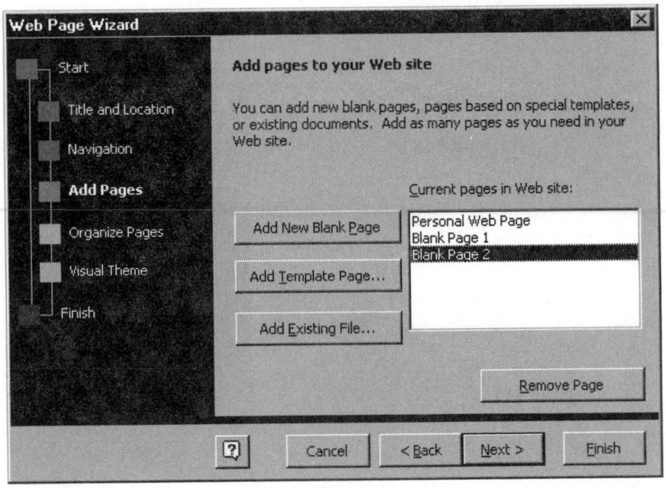

Figure 14-17.
The wizard allows you to add blank pages or template pages to your Web site.

The default option is a configuration of a Personal Web Page and two blank pages—Blank Page 1 and Blank Page 2. You can add additional blank pages or pages designed according to templates provided by the wizard.

8. Clicking Add Blank Page immediately adds a blank page to the Web site, but if you want to add a template page, click Add Template Page to see the list of templates shown in Figure 14-18, on the next page. When you click a template in this list, a sample of the page appears in the background.

9. When you have completed adding pages, click Next. You can now change the sequence of pages by selecting a page and then clicking the Move Up or Move Down button.

10. Click Next to display the next page of the wizard, which allows you to add a theme to your Web site, as shown in Figure 14-19, on the next page.

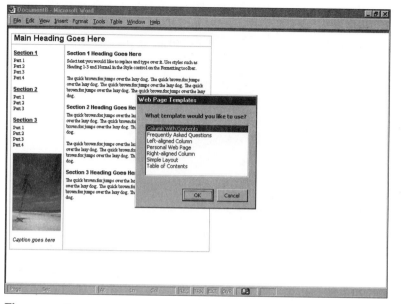

Figure 14-18.
Choose a page template from the list of templates.

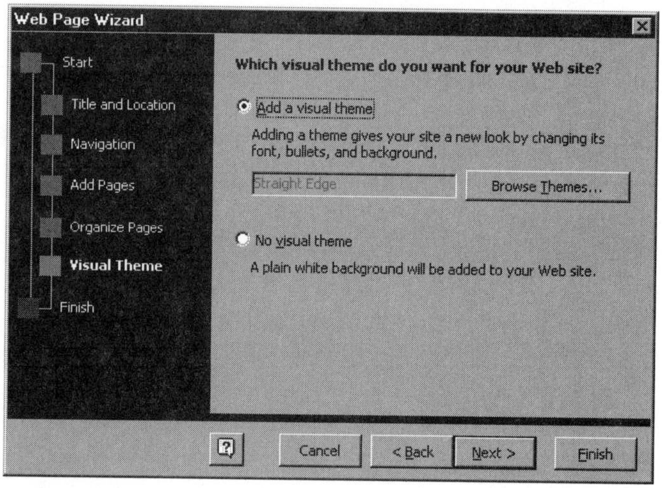

Figure 14-19.
Add a visual theme to your Web site.

11. To add a theme, click the Add A Visual Theme button, and then click Browse Theme to choose the theme.

Only some of the themes in the list are installed with Office 2000 when you perform the typical installation. If you select a theme that is not installed, a message appears asking whether you want to install the theme at this time. Insert your Office 2000 CD in the CD drive and click Install.

12. From the list of themes, select a theme, such as Artsy or Blends, and then click OK.

13. Click Finish to display the Web page on the screen, as shown in Figure 14-20.

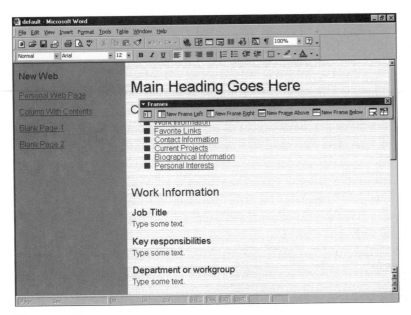

Figure 14-20.
After you add a visual theme to your Web page, click Finish to view the page.

Word adds sample text as a placeholder until you enter your own text on the page. Now you only need to fill in the sample text areas. You can click a link to another page or topic to move to that page.

Now It's Your Turn

Now that you've read how easy it is to use the Web Page Wizard to create a Web site, here's a step-by-step example you can try to create a Web page for yourself. Just follow these steps:

1. Start Microsoft Word.

2. From the File menu, choose New. Do not click the New Blank Document button on the standard toolbar.

3. In the New dialog box, click the Web Pages tab and then double-click the Web Page Wizard icon.

4. Click Next.

5. Enter a title for your Web page. I've entered *Alan's Family Web site*, but I'm sure you can be more creative.

6. Type *C:\Inetpub\Webpub* as the location for the Web site.

7. Click Next to select a navigation method.

8. Click the Horizontal Frame option button, and then click Next.

9. Click Next to accept the default number of pages, and click Next again to accept the default order of pages.
    You are now given the option of adding a visual theme.

10. Click the Browse button to display the list of themes.

11. Select Blueprint in the Choose A Theme list, and then click OK.

12. Click Next and then Finish to display your Web page, as shown in Figure 14-21.

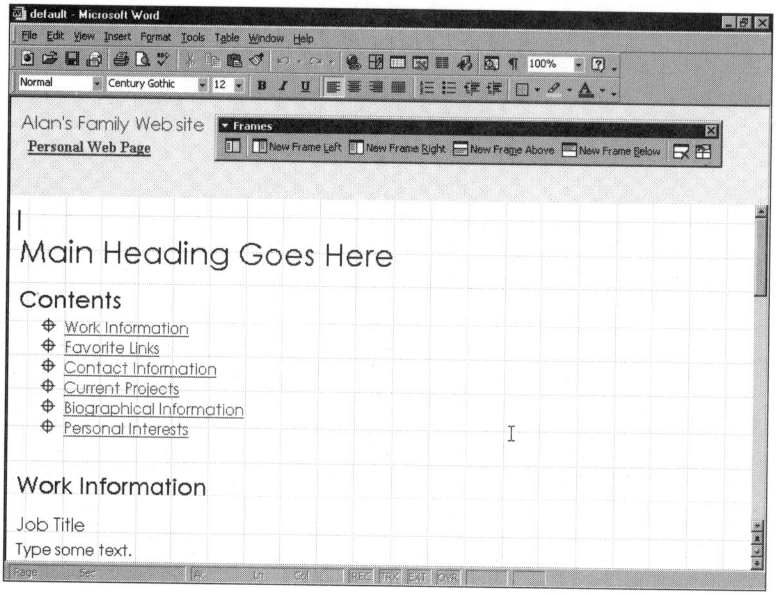

Figure 14-21.
The Web page you've created with the Home Page Wizard.

Working with Web Pages

Your Web page appears in Word's Web Layout view. In Web Layout view, your document appears just as it will when it's displayed in a Web browser. To actually use a browser to view your Word document, you can select Web Page Preview from the File menu. Office launches your Web browser, without connecting you to the Internet, and displays the document. Just close the browser to return to Word.

In Web Layout view, you also see the Frames toolbar. You can use this toolbar to change the way your page is divided into frames. A frame is a separate section of the page that contains its own text and hyperlinks, and it scrolls independently from the text in other frames. You won't be using the Frames toolbar in this example because your page already contains two frames, so click the toolbar's Close button to remove it from the screen.

When you are working in Web Layout view, you can continue formatting the document using Word's formatting commands. To change the theme, for example, choose Theme from the Format menu to see the Theme dialog box shown in Figure 14-22. Choose the theme you want to apply and then click OK.

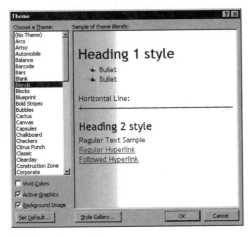

Figure 14-22.
Choose a theme in the Theme dialog box to change the look of your Web page.

In the Theme dialog box, you can also apply various *templates* to your text, which automatically format your text. Click the Style Gallery button in the Theme dialog box to display the Style Gallery dialog box shown in Figure 14-23, on the next page.

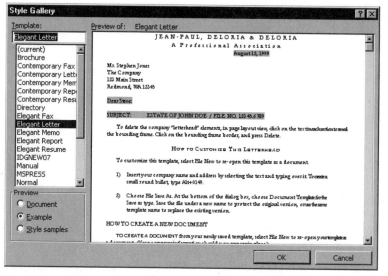

Figure 14-23.

Select a new style for your text from the Style Gallery dialog box.

Each template listed in the dialog box contains a collection of text formats that will be applied to certain areas of the document, such as titles, subtitles, and body text. To see how a template will affect your document, click a template in the list of templates, and then select the Document option in the Preview section. Your document will appear in the Preview Of panel. You can also select Example to see a sample document that uses most of the styles, or you can select Style Samples to see the name of each style set in that style. Click OK in the dialog box to apply the template to your document.

Of course, the sample text on the Web page is not exactly what you'd like for your own family home page. So you can start changing it by beginning with the text of the headlines, and then adjusting the hyperlinks.

1. Select the headline Main Heading Goes Here, and type *Get All of the News Here!*

2. Drag over the headline Work Information, not the underlined link, and type *Family Vacation.*

3. Select the next six lines, between Family Vacation and Back To Top, and replace them with some information about your most recent family trip.

   You can leave the Favorite Links section as it is for now. You'll add several hyperlinks later.

4. Select the heading Contact Information and type *How to Reach Me.*

5. Select the next six lines, between How to Reach Me and Back To Top, and replace them with your daytime telephone number.

6. Now for the sake of brevity, delete the remainder of the text, from the heading Current Projects to the end of the document.

Working with Hyperlinks

It's now time to tackle the hyperlinks on the page. Go back to the top of the page where you see a series of six underlined hyperlinks, from Work Information to Personal Interest. You want to adjust the links for the new text.

1. Select the last three links and press Delete to remove them.

    You can't click a link to select its text because clicking a link actually goes to its associated location in the document or Web page.

2. To change the text of the Work Information link, right-click it, point to Hyperlink on the shortcut menu that appears, and select Edit Hyperlink to see the Edit Hyperlink dialog box shown in Figure 14-24.

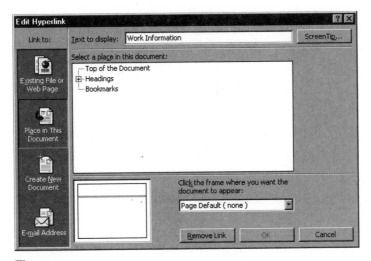

Figure 14-24.
Editing a hyperlink.

3. Change the text in the Text To Display text box from Work Information to Family Vacation.

    You now have to specify which heading in the document that clicking the link will jump to because you deleted the original heading, Work Information.

4. Click the plus sign next to Headings to see the item Get All of the News Here!

5. Click the plus sign next to Get All of the News Here! to see a list of the subheadings on the page.

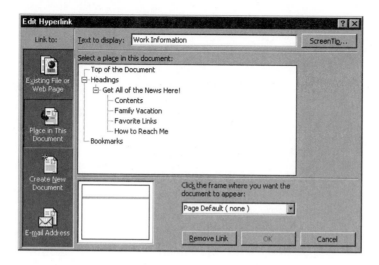

6. Click Family Vacation, and then click OK.

   When someone clicks the Family Vacation link in a browser, the section of the page starting with the heading Family Vacation will automatically scroll to the top of the page. Clicking the Back To Top link will scroll the window back to display the top of the page.

7. Change the Contact Information link so it reads How to Reach Me, and link it to the How to Reach Me heading.

   Now it's time to add your favorite Web pages to the Favorite Links section.

1. Scroll to the Favorite Links section of the page.

2. Select the first line, Insert a hyperlink here, and then click the Hyperlink button on the toolbar, which looks like a globe with a link of chain.

3. In the Insert Hyperlink dialog box, click Existing File Or Web Page to display the options shown in Figure 14-25.

   The Web site addresses shown in the list depend on the links you last inserted using Office.

4. In the Text To Display text box, type the text that will be the link.

5. In the Type The File Or Web Page Name text box, enter the address of a favorite Web site, such as *http://www.westerns.com*. If you do not know the address of the site, you can click Web Page in the Browse For section to go on line and locate the site.

6. Click OK to close the Insert Hyperlink dialog box.

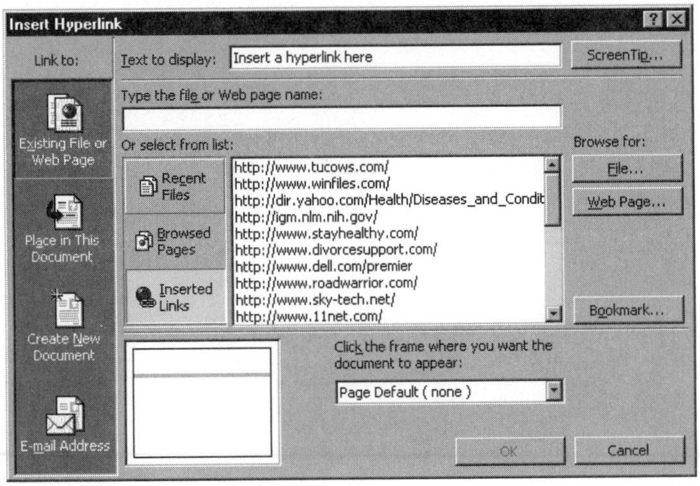

Figure 14-25.

Inserting a hyperlink.

Now let's add a link to a document that you've already created and saved on your disk.

1. Select the second line, Insert a Hyperlink Here, and then click the Hyperlink button on the toolbar.

2. In the Insert Hyperlink dialog box, click the Recent Files button to display a list of recently opened files. If the document you want to link to is not shown, you can type its path and name, or click File in the Browse For section to locate the document.

3. In the Text To Display text box, type the name of a document.

4. Click one of the documents in the list of recent files, and then click OK. When someone clicks this hyperlink, the linked document will open.

   Now let's add a link to a Web site that you've recently visited with your Web browser.

1. Select the third line, Insert a Hyperlink Here, and then click the Hyperlink button on the toolbar.

2. In the Insert Hyperlink dialog box, click the Browsed Pages button to display a list of recently visited Web sites.

3. In the Text To Display box, type the name of the Web site.

4. Click the site you want in the list of browsed pages, and then click OK.

The Web page also has hyperlinks in the top frame. These links jump to the pages of the Web site, and return to the page that serves as the site's home page, Personal Web Page. Let's change the text of these links and then look at one of these other pages.

1. Right-click the link Blank Page 1, point to Hyperlink in the shortcut menu, and click Edit Hyperlink to open the Edit Hyperlink dialog box.

2. In the Text To Display text box, change the text from Blank Page 1 to Family News, and then click OK.

3. Now click the Family News link to open the Web page.

The Family News page has the same upper frame as the Personal Web Page but the lower frame contains only the text This Web Page is Blank Page 1. The actual name of the file in which the page is stored is Blank Page 1.htm. You can leave the file name the same, because it's the content of the page that you're interested in.

You can now add and format any text and hyperlinks that you want to appear on the Family News page. When you're done designing the page, click the link Personal Web Page to return to the site's home page.

Using the same procedure, you can change the text of the link Blank Page 2, and the contents of that page.

Adding Graphics

Microsoft Office also includes a collection of graphics, called *ClipArt,* that you can use to illustrate your Web pages. To insert a ClipArt graphic, follow these steps:

1. Click the Personal Web Page link to display the home page.

2. Click in the document to place the insertion point where you want the graphic to appear.

3. From the Insert menu, point to Picture, and then click ClipArt to display the Insert ClipArt dialog box shown in Figure 14-26.

4. Click a category to display the ClipArt choices in that category.

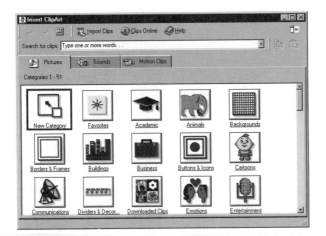

Figure 14-26.
The Insert ClipArt dialog box allows you to view and select graphics for your Web pages.

5. Click the graphic you want and then click one of the four options on the shortcut menu:

- **Insert Clip** places the ClipArt selection in the document.

- **Preview Clip** displays the ClipArt selection in a separate window.

- **Add Clip To Favorites Or Other Category** adds the clip to the Favorites category, where you can keep the clips you use most often. It also lets you place a copy in a different category.

- **Find Similar Clips** displays ClipArt selections that are similar in theme to the clip you've chosen.

You can also insert a graphic from your hard disk, perhaps a picture that you downloaded from the Internet. To do so, point to Picture on the Insert menu and click From File to open the Insert Picture dialog box. Locate the picture you want to insert, and then click the down arrow on the Insert button to pull down the Insert list and choose from these options:

- **Insert** places the graphic in the document so that it will be saved within the Word file.

- **Link To File** saves a link to the graphic in the Word file, but not the graphic itself. This reduces the size of the file and lets you use graphics that you might want to change later on. When you open the document, Word automatically displays the current version of the graphic that's on your hard disk.

- **Insert And Link** inserts the graphic and saves a link to it. The graphic is actually saved in the Word file.

After you insert a graphic in a document, you can customize it in a number of ways. To work with a picture, click it so that small boxes, called *handles*, surround it. The Picture toolbar also appears, as shown in Figure 14-27. If the Picture toolbar does not appear, right-click any other toolbar and choose Picture from the shortcut menu.

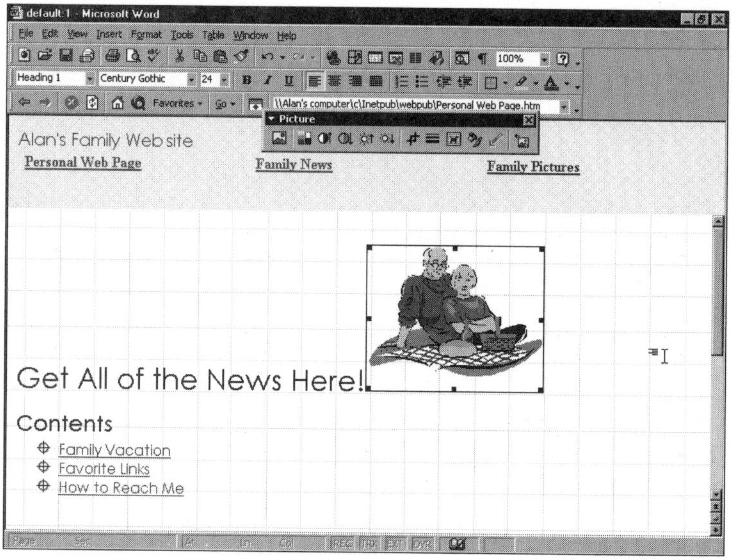

Figure 14-27.
Use the tools on the Picture toolbar to customize an inserted graphic.

To delete a picture from your document, select it and then press Delete or choose Clear from the Edit menu. To deselect the picture, click elsewhere in the document.

To change the size of a picture, place the mouse pointer on one of the handles so that the pointer changes to a two-headed arrow, and then drag the handle. Which handle you drag depends on how you want to change the picture's dimensions (a dotted box will show the size of the picture as you drag):

- Drag the handle on the left or right side to change only the width of the picture.

- Drag the handle on the top or bottom to change only the height of the picture.

- Drag a corner handle to change the height and width of the picture while maintaining its original proportions.

Just to see the number of files that actually make up a Web site, you can open the C:\Inetpub\Webpub folder. You'll see all the files shown in Figure 14-28. There will be a separate folder containing the graphic elements that were part of the theme for each of the pages, a separate file for each frame, and a file for each page. All of the files are linked together by the hyperlinks on the page.

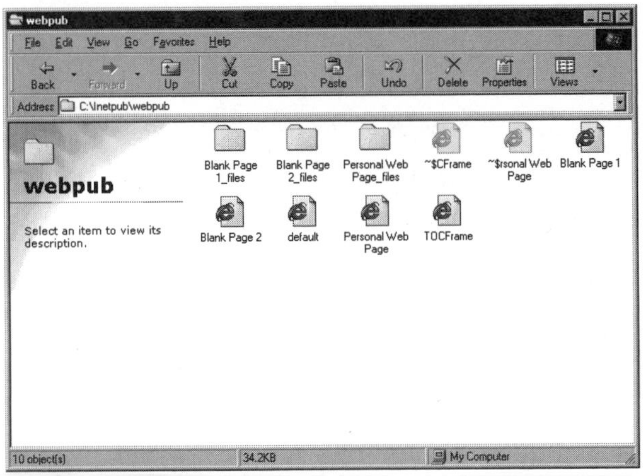

Figure 14-28.
The files that comprise a typical Web site created in Word.

To view the Web page you created in Word and access all its links, click the View My Published Documents link on your Personal Web Server home page, and then click the link for default.htm.

We've just touched upon the formatting features of Word that you can use to create your Web site. By using other formatting techniques and features, such as WordArt, you can develop your Web page further, as shown in Figure 14-29.

Figure 14-29.
Formatted Web page in Word.

Converting a Word Document to a Web Page

If you've already created a document that you'd like to add to your Web site, but it is not in HTML format, you can easily convert it to a Web page. Just follow these steps:

1. Open a document that you've typed and formatted.

2. From the File menu, choose Save As Web Page.

3. In the Save As dialog box, click in the Save In box and locate the C:\Inetpub\Webpub folder.

4. In the File Name text box, enter the file name you want for the Web page.

5. Click Save.

   Word converts the document to Web page format and displays it in Web Layout view. A message appears whenever there are Word formats in the document that do not have HTML equivalents. Click OK to convert the document anyway, displaying the formatted text as plain text.

   The file will be stored in the C:\Inetpub\Webpub folder so it can be accessed using the View My Published Documents link on your Personal Web Server home page.

Home Web pages are a great way to share information and opinions over your computer network. But when you are not at home, such as on a business trip, vacation, or away at school, you can still keep in touch with the family network remotely, as you'll learn in the next chapter.

Chapter 15

Networking for Road Warriors

Whether you work in an office or out of the home, at some point, you'll probably hit the road for business. As you'll learn in this chapter, even when you're traveling, you can still communicate with the folks back home on the home network and take advantage of all the benefits the network offers, such as sharing files and printing documents.

As countless computer-toting business travelers—road warriors—already know, it's easy to stay in touch with a home or office computer from any place that's within reach of a telephone. In this chapter, you'll learn how to set up and use a process called remote computing to dial in to your home network to access its resources the same way you dial into an ISP to access the Internet.

You'll also learn how to use Microsoft NetMeeting, a program that allows you to talk to and even see a family member on your home network or at a remote location, as long as each computer is equipped with a video camera (can be inexpensive and is easily added), and a microphone.

NetMeeting not only allows you to hold long-distance meetings, it also provides a handy feature, called remote desktop sharing, that allows you to take over another computer on the network and actually operate it from your keyboard and screen, no matter where you are. As you'll see later in this chapter, remote desktop sharing lets you troubleshoot problems a family member might be having with a computer or even show someone how to perform a specific task on the computer.

Packing for the Road

Suppose you're on a business trip away from home and you're relaxing in your hotel room going over the day's events. You'd like to dial in to your home computer to check e-mail messages from your family, send a file home, or perhaps print a note to your spouse on one of your home printers. At home, your modem is probably already plugged into the phone jack, so going on line is simple. But when you're away from home, connecting to a phone line isn't always that easy. Even if the hotel room or conference center where you want to plug-in has a standard, modular phone jack, which should be easy to plug in to, the jack may not be conveniently located or close enough to the spot at which you'd like to use your computer.

To avoid some potential hassles, you should start by packing a few road-wise essentials along with your laptop:

- Two six-foot or longer telephone extension cables
- A telephone cable coupler
- A two-to-one or three-to-one telephone adapter

The telephone cables, coupler, and adapter weigh practically nothing and they take up little space in your computer case or briefcase, but they can be lifesavers when you want to connect to a home network or to the Internet. You can purchase all of these items at a hardware store, your local Radio Shack, or at your local "Nothing over $1.00" store. They'll allow you to reach a phone jack, even one that's in an out-of-the-way place.

The coupler lets you connect two lengths of telephone cable to lengthen your reach even further. If a telephone is already connected to the phone jack, the two-to-one adapter lets you plug in both the phone and your modem.

Note

In a pinch, the adapter can also be used as a coupler—just plug both extension cables into the adapter and plug one end of the cable, rather than the adapter, into the jack.

Most hotels cater to business travelers who are now, more than ever, equipped with laptop computers. But not every hotel you stay in will be set up to facilitate remote computing.

The first hurdle you might encounter, especially if you are traveling abroad, is the lack of a standard, RJ-11 modular phone jack in your room. This is the standard type of receptacle that's used as a phone jack in the U.S. Even with the extra cables, couplers, and adapters that you've packed, you'll be stuck if there's no place to plug in your modem.

The second hurdle might be the phone line itself. The telephone lines in your home are regular analog lines. Your modem converts the digital information in your computer to analog signals that these regular phone lines can carry. But many hotels and offices have special, digital telephone systems. In a digital system, voice and fax communications are transmitted through the system as digital information so your analog modem won't work on it. What's worse is that if you connect your laptop to a digital network, the voltage from the digital lines might damage your laptop's modem permanently.

With a little preparation before your trip, however, you can overcome both of these hurdles.

When you make hotel reservations, find out whether the hotel's telephone system is analog or digital. Even if it is digital, you may be able to request a room with an analog phone connection and an RJ-11 jack that you can use with your laptop. Such rooms are frequently available to business travelers.

You can also purchase an *acoustic coupler*, a device that fits over the telephone handset and connects to your modem. Instead of plugging directly in to the phone system, you connect to the acoustic coupler, which sends and receives signals through the telephone handset. Another device that you can use with a digital system allows you to connect your modem to the jack into which the phone's handset is plugged in. Both of these devices take care of two problems at the same time: the lack of a jack and the digital phone system. Devices such as these are sold by Road Warrior (*http://www.warrior.com*), and are shown in Figure 15-1. These devices enable you to connect easily and safely to digital phone lines when you're on the road.

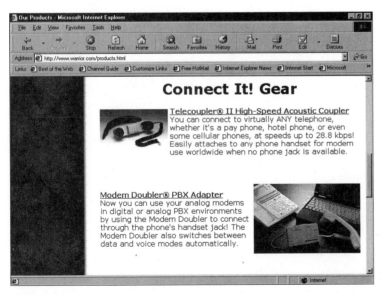

Figure 15-1.
These Road Warrior devices allow you to connect your modem to digital phone lines when you're traveling.

If you are traveling abroad, you can purchase jack adapters, which let you connect your modem to the type of jack used in the country you are visiting. To order the correct adapter, you'll have to find out what type of jack you'll be using, but most mail-order companies that specialize in remote computing hardware, such as Hello Direct (*http://www.hello-direct.com*) and Road Warrior, can help you with that.

For maximum protection, you might want to consider buying and bringing along a line tester, a device that indicates whether a line is analog or digital, and a surge protector, which protects a modem against power surges while you are connected. Road Warrior, for example, offers a product called the Modem Saver Plus. You plug this device into the phone jack before plugging in your modem. A green light indicates that the jack is safe to use, a red light indicates that it could damage your modem. A surge protector is also built into the Modem Saver Plus.

Dialing In to Your ISP

One other important item you should have for your trip is a local phone number for your Internet service provider in the area in which you'll be staying.

You've probably set up your computer to dial in to your ISP from home using the local number that's available where you live. You can use that same number when you travel, but you'd have to do two things first:

- Adjust Microsoft Windows so that it dials the area code as well as the number

- Take out a loan to pay the long distance charges, especially at hotel rates

Fortunately, large ISPs that are nationwide have local phone numbers in or near most major cities, so you should find out from your ISP ahead of time the local phone numbers for the areas in which you'll be staying. Call the ISP's support number and request the local access numbers or connect on line before you leave and look for the numbers on the ISP's Web site. When you arrive at your destination, you can change the phone number that your system dials to connect to the ISP. Be sure to make a note of the original number so you'll be able to restore it when you return home.

Note

Some ISPs require that you install special software to connect to them. If that's the case with your ISP, you'll need to follow the instructions that came with the software to change the access number your modem dials.

You can change the telephone number your computer dials by following these steps:

1. Double-click My Computer on the Windows desktop.

2. In the My Computer window, double-click the Dial-Up Networking icon.

3. Right-click the connection you normally use and choose Properties from the shortcut menu.

    You'll see a My Connection dialog box, much like the one shown in Figure 15-2.

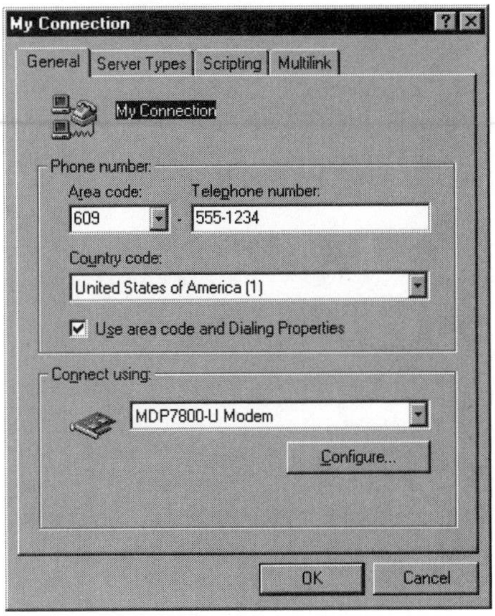

Figure 15-2.
Change your dial-up phone number to connect to your ISP from the road.

4. Replace the existing area code and telephone number with the new numbers.

5. If you must dial 9 or some other number to get an outside line, add the number and a comma before the phone number, as in *9,5551212*. The comma causes the modem to pause after dialing the number 9 so the outside dial tone can be obtained.

6. Click OK.

Note

Remember to change the phone number again when you return home.

Creating an Additional Dial-Up Networking Connection

If you travel frequently to the same location, such as a branch office in a different city, changing and restoring the telephone number of your ISP can be an annoyance. So instead of changing the number in your dial-up connection, you can create a new connection. The new connection will have all the settings required to dial into your ISP from the road. You can choose to use that connection when traveling, and then switch back to the original when you get home.

First, check your existing settings by following these steps:

1. Double-click My Computer on the Windows desktop.

2. In the My Computer window, double-click the Dial-Up Networking icon.

3. Right-click the connection you use to dial in to your ISP, and then choose Properties.

4. Click the Server Types tab in the dialog box for the new connection.

5. Make a note of the settings on the Server Types tab, including the Type Of Dial-Up Server setting, and the check boxes that are selected in the Advanced Options and Allowed Network Protocols sections.

6. Click the TCP/IP Settings button.

7. In the TCP/IP Settings dialog box, write down any numbers that appear in the Primary DNS and Secondary DNS text boxes.

8. Click Cancel to return to the Dial-Up Networking window, and click Cancel again to close the dialog box for the connection.

Now you can make a new connection by following these steps:

1. In the Dial-Up Networking window, double-click Make New Connection to open the Make New Connection dialog box.

2. Type a name for the connection, such as *Branch Office*.

3. If you have more than one modem, click the down arrow next to the Select A Device drop-down list and choose the modem you'll use to connect to the ISP.

4. Click Next.

5. Enter the ISP's local phone number at the remote location.

6. Click Next, and then click Finish.

While the Dial-Up Networking window is still open, you need to configure the connection for the proper protocol. Here's how to do it:

1. Right-click the connection you've just created and choose Properties.

2. In the connection dialog box, click the Server Types tab.

3. Set the options on the Server Types tab so they match the settings you made a note of earlier. Be sure to check that you've matched the Type Of Dial-Up Server, Advanced Options, and Allowed Network Protocols settings.

4. Click the TCP/IP Settings button.

5. In the TCP/IP Settings dialog box, enter the Primary DNS and Secondary DNS numbers that you copied down earlier.

6. Click OK to close the TCP/IP Settings dialog box.

7. Click OK to return to the Dial-Up Networking window.

Now when you're away from home and want to dial in to your ISP, you can choose the new connection you've just made. When you want to connect to the Internet, you can open the Dial-Up Networking window and double-click the connection to dial in to your ISP. The first time you connect with the new connection, you'll have to enter your user name and password. Select the Save Password box so Windows will remember the password for later connections. When you see a message reporting that the connection has been made, you can start your Web browser.

If you are using Microsoft Internet Explorer 5, you can easily change the default connection.

1. Right-click the Internet Explorer icon on the desktop.

2. Choose Properties from the shortcut menu.

3. On the Connections tab of the Internet Options dialog box, click the connection you want to use and then click the Set Default button.

4. Click OK.

Now whenever you start your browser, it will dial into the ISP using the new connection. Using this technique, however, means you'll need to change the connection again when you get home.

Note

If you use a program such as Microsoft Outlook Express to check your e-mail, you'll need to change the connection it uses to dial in to your ISP to send and receive mail.

Connecting to Your Home Network

As long as you can connect your modem to a phone line, you can dial in to your home network when you're away from home. But whether you want to connect to your home network to share or print files or just access your home computer to get messages, you need to set up your home computer so that it will allow you to dial in from the road. You do this by installing Dial-Up Server, a Windows feature that sets up a computer so that its modem answers the phone when you call in from a remote location, such as from a hotel room when you're traveling with a laptop computer.

When you set up your computers for dial-up networking, you can choose to password-protect your system so that only authorized persons can access your files. Password protection is optional but it's highly recommended. You should also consider using password protection to restrict access to sensitive folders, as explained in "Sharing and Accessing Network Resources," on page 144.

Installing Dial-Up Server

Although it comes with Microsoft Windows 98, and it's part of the Microsoft Plus! add-on for Windows 95, Dial-Up Server is not installed by default when you set up Windows. Installing Dial-Up Server, though, requires only a few simple steps.

Preparing to Install Dial-Up Server

Your first step is to make sure that all three network protocols are installed and that your hard disk is shared. If you haven't done this already, go back to "Installing Protocols" in Chapter 7 and "Sharing and Accessing Network Resources" in Chapter 9 of this book and follow the instructions there.

You'll need to install TCP/IP because Microsoft's Dial-Up Server software requires TCP/IP to connect to the remote computer. If your home network uses TCP/IP as its protocol, you can dial in to the dial-up server and access its files, but you will not be able to access the other computers on the network. In order to dial in to your dial-up server and access your entire home network, you must have installed either IPX/SPX or NetBEUI as a network protocol. In other words, you should install all three of the protocols—IPX/SPX, NetBEUI, and TCP/IP—on the computer you want to use as a dial-up server, but only IPX/SPX and NetBEUI on the other computers on the network.

You also need to set the Primary Network Logon to Windows Logon. Here's how you do this:

1. On the Start menu, point to Settings, and then click Control Panel.

2. In the Control Panel window, double-click the Network icon.

3. From the Primary Network Logon drop-down list, shown in Figure 15-3, choose Windows Logon.

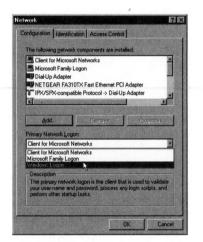

Figure 15-3.
Choose Windows Logon from the Primary Network Logon drop-down list.

4. Click OK to close the Network dialog box.

5. Click Yes when you are asked whether to restart your computer.

Installing the Dial-Up Server Software

To install the Dial-Up Server software, follow these steps:

1. On the Start menu, point to Settings, and then click Control Panel.
   If you are using Windows 95, you must first install the Windows add-on called Microsoft Plus! before you can set up and configure Dial-Up Server.

2. In the Control Panel window, double-click the Add/Remove Programs icon.

3. In the Add/Remove Programs Properties dialog box, click the Windows Setup tab.

4. In the list of components, click Communications, but be careful not to remove the check mark in the check box to its left.

5. Click Details.

6. In the Communications dialog box, select the Dial-Up Server check box, as shown in Figure 15-4.

Figure 15-4.

Select the Dial-Up Server check box to install Dial-Up Server.

7. Click OK to close the System Tools dialog box. *[Communications — handwritten correction above "System Tools"]*

8. Click OK again to close the Add/Remove Programs Properties dialog box.

At this point, you may need to insert the Windows CD. On some computers, the files that Windows needs are already stored on the hard disk. In either case, Dial-Up Server will be installed and you'll be ready for the next stage of the setup process.

Activating Dial-Up Server

Now that Dial-Up Server is installed, you have to activate it. This sets up your computer to answer the telephone when it rings and establish the connection to the remote computer. Follow these steps to activate Dial-Up Server:

1. Double-click My Computer on the Windows desktop.

2. In the My Computer window, double-click the Dial-Up Networking icon.

3. From the Connections menu, choose Dial-Up Server to open the Dial-Up Server dialog box shown in Figure 15-5.

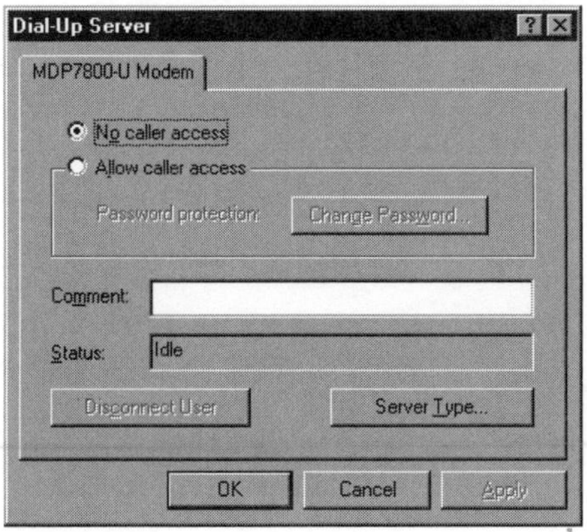

Figure 15-5.
The Dial-Up Server dialog box allows you to set up a modem to answer incoming calls.

If you have more than one modem, you'll see a tab for each modem in or connected to your computer. Click the tab for the modem you want to use to answer incoming calls.

4. Select Allow Caller Access.

5. To password-protect your system so that only authorized persons can connect to the network, click Change Password to open the Dial-Up Networking Password dialog box.

6. If you have not yet set a password, leave the Old Password text box blank. Type your password in both the New Password and Confirm New Password text boxes, and click OK.

7. Click Apply.

You'll now see a new icon next to the clock in your Windows system tray, indicating that Dial-Up Server is running.

Dialing In to the Dial-Up Server

Now that your home computer is set up for remote connection, you have to set up your laptop by creating a Dial-Up Networking connection that will call your home number. Just follow these steps:

1. Double-click My Computer on the Windows desktop.

2. In the My Computer window, double-click the Dial-Up Networking icon.

3. Double-click Make New Connection to open the Make New Connection dialog box shown in Figure 15-6.

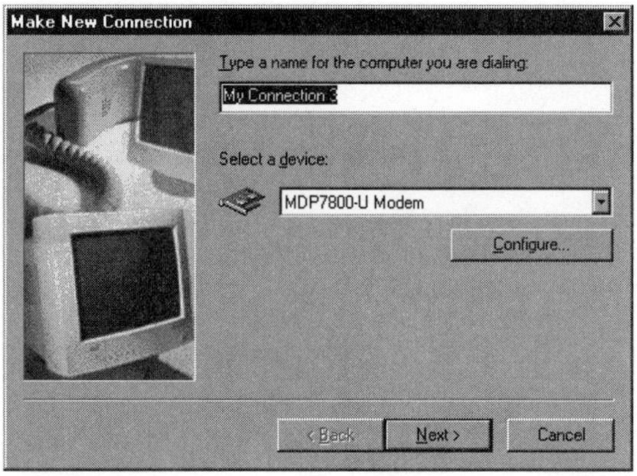

Figure 15-6.
The Make New Connection dialog box prompts you for a name of the new connection.

4. Type a name for your connection, such as *Road Warrior*.

5. If you have more than one modem, click the down arrow next to the Select a Device drop-down list and choose the modem you'll use to connect to your home computer.

6. Click Next to see the dialog box shown in Figure 15-7.

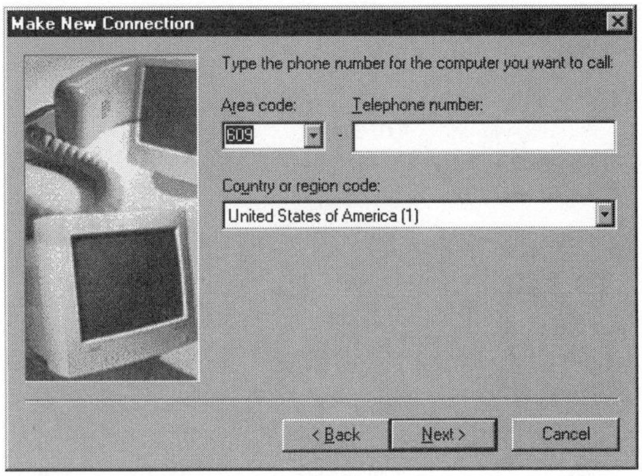

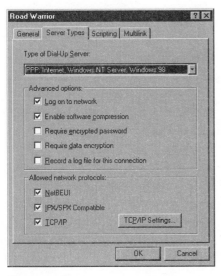

Figure 15-7.

Specify your home computer's telephone number.

7. Enter your home computer's area code and telephone number.

8. Click Next, and then click Finish.

While the Dial-Up Networking window is still open, you need to configure the connection for the proper protocol. Here's how to do it:

1. Right-click the connection you've just created and choose Properties.

2. In the connection dialog box, click the Server Types tab to see the options shown in Figure 15-8.

Figure 15-8.

Configure your dial-up connection from this set of options.

3. Make sure the Type Of Dial-Up Server option is set to PPP: Internet, Windows NT Server, Windows 98. If you are using Windows 95 rather than Windows 98, make sure it is set to PPP: Windows 95, Windows NT, Internet.

4. Select the Log On To Network check box.

5. Select all three of the protocols listed in the Allowed Network Protocols area of the dialog box: NetBEUI, IPX/SPX Compatible, and TCP/IP.

6. Click OK.

Note

You do not need to configure an IP address or set any other TCP/IP options.

You're now ready to dial in to your home computer from the road. Open the Dial-Up Networking window and double-click the remote dial-up connection. Click Connect to make the connection. Windows will dial in and make the connection to your home computer. Enter your password if you are asked for it.

To access the files on a computer on your network, you must enter its name.

1. On the Start menu, click Run.

2. In the Run dialog box, type two backwards slashes followed by the name of the computer you are dialing into, and then click OK.
    If the computer is named adam, for example, you'd enter *adam*.

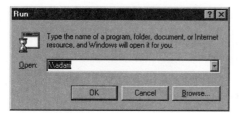

Now That You're Connected

After you enter the computer name, you can access the computer just as if you were at home and connected to the network. You'll see a window showing all the shared resources on the computer.

To access a file, double-click the shared drive and navigate to the file just as if you were using the My Computer window from home. Copy and move files by dragging them between windows. For example, to get a copy of a file from home onto your laptop, locate the file on your home computer and drag it to your laptop's desktop.

Printing a document on a shared printer that's connected to a home computer is just as easy. Locate the document using My Computer or Windows Explorer on your laptop, and drag it to the icon for the shared printer. The document will be waiting for you when you return home.

Keeping in Touch with Family

Microsoft NetMeeting allows you to communicate with your family in a variety of ways when you're traveling and away from home. It's also a good way to keep in touch with other family members who are at remote locations.

Let's say you're on a business trip or your child is away at school. Instead of simply sending and receiving e-mail, you can use NetMeeting to talk to each other just as you would over the telephone. You can also send and receive files, work on programs together, and share drawings, as shown in Figure 15-9. If your computers are equipped with video cameras, you can even see each other at the same time you talk.

Figure 15-9.
NetMeeting in action.

If you have version 4 or later of Microsoft Internet Explorer, NetMeeting is already installed on your system. If NetMeeting isn't installed, you can download a free copy of it from the Microsoft Web site at this address: *http://www.microsoft.com/windows/netmeeting/*.

The information in this chapter is based on NetMeeting 3.0, the version of the program that is installed with Internet Explorer 5 or later. If you have an earlier version of NetMeeting, you should download the newest version from the Microsoft Web site to obtain all the latest features.

To start NetMeeting, point to Programs on the Start menu, and then click Microsoft NetMeeting. The program might also be listed in the submenu that appears when you point to Internet Explorer on the Programs menu, or when you point to Accessories and then point to Internet Tools.

The first time you run NetMeeting, you'll see a series of dialog boxes that help you set up the program on your system. Depending on your system's configuration and on the version of NetMeeting that you're using, the order and content of these dialog boxes might be somewhat different from the following description, which is based on NetMeeting 3.0. Respond to the prompts in each dialog box, and then click Next to move to the next dialog box.

1. Click Next at the first dialog box, which explains the features available in NetMeeting.

2. In the next dialog box, enter your name, e-mail address, city, state, and country, and a brief comment about yourself that will identify you on screen to other NetMeeting users.

3. Click Next to continue.

4. In the next dialog box, shown in Figure 15-10, choose whether you want to log on to a server whenever NetMeeting starts, and select the default server. The server is a Microsoft computer or an Internet service provider's computer that handles communications among NetMeeting users over the Internet. The server acts like a gigantic telephone switchboard, maintaining a directory of everyone who is logged on and ready to accept calls. The member of your family that you plan to contact over the Internet with NetMeeting should choose the same server.

Note

When you are home, you can also use NetMeeting directly over your home network as a family intercom. Since you do not need to log on to a server if you'll be using NetMeeting over your home network, do not choose to log on to a server when NetMeeting starts.

5. Click Next to continue.

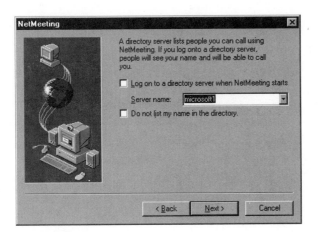

Figure 15-10.
This NetMeeting dialog box allows you to log on to a server.

6. If you have a video capture board installed in your computer, you'll see a dialog box that asks you to confirm its use.

7. Click Next to continue.

8. If a dialog box appears asking for the speed of your connection, select the speed of your modem and click Next.

   Now you're halfway there. Continue by following these steps:

1. To make NetMeeting easier to start, select both check boxes in the next dialog box to place shortcuts for NetMeeting both on your Windows desktop and on the Quick Launch toolbar, just to the right of the Start button, and then click Next.

2. Click Next at the next screen, when NetMeeting informs you that the Audio Tuning Wizard is about to help you tune your audio settings. It also instructs you to close all other programs that play or record sound.

3. You may now see a dialog box that asks you to select the devices that will record and play back sound on your system. Generally, your sound card performs both functions.

4. Select the sound card you have, and click Next.

5. Test the volume of your speakers by clicking the Test button in the dialog box shown in Figure 15-11, on the next page, and adjusting the slider to set a comfortable listening level. Click Stop to stop the sound, and then click Next.

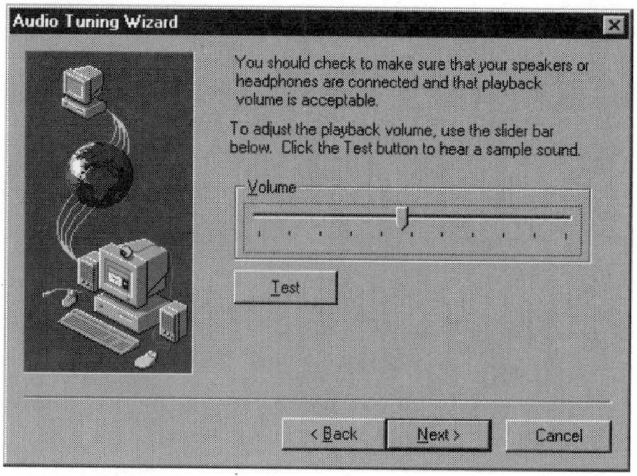

Audio Tuning Wizard
You should check to make sure that your speakers or headphones are connected and that playback volume is acceptable.
To adjust the playback volume, use the slider bar below. Click the Test button to hear a sample sound.
Volume
Test
< Back
Next >
Cancel

Figure 15-11.
Use the slider to adjust the sound volume.

6. To set the sensitivity of your microphone, speak into the microphone and watch the color bar that indicates the volume of your voice. Adjust the Record Volume slider so the bar reaches about the halfway mark, and click Next.
7. Click Finish when the Audio Tuning Wizard reports that you have successfully tuned your settings.

   When you click Finish, you'll see the NetMeeting window, shown in Figure 15-12.

NetMeeting - Not in a Call
Call View Tools Help
Windows NetMeeting
Name
Not in a call

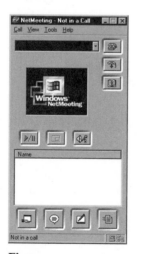

Figure 15-12.
The NetMeeting program allows you to call other network users.

Note

After you start NetMeeting, you can change all of the setup options and fine-tune calling, audio, and video settings by choosing Options from the NetMeeting Tools menu.

Starting a Meeting

If NetMeeting is set to log on to a directory server automatically, it will dial in to your ISP each time it is started. If it does not dial automatically, choose Log On To from the Call menu, which is followed by the name of the server, such as ils.Microsoft.com.

To place a call, choose Directory from the Call menu to open a dialog box listing the people logged on to the server. If many people are logged on, the list may take a few moments to appear while their names are downloaded. Scroll through the list to locate the person you want to speak with and double-click that person's name.

NetMeeting on a Network

Although NetMeeting is initially set to work across the Internet, you can call someone on your home network by adjusting the program so that it places the call through the network instead of through the Internet.

Note

If your computer tries to dial in to the Internet when you are placing a network call, just close the Dial-Up Networking box to stop the call.

1. Find out the IP address or name of the network computer you want to dial. You must be using the TCP/IP protocol on the network to make NetMeeting calls across the network.

2. Click the Place Call button or choose New Call from the Call menu to see the Place A Call dialog box.

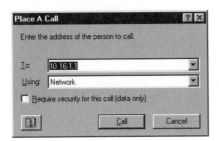

3. From the Using drop-down list, choose Network.

4. In the To box, enter the IP address or the name of the computer you are trying to reach, and then click Call.

The person at the computer you are calling will hear a telephone ring sound and a message box will open to ask whether the user wants to accept or ignore your call.

> **NetMeeting - Incoming Call**
>
> Incoming call from Barbara Neibauer...   [Accept]   [Ignore]

If the person chooses to ignore the call, a message appears on your screen reporting that the other user did not accept your call.

Note

NetMeeting might also display a message reporting that the person you've called is currently in another meeting and cannot accept your call, or it might inform you that the person is in a meeting and ask if you would like to join.

When your call is accepted, the names of the people in the meeting are displayed in the NetMeeting window and you can start communicating. If each computer has a microphone and speakers, you can each speak into the microphone to talk to one another. If your computer is equipped with a camera, the person you're talking to will also able to see you, as shown in Figure 15-13.

Figure 15-13.

In a NetMeeting, it's possible to see the people you're talking to.

To end the meeting, click the End Call button or choose Hang Up from the Call menu.

Using the Microsoft Internet Directory

Rather than log on to a directory server, you can connect to the Microsoft Internet Directory and search for the person you want to contact.

1. In NetMeeting, choose Options from the Tools menu to see the Options dialog box.

2. On the General tab of the dialog box, click the down arrow next to the Directory drop-down list, choose Microsoft Internet Directory from the list, and then click OK.

When you select Log On To Microsoft Internet Directory from the Call menu, you'll see the search form shown in Figure 15-14. Enter the name or e-mail address of the person you want to contact and click Search.

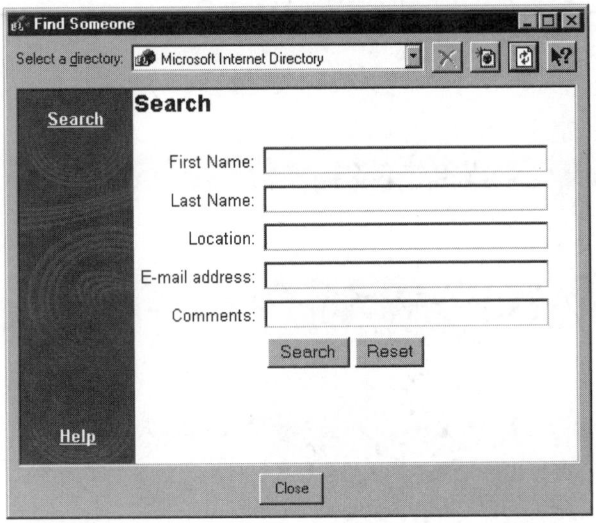

Figure 15-14.
Use the Microsoft Internet Directory to search for the person you want to contact.

You'll see a list of persons who meet your search criteria. To place a NetMeeting call, click the person you want to contact.

Chatting in NetMeeting

Even with the proper equipment, the audio quality of a NetMeeting call can be poor. Instead of actually speaking over the network, you may want to open a chat window and type messages to the other participants in the meeting. Follow these steps to open a chat window:

1. Click the Chat button or choose Chat from the Tools menu to open the chat window.

   The Chat window also opens on the other participants' screens.

2. Read the chat messages as they appear in the large text box, as shown in Figure 15-15.

Figure 15-15.
With NetMeeting, you can create your own chat room on the network.

3. Type your messages in the Message text box and press Enter to transmit them.

If you want to send a private message to a particular chat participant, select the participant's name from the Send To drop-down list before clicking the Send Message button.

To resume sending public messages to everyone in the chat, choose Everyone In Chat from the Send To drop-down list.

Note
_____

You can talk (speak) and chat (write) at the same time.

To exit a chat, close the Chat window or choose Exit from the File menu.

Using the Whiteboard

Sometimes you may need to communicate about something on line that you can't easily express in words. Suppose, for example, that you want the participants in the meeting to review a drawing. You'd like to give each participant the opportunity to comment on the drawing or even make changes to it as the meeting progresses. The solution in such situations is a handy NetMeeting feature called the whiteboard.

The whiteboard is a drawing window that you can share with everyone at the meeting. Whatever you draw on the whiteboard appears on the whiteboards of all the other participants. They, in turn, can use their whiteboards to add to your drawing, as long as you permit it. A NetMeeting whiteboard is shown in Figure 15-16.

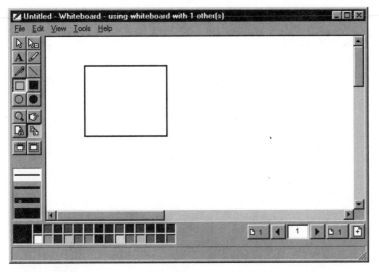

Figure 15-16.
The whiteboard feature in NetMeeting allows meeting participants to view and make changes to drawings.

To use the whiteboard, follow these steps:

1. Click the Whiteboard button or choose Whiteboard from the Tools menu.

2. Draw on the whiteboard using tools from the whiteboard tool palette, shown in Figure 15-17, on the next page.

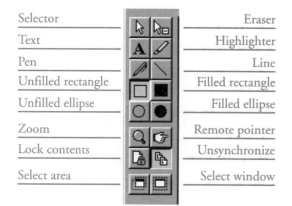

Selector	Eraser
Text	Highlighter
Pen	Line
Unfilled rectangle	Filled rectangle
Unfilled ellipse	Filled ellipse
Zoom	Remote pointer
Lock contents	Unsynchronize
Select area	Select window

Figure 15-17.
The items in the whiteboard tool palette allow you to work on shared graphics and text.

The tool palette contains everything you need to create and edit drawings and text on the whiteboard. The same features are also available on the Tools menu.

Here's how to use the whiteboard tools:

- **Selector** Click this tool on an object you want to select, choose Delete, Copy, or Cut from the Edit menu or drag the selected object to move it on the screen.

- **Eraser** Click this tool on an object you want to erase. You can also use it to drag a rectangle around an area. All objects even partially within the rectangle will be deleted.

- **Text** Clicking this tool enables you to use your keyboard to type on the whiteboard. Choose a color from the color palette, or click the Font Options button that appears when you select the tool to change the font, font size, and font style. The Colors and Font commands on the Options menu also allow you to change the color, size and style of your type.

- **Highlighter** Choose a line width and a color, and then drag this tool over the area you want to highlight.

- **Pen** Click this tool and then drag it in the whiteboard area to draw freehand on the screen.

- **Line** Click this tool to draw straight lines by dragging the mouse pointer from one point to the next. Select a line width and choose a color from the color palette shown in the whiteboard window. You can also use the Colors and Line Width commands on the Options menu.

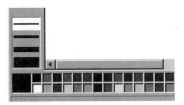

Note

You can use the Bring To Front or Send To Back commands on the Edit menu to change how objects overlap.

- **Rectangle** Choose a line width and color from the palette, and then click the Unfilled Rectangle button and draw the outline of a rectangle by dragging, or click the Filled Rectangle button and draw a solid rectangle of the selected color.

- **Ellipse** Click one of the two ellipse buttons and then drag on the whiteboard to draw filled or unfilled circles or ellipses in the line width and color of your choice.

- **Zoom** Click this tool, or use the Zoom command on the View menu, to switch between normal and enlarged views.

- **Remote Pointer** Select this tool to display a pointer, and then move it to the area of the whiteboard you want others to look at.

- **Lock Contents** Select this tool to prevent others from changing the whiteboard contents. Deselect it to allow others to change the whiteboard.

- **Synchronize/Unsynchronize** This tool lets you determine whether other whiteboard users can see the same pages you are viewing. To synchronize the pages click the tool so that it appears pressed down. To unsynchronize the pages, click the tool so that it appears released.

- **Select Area** Use this tool to drag a rectangle over an area of the screen outside of the whiteboard you want to copy to the whiteboard.

- **Select Window** This tool works in much the same way as the Windows clipboard. Click any window on your screen, even a partially obscured one, to copy the contents of the window to the whiteboard. The whiteboard will show the contents of the window inserted as a graphic.

Adding and Changing Whiteboard Pages

If a meeting you were conducting was held in person, you might use a flip chart to draw images and highlight important points. When you fill up one page, you just flip it over and start a fresh sheet. You can use the whiteboard in the same way, adding pages and changing them as needed.

Use the buttons at the lower-right corner of the whiteboard window to insert a page and to switch from page to page.

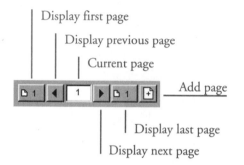

Display first page

Display previous page

Current page

Add page

Display last page

Display next page

Choose Clear Page from the Edit menu to erase the current page, or choose Delete Page from the Edit menu to delete the page. Erasing a page removes the page's contents on the screen of all NetMeeting participants, but leaves the page in place. Deleting a page actually removes it from your whiteboard and from those of other participants as well.

Note

Normally, everyone in the meeting can see the same page that you have displayed on your screen. If you want to change pages without letting everyone see what you are doing, deselect Synchronize on the View menu.

Saving and Printing the Whiteboard

When your meeting is over, you don't have to lose the contents of the whiteboard. While the whiteboard is still displayed, each participant in the meeting can print a copy of the whiteboard by choosing Print from the File menu. Each participant can also save the whiteboard by choosing Save from the File menu. Whiteboards are saved in a special format, with a .wht extension. To reopen saved whiteboard files, choose Open from the File menu.

Note

Closing your own whiteboard does not close the whiteboards of other participants, who can continue to draw on theirs. If you open the whiteboard again, NetMeeting will locate and display the same whiteboard the other participants see. If you try to close a whiteboard before saving it, NetMeeting asks if you want to save it.

Working Together on Programs

In addition to sharing a drawing on the Whiteboard, you may want meeting participants to share a program as well. When you share a program with others, the meeting participants can see the program, but they cannot control it, unless you specifically allow them to do so. The person running the program is called the *owner,* and only the owner has control over who can work with the program. Here's how to use NetMeeting to share a program:

1. Start the program you want to share, and then switch back to NetMeeting.

2. Click the Share Program button or choose Sharing from the Tools menu to see the dialog box in Figure 15-18.

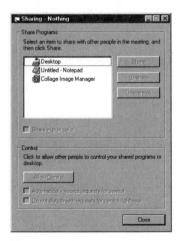

Figure 15-18.
The Sharing dialog box allows you to share programs with other meeting participants.

3. In the list of programs that are running, select the program you want to share, and then click Share.

Other meeting participants will now be able to see exactly what you are doing with the shared program.

If you want to allow meeting participants to use the shared program, rather than just view it, click the Allow Control button in the Sharing dialog box. You'll be offered these two options:

- **Automatically Accept Requests For Control** lets a meeting participant use the program without your express permission.

- **Do Not Disturb With Requests For Control Right Now** prevents requests for sharing from appearing on your screen.

To gain control of a program, a meeting participant must double-click the program window on the screen. This either takes control of the program or, if you have not turned on automatic acceptance in the Sharing dialog box, displays a dialog box asking if you want to Reject or Accept the request.

By clicking Accept, you transfer control of the program to the participant, and you will no longer be able to use your pointer on screen.

To regain control over the program and your cursor, and to stop any participant who is currently working with the shared program, press Esc or click the mouse button.

To stop sharing the program, click Unshare or Unshare All in the Sharing dialog box.

Sending and Receiving Files

While you are in a meeting, you can exchange files with other participants. Click the Transfer Files button or choose File Transfer from the Tools menu to view the File Transfer dialog box.

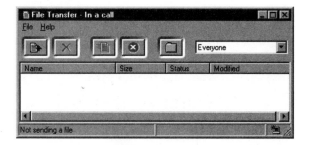

Click Add Files and, in the Choose Files To Send dialog box, choose the files you want to transfer. Then click Send All to send the files to everyone or, from the drop-down list of meeting participants in the File Transfer dialog box, choose the participant to whom you want the files sent, and then click Send All.

When you receive a file from someone else, you'll see a dialog box, similar to the one shown here, giving you the option to close the dialog box, open the file, or delete the file.

Files that you receive are stored in the C:\Program Files\NetMeeting\Received Files folder. Click the View Received Files button—the one that shows an icon of a folder—to open that folder.

Controlling a Home Computer Remotely

NetMeeting includes a powerful feature that lets you actually control one of the other computers on the network. For example, suppose a family member is having trouble changing a setting in the Control Panel or needs help performing some Windows task. You can take control of another person's computer from your own system and perform tasks as though you were sitting in front of the other computer.

To set up a computer to accept remote control, you have to use the Remote Desktop Sharing Wizard on that computer.

1. Start NetMeeting on the computer you want to be able to control and choose Remote Desktop Sharing from the Tools menu.

2. Click Next after reading the first Remote Desktop Sharing Wizard page.

3. Enter a password of at least seven characters that will allow access from the controlling computer.

4. Reenter the password to confirm it, and then click Next.

5. You can now choose to password-protect a screen saver as an extra security feature. Make your choice and click Next.

6. Click Finish.

7. Close NetMeeting.

The Remote Desktop Sharing icon will appear in the computer's system tray, to the left of the clock on the taskbar.

8. Right-click the Remote Desktop Sharing icon and select Activate Remote Desktop Sharing from the shortcut menu.

9. Start NetMeeting on the computer that will be in control and call the computer you want to share.

10. In the Place A Call dialog box that appears, select the Require Security For This Call (Data Only) check box, and then click Call.
You'll be asked to enter the password.

11. Enter the password and click OK.

You'll see a window that contains the other computer's desktop, as shown in Figure 15-19. You can now control the remote computer just as if you were sitting at its keyboard.

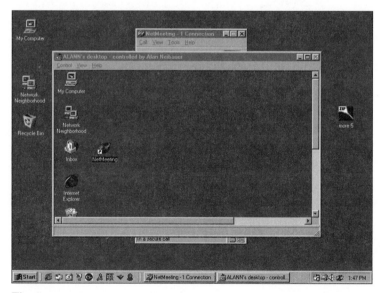

Figure 15-19.
With Remote Desktop Sharing, you can operate a remote computer from your own keyboard and screen.

To stop sharing, right-click the Remote Desktop Sharing icon on the desktop of the computer you are sharing and select Exit.

Dialing in from the road, remotely controlling a computer, and seeing the folks you are talking to over the Internet—it all seems like something out of the future, but these options are available to you today. In the next chapter, you'll learn what other futuristic features are available right now or are soon headed your way.

Chapter 16

Your Future Home Network

In previous chapters, you learned how to set up a home network using the latest available technologies: Ethernet networks, telephone and power line networks, and wireless technologies. While computers and their peripherals are constantly changing, the technologies and techniques described in this book will see your home network well into the future.

In this chapter, however, you'll take a look at some emerging and alternative technologies, and what the future may hold for you and your home. A wired home, as you will learn, will no longer be one that simply has an Ethernet network.

Controlling Your Wired Home

Imagine controlling every appliance, light, and security device in your home from your computer, or walking through the front door and saying, "Lights on. Television channel 6." Before going to sleep, you'd check that the lights and stove are turned off, that the refrigerator is working, and that your pet has come in for the night. You'd feed the dog, cat, or fish by calling in from the office or while on vacation, and you'd turn on the heating or air conditioning from your car phone on the way home.

Well, if you think complete home automation is a thing of the far-distant future, think again. The technology for home automation is here today, and thousands of homes have already led the way to the future.

Much of today's home automation is performed through a power line technology called *X10*. The communication between automated devices is carried through your existing home wiring, much like the power line network discussed in Chapter 6. You simply plug the X10 devices into wall outlets, and control the system from a control station or computer interface.

Note

You can use several other types of interfaces besides X10—CEBus is one example—but the X10 system is the most widely available.

An X10 controller, either a wall-mounted device or a program that runs on your computer, can individually direct the operation of up to 256 devices. In addition, the technology is standardized, so you can control devices from various manufacturers through the same wiring and with the same controllers.

In an X10 system, you can use three types of units:

- A *transmitter* sends signals from a controller to another X10 device. An X10 switch, for example, sends a signal to an X10 device that turns on a light.

- A *receiver*, such as a device that turns on a light or television, accepts signals from X10 controllers.

- A *transceiver* can both send and receive signals. These are usually controllers that can send signals to units and simultaneously receive status information from other units.

X10 receivers can be given one of up to 256 different codes. The controller uses the code to send a signal to the receiver telling it to switch on or off. You can have up to 256 separate devices, each controlled separately. You can also set several devices to have the same code so you can control them as a group with one signal from the controller.

You can control almost any electrical device with an X10 system. For example, X10 can underpin a security system that monitors access to your home and detects unauthorized entry. X10 security devices can include underground driveway sensors that alert you when a car enters the driveway, remote controlled doors and gates, and video surveillance and alarm systems.

The system is ideal for controlling internal and external lights and appliances such as coffee makers, microwaves, ovens, and refrigerators. X10 can also automate television and stereo home entertainment systems and communications devices such as telephones and intercoms. Just some of the X10 devices that are available from SmartHome (*http://www.smarthome.com*) for home entertainment are shown in Figure 16-1.

Figure 16-1.

The SmartHome.com Web site shows a number of X10 home entertainment devices.

An X10 product named DVD Anywhere (available at *http://www.x10.com*) lets you broadcast DVD movies from your computer's DVD player to any television in the house. The system requires that your PC DVD player or video card have an output jack that is RCA-type. Another product from X10.com, VideoSender, can broadcast cable, DSS, or VCR signals to any room in the house.

Note

The Leapfrog Home Network System, available at the SmartHome.com Web site, can transmit video signals through your existing telephone lines.

You can also use X10 to control heating and air conditioning systems that automate temperature and ventilation control and that compensate automatically for changing weather conditions. You can install systems that will open and close windows, drapes, and blinds at the touch of a switch or by voice command.

X10 devices can also perform the following tasks:

- Alert you when mail has been delivered to your mailbox or when packages have been dropped off at the doorstep

- Dispense food to a dog, cat, or fish

- Water your house plants

- Control lawn sprinklers by sensing heat and dryness

- Monitor and report current weather conditions

To get started with an X10 system, you can purchase X10 starter kits that control a few lights from a small panel for about $25. You can then add individual devices to build a complete home automation system. The most common and inexpensive of these (about $6) are switches, dimmers, and lamp modules that allow you to turn on or off lights and small appliances. Heavy-duty modules for 220-volt appliances such as air conditioners, dryers, hot water heaters, and pool pumps cost about $15.

Controllable thermostats are more expensive, costing over $100. Among the available models is a telephone-controlled thermostat that you can remotely control from any phone. There are also multiple switch boxes for controlling speakers, sprinkler systems, and window treatments. For drapes and blinds, you'll need a motorized control that opens or closes the drapes or blinds when the X10 signal is detected.

An X10 system can be self-contained; wall-mounted or tabletop panels can control the devices on the system. But for the ultimate in control, you can use your computer to control the entire system from your network. In fact, when you use a computer to automate your home, you can turn on the coffee pot so that the coffee is ready when you wake up, turn lights on and off according to a predetermined schedule, control a DVD player from any computer in the house, or check for mail. To achieve all this, you have to install software and then connect a special controller to your computer that connects it to the X10 system. You can then work with the controller from any networked computer.

You can choose from among several programs that connect your computer with the X10 devices in your home. This control panel, for example, is from the program Plato for Windows.

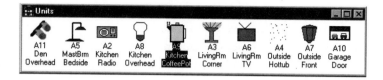

The icons on the control panel show that the coffee pot has been turned on to make coffee, the living room corner light is turned on, and the garage door is open. To add X10 units to the system, you use the Add An X10 Unit dialog box shown in Figure 16-2.

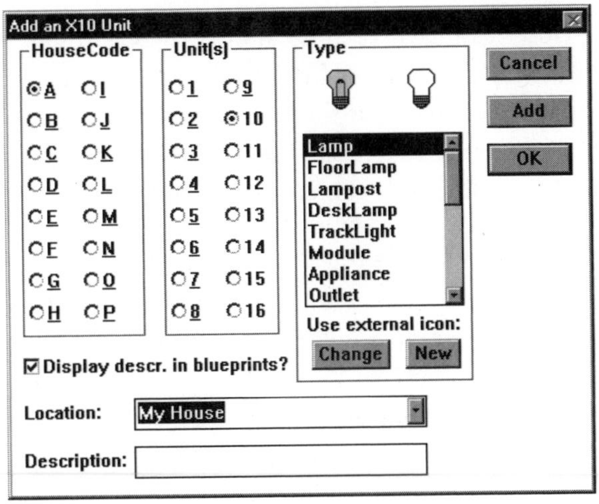

Figure 16-2.
You can add new X10 units in this dialog box.

So that you can control a particular device, you set its house and device codes. These codes identify the device and designate its type and location so it is controllable by the software. You can also create an onscreen blueprint of your home with icons representing each X10 device so you can visualize the location of each of the X10-controlled items in your house.

Getting Wired for the Future

In previous chapters, you learned how to run network cable through your home to create an Ethernet network. If you are building a new house or remodeling your current home, however, you may want to wire it for the future. Ethernet cable is certainly fine for a home computer network, but the future of your wired home goes far beyond Ethernet.

In addition to a computer network, you can wire your home for

- Home entertainment
- Telephone and intercom
- Security
- Home automation
- Environmental controls

First, plan to have a central "wiring closet" somewhere in the house where all the wires can converge. This can be any standard closet that provides enough space for you to get in and manipulate the wiring. As long as we're looking at the future, you might want to plan to use a small room, about the size of a powder room, that has heating and cooling vents and enough space for you to access all four sides of a central wiring cabinet.

In this wiring cabinet, you could have

- An Ethernet hub

- A LAN modem for sharing an Internet account (*see Chapter 9 for a note about sharing accounts*)

- A video distribution panel for a home entertainment system

- A telephone system

- A security panel

- Central home automation controllers

- A controller for multiple zone heating and air conditioning

Make sure the wiring closet has enough electrical outlets, and that all electrical outlets, telephone lines, and video cables are protected against surges.

When you plan the electrical system for your home, make sure your plan includes plenty of wall outlets. Carefully mark which outlets are connected to wall switches because you don't want to plug certain pieces of equipment into switched outlets. Accidentally flipping the switch to turn off a light might also then turn off a computer or hub.

If you plan on using X10 for home automation, have the electrician run a neutral wire to all wall switch boxes. While some contractors don't bother running the neutral wire to all switches, the neutral wire is needed for some X10 devices. Also make sure that the boxes themselves are extra deep to accommodate X10 switches, which are usually bulkier than standard switches.

Now run the following wires to each bedroom, den, and living room:

- Two coaxial video cables. You can use one for the television signal and the other for video cameras, VCRs, or DVD players. You can then watch a video or DVD playing from any other room in the house, or set up your own closed-circuit video system.

- Three Category 5 UTP cables. You can use one cable for your basic home network, and reserve the others are for maximum expandability so you can add networked printers, modems, and other equipment, as well as an intercom.

- Telephone cable for your telephone system, sufficient for two lines.

- Speaker cable for connecting stereo speakers throughout the home.

- Thermostat cable for use with a multiple-zoned heating and cooling system.

- Fiber optic cable for future expansion.

Terminate all the cables into wall jacks, and label each of the jacks to identify its use. Plan the arrangement beforehand for each room, based on where you intend to place computer desks, entertainment units, and other furniture. You may decide, for example, to have speakers built into the walls or ceilings. You'll need to plan their location so the speaker wire can be properly run. Thermostats are usually located away from windows and other sources of drafts. Plan their location carefully with a heating contractor.

Home entertainment networks provide a centralized source for video and audio. For example, you might plan for a thin, wall-mounted television display and hidden speakers in every room. Using a universal, hand-held remote control, you will be able to tune in your favorite music or television show, or watch a video or DVD. A video distribution panel will serve as a switchboard for video signals from your cable provider and also from your in-house video cameras and players. Much of this technology is available today. There are devices, for example, that let you broadcast cable television signals, or output video from a VCD or DVD player, even a device in your computer, to any television in the house.

Fiber Optics

One day you may need only one type of cable throughout your home for computer networking, a telephone system, home security, and video. That cable will be fiber optic. Fiber optic cable consists of a thin glass wire through which light passes in pulses. Fiber optic cable has a very low error rate, it's not susceptible to electromagnetic interference, it's more secure than copper wire because taps can be detected, and it's lightweight.

Fiber optic cable can transmit signals at speeds in the tens of gigabits per second and can handle several different gigabits of channels simultaneously, each channel using a different wavelength of light. The fiber optic cable contains five parts:

- The glass core that carries the light

- Glass cladding surrounding the core that reflects the light back to the core so it travels without signal loss

- A buffer layer that protects the core and cladding from damage

- A layer of material that strengthens the cable

- An outer jacket, such as PVC plastic

Normal electrical signals become weak over distances. To maintain signals over a distance, you need to add devices called repeaters every mile to boost the signals back to their full strength. With fiber optic cable, however, the reflection of the light back to the cable's core off of the cladding that surrounds the core keeps the signal strong for longer. Fiber optic repeaters are needed only every 60 miles or more.

To prepare for the day when you'll be able to replace all the network, telephone, and video cables in your home with fiber optic cable, consider having fiber optic cable run through your home in addition to other cables.

Wiring for High-Speed Internet Access

Most homes still connect to the Internet through a modem and standard telephone lines. Since standard telephone lines are already wired into your home, they are the easiest and least expensive option. But when you plan your wired home, you can consider other options.

In the best of circumstances, when you've got good, clear phone lines, the maximum speed of a standard modem is 56 Kbps, but most connections are considerably slower. If you spend a lot of time surfing the Net and downloading software, these slow speeds may not be acceptable to you, so you may be willing to consent to the higher cost of a faster connection. Even though you may pay more per month, your Internet experience will be much more pleasurable, and you can share one high-speed connection among all the members of your household.

Fortunately, if you want a faster connection, one or more of several technologies may be available in your area.

- ISDN

- Satellite Internet access

- DSL

- Cable modem

Of these, cable modems offer the fastest connections, but like DSL, they are not yet available at every location. ISDN connections are more widely available, and satellite Internet connections are available just about anywhere, but they offer slower connections than cable and DSL, and are more expensive to install and use. Table 16-1 compares these Internet access methods.

Table 16-1. **Comparison of Internet Access Methods**

Device	Initial cost	Monthly cost	Download speed	Pros	Cons
Analog modem	Included with most computers, less than $100 to purchase and install otherwise	ISP charges about $20, in addition to monthly telephone line charges	56 Kbps or less	Least expensive option, most widely available service, wide choice of ISPs	Requires a telephone line; slowest Internet option
ISDN	Up to $800	Phone line, $19–$50 for the ISDN line, plus a per-minute usage charge in some locations, plus ISP charges	128 Kbps	Next widely available option	You must be located near the phone company's central office
DirecPC satellite	$300–$800	$30–$100	400 Kbps download, 56 Kbps upload	Widely available	Requires outside satellite dish; uploading via standard modem and telephone line
DSL	$500–$1000	$40–$200	128 Kbps– 4 Mbps	Always connected to the Internet	Costly; not universally available; you must be located near the phone company's central office
Cable modem	Up to $600 with Ethernet card and modem	$30–$59	500 Kbps– 20 Mbps	High speed, always connected to the Internet	Not universally available

Integrated Services Digital Network (ISDN)

The original attempt to provide a faster connection speed was a service called Integrated Services Digital Network (ISDN). ISDN uses three separate frequencies, called *channels*, on a special, dedicated telephone line. One channel (called the D channel) operates at a slow 16 Kbps, while the two remaining channels (the B channels) connect at up to 64 Kbps each. By binding the two B channels together, ISDN can achieve speeds of up to 128 Kbps.

ISDN is available at many locations in the United States, but your home must be within 20,000 feet of the local telephone company switching equipment. You'll also need a special modem or network interface that can cost between $200 and $500. With installation costs of $100 to $300, the total initial cost for setting up an ISDN line can be as high as $800. In addition, you must pay a monthly service fee to the phone company for the ISDN line and you may have to pay the phone company a penny or two for each minute you use the line. On top of that, many ISP's charge a premium for an ISDN connection.

Unless you set up your network for modem-sharing, you'll need to buy a special ISDN modem for each computer you want to connect to the Internet and install a separate ISDN telephone line for each, which can get quite expensive.

For most people, the increased speed of an ISDN connection does not justify the additional cost, especially when there are other, faster alternatives available.

Satellite Internet Access

Hughes Network Systems, the company that offers DirecTV for satellite television, also offers DirecPC for your Internet connection, which provides downloads of up to 400 Kbps, quite a bit faster than ISDN. You must have a DirecPC dish installed on your roof, though, and a cable that runs from the satellite dish to your computer. The cable connects to an internal card or to an external USB modem. Unless you share the modem over a network, which requires a more expensive network option, you'll need a separate satellite dish, cable connection and an internal card or nn external USB modem for each computer you want connected to the Internet.

DirecPC works in conjunction with the modem and phone line you already have. You establish a modem connection to your regular ISP or to Hughes, which can be your ISP if you don't already have one. When you enter a Web site address into yo'·r browser, the request goes through your phone line at regular speed to Hughes. Then t..ᵉ data is sent back to your system by the satellite at high speed.

The great advantage of DirecPC is that you can use it anywhere in the continental United States, even in remote, rural areas. The dish and the card or USB modem costs about $200 plus an installation fee, and you must pay a monthly charge for a certain number of hours each month. This fee ranges from about $20 to $100, depending on the number of hours you choose. Hughes also sells DirecDuo, which combines DirecPC and DirecTV in one satellite dish. You may also be able to find a promotion that gives you free installation if you sign up for the DirecPC ISP service. You can also save money by installing the dish yourself, but it's not easy. You'll need an installation kit, costing about $30 to $40, the ability to climb onto your roof, and the patience to aim the dish and find the satellite. It's possible to do yourself, but you're better off leaving it to your local expert.

The main disadvantage of DirecPC is that it offers high-speed access in only one direction, relying on your regular modem for uploading data and sending e-mail. So although you can download Web sites and software over the satellite at high speed, you can upload no faster than your regular modem connection. If you play games over the Internet, which requires fast two-way communication, the combination of DirecPC and a regular modem will not be any faster than a regular modem by itself.

Digital Subscriber Lines

Another high-speed Internet option is a Digital Subscriber Line (DSL). DSL can let you download from the Internet at speeds up to 3 to 4 Mbps, although about 1 Mbps is more common. DSL lines are asymmetric, though, which means that the downloading speed is much faster than the uploading speed. Usually, the uploading speed of a DSL line is limited to about the speed of an ISDN line, 128 Kbps.

DSL modems are always connected to the Internet; you do not have to dial in to make a connection. As long as your computer is turned on, you are online and ready to send and receive mail and surf the Internet. They also have a fixed bandwidth, which means that the speed of your connection will not vary with the number of other people also connected to the Internet through their own DSL lines.

DSL is only available in certain locations, however, and it works only when you live very close to the local telephone company's office, within a few miles. In fact, the farther you are from the local phone company, the slower your connection speed. If you're a few miles from the nearest office, your connection speed may be no faster than the speed you get with a regular modem.

To get DSL service, you'll need a special line installed, a special telephone jack, a DSL modem, and an Ethernet card to which the modem connects. Installation costs are generally from $100 to $500, and the modem can cost up to $400, although many DSL companies will rent the DSL modem to you for a minor fee each month. Companies that provide DSL connections generally charge around $40 to $50 per month for the connection, plus the cost of ISP service.

As with ISDN, you'll need a special DSL line and modem for each computer you want to connect to the Internet, which can get quite expensive, or you'll need to set up your network for modem sharing. Having a high-speed, full-time connection to the Internet, though, is a great benefit to any family.

Cable Modems

If you have cable television service in your area, you may also be able to get cable Internet access. The Internet connection is made through the same coaxial cable that brings the television signal into your home, at two-way speeds between 500 Kbps and 20 Mbps, although about 1 Mbps is most common. The coaxial cable connects to a special cable modem that connects, in turn, to an Ethernet NIC in your computer. Because you are permanently connected to the Internet through the cable modem, you don't have to dial in to reach your ISP. Unlike ISDN and DSL, you can have cable modem service regardless of how far you live from the telephone company switches.

Installation usually costs less than $100, not including an Ethernet NIC, if you need to buy one, and the cost of buying or renting the cable modem. You can purchase Ethernet NICs for less than $50, but cable modems can cost up to $400. Monthly charges are usually about $30, and you can often pay for the cable modem with a month-to-month rental fee. You can set up your home network to share the Internet connection (subject to your ISP agreement), or you can purchase additional IP addresses to allow more than one computer to log on at the same time. The number of additional IP addresses you can buy varies with the cable provider and may cost an additional $10 or so per month for each address.

Not every cable TV provider currently offers cable modem service, and those who do may not yet offer it in their entire service area. In addition, the speed of your Internet connection depends on the number of other subscribers in your area who are on line at any given time because everyone in the neighborhood, and possibly surrounding neighborhoods, shares the same bandwidth. Still, cable modems are a good alternative if you want a high-speed Internet connection. Call your local cable company to find out if they offer cable Internet service, or to inquire about when the service will become available in your area.

The Device of the Future: The Teledevice

The home of today has at least six devices for communications and entertainment:

- Telephone
- Computer
- Television, along with VCR and DVD
- Radio
- Stereo
- Alarm system

As we approach the future, these devices may merge into a single communications and entertainment device some futurists call the *teledevice.*

Straight out of a sci-fi movie, the teledevice will connect you to the Internet, serve as a videophone and answering machine, and bring movies, information, and music into every room of your home. It will be integrated into every major appliance in the home, including a home control and security system, and even your refrigerator and coffee maker.

Barcode readers, for example, will be able to detect when you've removed the last bottle of something from the refrigerator or pantry, and automatically order more from your local store. You will use the same display screen to watch movies, surf the Internet, and to see your friends and relatives as you speak with them.

The teledevice falls right in line with Microsoft chairman Bill Gates's vision of a future in which "the boundary between what is a TV and what is a PC will be completely blurred" and "Americans will live a Web lifestyle." This means that you'll be able to get your entertainment and communications needs through one device. You will no longer need a television to watch movies and entertainment programs, and a computer to run programs, send and receive mail, and surf the Internet. One device will serve all of these functions.

In a "Web lifestyle," getting information online and communicating through e-mail will become a standard fact of life. Just as most people consider the telephone a basic necessity today, the teledevice will become a ubiquitous household fixture.

Currency and charge cards may eventually be replaced completely by smart cards that automatically debit your accounts for purchases and identify your personal needs. When you come home, you'll swipe your smartcard through the reader on the teledevice to automatically get your e-mail and other messages, update your bank accounts and portfolio, get the latest headline news that matches your interests, and set the temperature for your personal comfort level. You can see examples of personalized news, investment information, and retailing on the Internet today. Amazon.com, for example, can track your interests and buying habits and use that information to recommend new books as they are published.

Smart card technology promises to extend this personalization into many other areas of your life. In fact, some of the technology is already available. Microsoft's Smart Card for Windows provides a smart card interface for the Windows environment. It can be used, for example, to authorize logon to a PC or to a computer network.

All this future technology will be possible because of advances in hardware and home wiring. In the future, homebuilders will probably routinely install Ethernet, coaxial cable, or perhaps fiber optic cable in all new houses. The home network you're setting up now is just the beginning. You'll have a jump on the future by planning for the complete wired home today.

Index

Alan Neibauer

Alan Neibauer is a veteran computer book author, with several bestsellers to his credit, including *Running Outlook* and *The Official Guide to the Corel WordPerfect Suite*. Neibauer has a degree in Journalism from Temple University and a master's from the Wharton School of the University of Pennsylvania. He served as Chairperson of Management Information Systems at Holy Family College, in Philadelphia, and consults to companies large and small. He lives in Longport, New Jersey with his wife Barbara. The two Tae Kwon Do black belts enjoy practicing on the beach.

The manuscript for this book was prepared and galleyed using Microsoft Word 2000. Pages were composed by Studioserv (www.studioserv.com) using Adobe PageMaker 6.52 for Windows, with text in AGaramond and display type in Garamond Condensed. Composed pages were delivered to the printer as electronic prepress files.

Cover Art Director:	Patrick Lanfear
Cover Illustrator:	Todd Daman
Cover Designer:	Tom Draper Design
Interior Graphic Designer:	James D. Kramer
Illustrator:	Steve Hussey
Principal Compositor:	Sharon Bell, Presentation Desktop Publications
Principal Proofreader:	Tom Speeches
Indexer:	Steve Sagman

Proof of Purchase

0-7356-0847-4

Do not send this card with your registration.
Use this card as proof of purchase if participating in a promotion or
rebate offer on *This Wired Home: The Microsoft® Guide to Home Networking*. Card must be used in
conjunction with other proof(s) of payment such as your dated sales receipt—see offer details.

This Wired Home:
The Microsoft® Guide to Home Networking

WHERE DID YOU PURCHASE THIS PRODUCT?

CUSTOMER NAME

mspress.microsoft.com

Microsoft Press, PO Box 97017, Redmond, WA 98073-9830

OWNER REGISTRATION CARD

Register Today!

0-7356-0847-4

Return the bottom portion of this card to register today.

This Wired Home:
The Microsoft® Guide to Home Networking

FIRST NAME

MIDDLE INITIAL

LAST NAME

INSTITUTION OR COMPANY NAME

ADDRESS

CITY

STATE

ZIP

(   )

E-MAIL ADDRESS

PHONE NUMBER

U.S. and Canada addresses only. Fill in information above and mail postage-free.
Please mail only the bottom half of this page.

For information about Microsoft Press® products, visit our Web site at mspress.microsoft.com

BUSINESS REPLY MAIL
FIRST-CLASS MAIL   PERMIT NO. 108   REDMOND WA

POSTAGE WILL BE PAID BY ADDRESSEE

MICROSOFT PRESS
PO BOX 97017
REDMOND, WA 98073-9830